Brian Charles MacDermot, editor

THE IRISH CATHOLIC PETITION OF 1805

THE IRISH CATHOLIC PETITION OF 1805

THE DIARY OF DENYS SCULLY

Brian MacDermot, Editor

IRISH ACADEMIC PRESS

Published by
Irish Academic Press Ltd,
Kill Lane, Blackrock, Co. Dublin.

A catalogue record for this book
is available from the British Library.

ISBN 0-7165-2497-X

Printed in Great Britain by
Antony Rowe Ltd, Chippenham, Wilts

CONTENTS

EDITORIAL NOTE AND ACKNOWLEDGEMENTS

Among the Scully Papers held by the National Library of Ireland are three small notebooks (MS 27,514 i-iii) the contents of which, all in the hand of Denys Scully, record the activities of the Irish Catholic deputation that took a petition to London in March 1805. The first, which contains Scully's own draft/copies of the minutes of the deputation's meetings, was lent in 1809 to Francis Plowden, who however made but scant use of it in the *History* which he published in 1811. The other two contain a personal diary which Scully kept from the date of his departure for London to that of his return to Dublin. The existence of this was drawn to the attention of historians in 1908 when the Revd William Hunt, to whom Denys Scully's grandson, Vincent Scully, had submitted a selection of the Scully papers for appraisal, made it the main subject of a presidential address to the Royal Historical Society, subsequently published in its *Transactions*. It was then returned to Vincent Scully with the other papers and remained inaccessible until the whole collection was deposited with the National Library in 1983.

When I published a collection of Denys Scully's papers in 1988, under the title of *The Catholic Question in Ireland and England 1798-1822*, I was unable to to include the diary, partly because of its own length and partly because still more space would have been required to set it in the context of a considerable body of other evidence bearing on Scully's role in the proceedings of the 1804 Committee, including three documents in the Home Office files which may be regarded as having emanated from Scully himself. Separate publication now makes it possible to include these together with the greater part of the correspondence between Dublin Castle and Whitehall over the government's attempt to get the petition suppressed, and present an account of the origin of the Committee contributed to the *Freeman's Journal* in 1810 by its begetter, James Ryan. Room is also provided for a text of the petition, of which Scully says he was the author, some notes on the Irish Catholics composed by his friend Robert Marshall in 1806 and other appendices which may be found useful in filling in the background to the events described.

Of the contents of the first notebook I have omitted some redundant material and moved the opening Instructions to the Deputation to a more convenient location immediately preceding Scully's departure for London. Except for the occasional amalgamation of short paragraphs I have left the diary as I found it. To the petition, taken direct from the surviving manuscript belonging to the House of Lords, I have added paragraph numbers and amalgamated its seventy-five signatories with the ninety-eight of the petition to the House of Commons into a single list, which I have arranged in alphabetical order.

While there are two or three obvious interpolations in the first notebook, perhaps inserted for the benefit of Francis Plowden in 1809, it will be seen that in the diary Scully entered his afterthoughts (prefixed by 'N.B.'), either later on the same day or very soon after. Examination of the manuscript reveals only one revision: failing even by the use of smaller handwriting to fit an expanded account of the interview with Pitt into the space he had made for himself Scully had to complete the passage twenty-two pages later, between his entries for the next day and the following one.

In my transcription of the texts I have left punctuation and spelling as I found them, but superscripts in abbreviations have been put in the lower case and in the headings I have rendered the dates in a standardised form. Sparing use has been made of of the suffix *sic* after faulty or variant spellings. In some cases miswritten names are silently corrected in the index. As regards regards ecclesiastical titles I have left it to the context to show which bishops or priests were Roman Catholic and which belonged to the established church.

Apart from Robert Marshall's notes, names, place-names and subjects in the appendices have not been indexed unless they have been previously mentioned in the main body of the work. Even so the Index of Persons contains close on 350 names. Brief information about some two hundred of these will be found in the last appendix or occasionally in a footnote. Of the remainder the great majority can be identified to the extent of their first names or initials being mentioned in the text or suppliable from other sources.

I am indebted to the following for permission to publish documents copied from from their archives: the the Trustees of the National Library of Ireland; the Controller of Her Majesty's Stationery Office, for Crown copyright material in the Public Record at Kew; the Board of the British Library; the Clerk of the Records, House of Lords; and His Grace the Most Reverend Dr Desmond Connell, Archbishop of Dublin. This work being the outcome of research which was for the most part completed before the publication of *The Catholic Question* I need only repeat my thanks to the individuals listed therein, while adding the name of Julian Walton, who was inadvertently omitted.

B. C. MacDermot, May 1992

ABBREVIATIONS

ADD.MSS	Additional Manuscripts in the British Library
DDA	Dublin Diocesan Archives
HO	Home Office
NLI	National Library of Ireland

Note

For sources cited by short titles see the Select Bibliography.

INTRODUCTION

To see the Irish Catholic petition of 1805 in its historical perspective we must go back to the events immediately connected with the last relief act, that of 1793, which would have been still fresh in the memories of nearly all the petitioners and in which some of them had played an active or even a leading part. As the starting point we may choose the split in the Catholic body which occurred at the end of 1791, when the aristocracy, followed by some of the leading gentry, became distrustful of the republican tendencies they discerned in the Catholic Committee of that time and publicly dissociated themselves from it, becoming known in consequence as 'seceders'. The rest of the Committee, going ahead on their own, appointed a sub-committee to organise a network of local committees who were to send delegates to join the members of the committee resident in Dublin and form an assembly representative of the whole country.[1] In July 1792 fresh impetus was given to this operation when Wolfe Tone was taken on as Secretary of the Committee, and the so-called Catholic Convention (of merchants and country gentlemen, with a few doctors and lawyers), duly assembled in Dublin in December, at a time when the recent victories of the French armies on the continent had created alarm in London. Two hundred and thirty-three delegates then subscribed their names to a petition for total repeal of the penal laws, on behalf of themselves and their respective constituents, while the Archbishop of Dublin, Dr Troy, and the Bishop of Cork, Dr Moylan, who had attended one of the meetings, signed for themselves and the clergy of Ireland.[2] By-passing the Irish government in Dublin Castle, five delegates nominated by the Convention (among them John Keogh and Sir Thomas French) took the petition to London and at a levee on 2 January 1793 placed it in the hands of King George III himself.

Although Henry Dundas, the Home Secretary, told Hobart, Chief Secretary at Dublin Castle, that he would have preferred to postpone the presentation of the petition until the arrival of the Irish ministers in London (for the beginning of the parliamentary session), there seems to be no evidence that he tried to prevent the

[1] Counties were represented in two ways: by chosen members of the General Committee resident in Dublin; and by two members of each county committee who were ready to go up to Dublin when occasion required (Tone, *Life*, I, p.62).

[2] For the text and list of signatories see Tone, *Life*, I, p.451. The original on vellum is at the Public Record Office (HO 100/38.f.333).

delegates seeing the King.[1] The delegates, however, suspected that this was his object and their supposed frustration of his designs as well as the benevolence with which the King had politely addressed them induced a feeling of triumph which communicated itself to Ireland and encouraged a belief that the Catholics' demands were to be met in their entirety. In the dismay that followed the publication of a bill falling short of the Sub-Committee's expectations, principally by the exclusion of Catholics from parliament and the higher state offices, the delegates to London were pressed into admitting that the Home Secretary had made no specific promises and one of them, James Edward Devereux of Wexford, brought to light a curious incident in which one of the figures who was to play a leading part in the handling of the 1805 petition made a brief appearance on the scene. While the delegates were waiting for a final interview with Dundas, Evan Nepean, Undersecretary at the Home Office, came into the antechamber, invited John Keogh to follow him and kept him forty minutes in his office. As Keogh. when interrogated in the Sub-Committee, was evasive as to the subject of the conversation and volunteered only the unconvincing explanation that Nepean had told him "strong language would be most efficacious", the suspicion arose that he had signified the willingness of the Catholic body to accept a measure falling short of complete emancipation.[2]

At this point we find another prominent member of the 1804 committee already playing his characteristic role of mediator. Pointing out that the delegates had been instructed to get the King's answer to their petition, that the answer had been favourable and that they had therefore done their duty, the merchant Randal MacDonnell secured for them a vote of thanks rather than censure. With a lavishness that the committees of 1804 and later were neverable to emulate, the Sub-Committee then drew on funds raised by the convention to award each delegate a service of plate worth £150, to pay Wolfe Tone £1500 for his services, to order other disbursements amounting to £1500, to commission portraits of their leaders, and to vote for the erection of a statue of George III on the lawn of Leinster House.[3]

Hobart's bill, in addition to giving the elective franchise to Catholic forty shilling freeholders, enabled Catholics to bear arms, to become members of corporations, to serve on Grand Juries, to take degrees at Dublin University, to hold minor offices and to obtain commissions in the army below the rank that of 1792, it left Catholics on a footing of equality before of general—in short, coming on top of the previous relief acts, particularly the law with their Protestant fellow subjects in most spheres of everyday life and was regarded by the majority as a triumph rather than as a betrayal of their hopes.

[1] Dundas assured Hobart on 3 January that nothing material had passed between the delegates and the King (HO 100/46 f.1) but claiming pressure of business he did not write again until the 12th, when he said that he had read a (missing) paper to the delegates on the 7th (HO100/42 f.55).
[2] Tone, *Life*, I, p.256.
[3] Ibid. pp.264, 267.

An additional inducement to accept the bill as it stood was the belief that sooner rather than later it was bound to be followed by a further and perhaps final act of emancipation. That moment seemed to have come in January 1795, when Lord Fitzwilliam arrived in Ireland as Lord Lieutenant with instructions encouraging him to follow a conciliatory policy towards the Catholics, a policy which took on a more urgent aspect when in the same month the French captured the Dutch fleet and raised the prospect of an invasion of Ireland. The seceders of 1791 now threw their weight behind the Catholic Committee, petitions were organised throughout the country and Henry Grattan brought in a bill which was given a first reading in the Irish House of Commons. Had Lord Fitzwilliam not provoked his own recall to London by overplaying his hand in other ways this bill might have been passed, with or without modification in the committee stage. In the long term however the impetus that had carried the Catholics thus far was doomed to falter and it was not until 1813 that an emancipation bill (also tabled by Grattan) again secured a hearing in parliament.

The extension of the franchise to Catholic as well as Protestant forty shilling freeholders, striking though it was as a gesture of conciliation, in practice opened no constitutional path to further reform. The Catholic vote preponderated only in the countryside and then only in a portion of the sixty-four county seats, which in turn formed a minority in a parliament of 150 members; there were few contested elections; and Catholic tenants had only been given the vote because they could be counted upon to follow their landlords. Outside parliament the scope of legal agitation was drastically curtailed in August 1793 by the passage of the Convention Act, prohibiting delegated assemblies. The establishment of an Irish militia in the same session of parliament, followed in 1796 by the creation of a force of yeomanry, in time reduced the government's dependence on regular forces which might be withdrawn at any moment for foreign service. When from 1796 onwards Wolfe Tone and the leaders of the United Irishmen turned to revolution in complicity with the French the Catholic body ceased to profit from the general agitation against the English connexion that had hitherto encouraged the government to make concessions. With the foundation of the Orange Order in 1796 the spirit of eighteenth century religious indifference, from which too the Catholics had benefited, increasingly gave way to a new sectarianism that was exacerbated when the rebellion of 1798 (put down though it largely was by the Catholic soldiery of the militia) whipped up animosities on the Catholic side. To these factors may be added the debilitating effect of the 1793 act itself. As Charles Ryan, one of the leaders of the Convention, pointed out at the time,[1] the "remnants of the popery laws" were not enough to interest the people, "for men would not exert themselves just to make such a man a judge or such a man a member of parliament". On the Protestant side it blunted sympathies hitherto evoked by such catchwords as

[1] Ibid. p.265.

'religious toleration' and 'freedom of worship', and the continued use of the emotive word 'emancipation' became increasingly resented. Comparison with the lot of the English Catholics invited the reflection that the Irish had little to complain about and much to be thankful for. In Ireland Catholic marriages had always been recognised, the Catholic tenantry now had the vote and the younger sons of the gentry could make careers in the army, whereas English Catholics could be married only by ministers of the established church, had no share in the elective franchise and were denied commissions in the forces.

After the rebellion a new opportunity to press Catholic claims from a position of some advantage arose when the long contemplated plan for a union of the Irish and British legislatures was put before the Irish parliament and Pitt's government feared that the measure could not be carried without at least the tacit acquiescence of the Irish Catholics. At the time of the recall of Lord Fitzwilliam, in April 1795, when it was learnt that a final act of relief might have to be postponed until such a union, a Catholic meeting had declared that they would rather forgo their own emancipation than acquiesce in a surrender of the liberties of their country.[1] In the meantime, however, Ireland had been convulsed by the rebellion fomented by the leaders of the United Irishmen, much repressive legislation remained in force and those leading Catholics who had been United Irishmen themselves or connected with them found it prudent to lie low—John Keogh to the extent of settling temporarily in England. There no longer existed therefore any representative body capable of uniting the Catholics on the question and making a deal either with the opposition in the Irish parliament or with the government. As private individuals Catholics were as likely as their Protestant fellow subjects to hold different opinions on a measure which had political and economic implications extending beyond the consideration, also a matter of personal judgement, whether it would make a final relief act more or less likely. The die was cast at a meeting in Lord Fingall's house in December 1798, when in the absence of unanimity the decision was taken that it was inexpedient to adopt any resolution. On 13 January 1800 a meeting[2] at which the young Daniel O'Connell was the leading speaker, passed a resolution indignantly challenging this determination "not to come forward in the distinct character of Catholics", but this was not a view commanding wide support and it was put forward too late, for the Union bill was to be passed by the Irish House of Commons six weeks later. In the meantime Marquis Cornwallis, Lord Lieutenant and Commander-in-Chief, and Viscount Castlereagh, Chief Secretary, had been left free to neutralise opposition or win active support by the judicious use of arguments *ad hominem,* in some cases hints of future reward, discreet approaches to the Catholic prelates and a persuasive pamphlet literature to which Edward Cooke, Theobald McKenna and Pitt himself, in a reprint of his speech in the House of

[1] Lecky, III, p.319.
[2] Plowden, *Historical Review*, III, p.983.

Commons, made the most effective contributions. Making much of the point that emancipation could be achieved with less danger to the constitution in a united parliament, they managed to let most Catholics believe that a relief measure was certain to follow the act without entering into any commitment binding on the existing government or a future administration.

Pitt nevertheless saw a settlement of the Catholic question as one of the chief benefits to be reaped from the Union, and for the sake of political consistency if not of honour it was now up to him to tackle it. Striking while the iron was hot he therefore induced his cabinet in January 1801 to adopt the outlines of a new Catholic relief act—only to have his proposals immediately turned down by the King. Pitt must have known that the latter had believed or professed to believe since 1795, when Lord Fitzwilliam's enemies put the idea into his head, that he would be breaking his coronation oath to protect the established church if he sanctioned the admission of Catholics to parliament or the higher office of state, but he may have hoped that in the context of the Act of Union, a clause of which entrenched the Protestant church as the established church of Ireland, the monarch would take the advice of his ministers on the matter. However Pitt's opponents on the Catholic question now brought in the Archbishops of Canterbury and Armagh and the Bishop of London to add their endorsement to the King's interpretation of his oath, a division arose in the cabinet and Pitt had to yield to a scruple which not only demanded the respect due to a matter of conscience but embodied the prejudices, open or unavowed, which the popular monarch shared with most of his subjects, inside as well as outside parliament.

Pitt having tendered his resignation, Lord Castlereagh wrote to Lord Cornwallis on 9 February to explain why Pitt did not think it expedient to press the measure "in present circumstances" and to brief him on what he was to say to the Catholics.[1] The reason that most strongly operated on Pitt's mind, he said, was the conviction that were the measure to be carried against the opposition of the House of Lords and the King it would be deprived of all its benefits (i.e by failing to bring about the desired reconciliation between the Catholics and their Protestant fellow subjects). Without bringing forward the King's name, Lord Cornwallis was to tell the Catholics that an obstacle which ministers could not surmount precluded them from bringing forward the measure while in office, that they were retiring from the King's service in the belief that this was most likely to contribute to the ultimate success of the measure and that they could rely on the zealous support of those now retiring, and many who remained, when it could be given with any prospect of success. He went on to say that while Pitt could not concur at the moment in any hopeless attempt to force the question, he would in the meantime do his utmost to establish their cause in the public favour. Exceeding his instructions, Lord Cornwallis gave Lord Fingall and the Catholic Archbishop of Dublin a declaration

[1] Cornwallis, *Correspondence*, III, p.33.

of his personal sentiments (subsequently published in the press) urging the Catholics "to be sensible of the benefit they possess by having so many characters of eminence pledged not to embark in the service of government, except on the terms of the Catholic privileges being obtained".[1] Within a month, however, Pitt secretly conveyed an assurance to the King, when he was stricken by a recurrence of his mental illness, that he would not raise the Catholic question again in the King's lifetime, whether in or out of office; he openly lent his support to the formation of a new government under an avowed anti-Catholic, Henry Addington; and in the following year consented to Lord Castlereagh's joining that administration.

In addition to the King's coronation oath another obstacle to future progress had taken shape which only became fully apparent in 1808, when the so-called veto controversy broke out, but was already looming up when the petition of 1805 came before parliament. Up to Grattan's bill of 1795 successive relief measures had taken the form of a simple repeal of particular penal laws. In the run-up to the Union, however, the prospect of the incorporation of Catholics into the body politic naturally invited closer attention to the influence which their Bishops and the Pope in Rome were believed to exercise upon the laity. In January 1799 Lord Castlereagh entered into an agreement with the four Archbishops and six Bishops which, subject to the approval of the Holy See, provided on the one hand for salaries for the clergy, on the other for a government voice in nominations to vacant sees. Two years later the veto became in effect linked with the restoration of full political rights to the laity when a role for the crown in nominations to vacant sees was included in the measure that Pitt submitted to the King, a measure endorsed by a cabinet of which Lord Grenville, the future leader of the opposition to Pitt, was a prominent member.[2]

In the light of our present knowledge of Pitt's commitment to the King it is tempting to dismiss the expectations aroused by his return to power as mere wishful thinking. For contemporaries, however, the situation was not so clear-cut. While the nature of the King's scruples was generally known, it was not unreasonable to suppose that they might yield to argument and in any case they did not necessarily preclude concessions falling short of seats in parliament and the highest offices, for instance payment of salaries for the clergy and equal religious rights in the armed forces. Rumours of Pitt's promises to the King had indeed passed into circulation, as Charles Butler informed Lord Fingall in a letter of 6 February 1804, [3] but in the nature of the case they could be neither avowed nor denied, it being an essential feature of the constitution that the King acted only on the advice of his ministers,

[1] Ibid. p.347.

[2] Ward. *Dawn of the Catholic Revival*, II, p.216, citing an entry in the diary of Dr. Douglass, Vicar Apostolic of the London district.

[3] Fingall Papers, NLI MS 11,294.

and it remained uncertain what his attitude might be if the Catholic question were brought up by others. It is not to be wondered at that Irish Catholics, who remembered Lord Cornwallis' assurances, should have taken the straightforward view that, having gone out on the Catholic question, Pitt was bound to take it up again on his coming back, but it is surprising to find Lord Hardwicke taking a similar line in a letter which he wrote to his half-brother a few days before Pitt announced the formation of his new government:

> I have no doubt that Pitt will bring on the Catholic question during the present reign; and whenever he does bring it on, I am sanguine enough to hope from his judgement and discretion as well as from the peculiar talent he possesses of comprehending all the bearings of the most difficult questions, that he will be able to frame and enforce such a measure as will either give general satisfaction or at least have the advantage of setting the question at rest, by proving that satisfaction cannot be given. The sitting in Parliament seems almost to follow from the privilege of voting for Members of Parliament which was conceded by the act of 1793. There are many offices which might be held by Roman Catholics without inconvenience or danger—but it would fairer if limitations were defined by the law and not left to the discretion of the King.[1]

Lord Hardwicke, while dwelling more on what he saw as the difficulty of making arrangements for the Irish Catholic church, went on to say that "the laity might be easily satisfied." Whatever he meant, it is clear from his archives that he was far from expecting any initiative from the latter, who had given him no trouble since the autumn of 1803, when a solitary committee in Galway had easily been persuaded to drop a petition.[2] As against this. however, apprehensions were aroused in him by reports from London of the intentions of Charles James Fox. Whether or not he was aware that Fox was trying to entice Grattan to come out of his retirement in County Wicklow in order to give a lead on Ireland in parliament,[3] he was from 12 October 1803 onwards expecting Fox to bring the Catholic question up in the House of Commons, for the sole purpose, as he thought, of creating embarrassment for the Addington government. When in the end Fox desisted it was perhaps partly because of his failure for the moment to bring Grattan back to public life, but more directly because of the evident futility of asking for the Catholics something that they had not yet demanded themselves. By the beginning of February 1804, when it when it was announced in the *Morning Chronicle* that the question was not to be stirred

[1] Hardwicke Papers, Add.Mss. 35,709 f.1.
[2] MacDonagh, *The Viceroy's Postbag*, p.191.
[3] Cf. Grattan, *Life and Times*, V, p.239.

owing to the "moderation of the Catholics themselves" it was too late to organise an Irish petition for the current session, but, as the first document in the present collection shows, preparations were started in good time for that of 1805.

In the forging of links between the Foxite opposition and the Irish Catholics the key figure seems to have been William Parnell, grandfather of Charles Stewart Parnell. He was, on the one hand, a friend of Grattan and a neighbour in Co. Wicklow of the young Lord King who sat with the opposition in the House of Lords; on the other, it is likely that he was already on terms of friendship with George Evans of Portrane, who was to marry his sister in August 1805. George Evans in his turn knew the Dublin businessman James Ryan, who in addition to having an aggressive personality enjoyed the qualification of having been Secretary to the last public Catholic meeting held in Dublin, the ad hoc one called on 13 January 1800 to urge Catholics to oppose the Union. To guard against the danger of the project being nipped in the bud either by the Irish administration in Dublin Castle or by defeatists among the Catholics themselves, Ryan on his part necessarily confined his preliminary soundings to those in his own business community most likely to support him, but as a petition from which any important part of the Catholic body dissociated itself would not have served the purpose of the opposition it may be assumed that the intention from the beginning was to bring in also the nobility, gentry and professional classes.[1] This second stage was reached on 27 October 1804 when the senior Catholic peer, the eighth Earl of Fingall, was pressed into the chair, and the central figure of the present work made his first appearance in a Catholic committee.

Denys Scully, the eldest surviving son of James Scully of Kilfeacle in County Tipperary and now in the thirty-second year of his age, was one of the first batch of Irish Catholics to take advantage of the 1792 act allowing Catholics to become barristers. Having eaten his dinners at the Middle Temple and attended Trinity College, Cambridge, in 1794 and 1795, he had been called to the Irish bar in 1796. He may have returned to London for further studies as a special pleader and he was perhaps absent from Ireland during the rebellion of 1798. From the end of that year we find him enrolled as a member of the Lawyers Corps of yeomanry; following his profession on the Leinster circuit; visiting Moira House (in its heyday the meeting place of the Irish Whigs); and corresponding with Lady Moira, her daughter and her chaplain, all three of them fierce opponents of the Union. Scully's family, "to a man" he tells us, supported that measure and he himself would appear to have at least passively accepted it.

[1] The petition being for the restoration of civil rights there was no reason for the Irish Catholic hierarchy to let themselves be involved until, when it was about to come before parliament, Lord Grenville tried to assuage Protesant fears by seeking an expression of their consent in principle to a role for government in the nomination and supervision of bishops.

Despite his previous Whig contacts, when Scully first ventured into public life, immediately after the Emmet rising in 1803, he had become to all outward appearances a 'Castle Catholic', not afraid to bestow praise on Lord Hardwicke and Lord Redesdale in a long pamphlet urging his countrymen not to side with the French upon the renewal of the war with France, nor in a second pamphlet to link his name with that of the well known Castle Catholic, Theobald McKenna. Perhaps still more significantly, he had formed a social connection with the Lord Lieutenant by his marriage in London on 25 November 1801 to Mary Huddleston,[1] the elder daughter of Ferdinand Huddleston, whose manor of Sawston Hall was less than ten miles distant from Lord Hardwicke's magnificent demesne of Wimpole Park, near Cambridge. The Huddlestons were a respectable old Catholic family which could boast of Plantagenet descent but could at this time barely afford a dowry of £2000, payable in instalments. However, if disparity in wealth, worldly status and religion ruled out any close degree of intimacy, relations between the two houses went rather further than a grateful acceptance by the poorer one of a haunch of venison in winter. On being invited to raise a militia regiment in 1793 Lord Hardwicke had written to Ferdinand Huddleston offering commissions to two of his sons and the surprised Ferdinand, after checking that Lord Hardwicke realised they were Catholics, had accepted for Richard and Edward. In 1799 Richard had gone with him in the Cambridgeshire Militia to Dublin, and had since risen to be the regimental Major: as Colonel of the regiment Lord Hardwicke corresponded with him on regimental affairs, addressing him as "Dear Huddleston." Moreover, in March 1800 the younger daughter, Jane, dined at Wimpole and met Prince William, and in the following May she was there again, this time meeting Lord Hardwicke's half-brother, Charles Yorke. In May 1805 Lady Hardwicke, in London for her husband's Garter ceremony, returned Jane's call in Thayer Street and made polite enquiries about her aunt, Mrs Bostock.[2]

Thus when Denys and Mary Scully returned to Dublin after their marriage and set up house at 34 Baggot Street they could expect to receive a modicum of attention from the Hardwickes and there is enough evidence to show that they were not disappointed. By 1 March 1802 Lady Jerningham in London had heard that "Mrs Skully is . . . on a very agreeable footing in Dublin; Lady Hardwicke has put her in fashion with the nobles, and Lady Moira . . . says the Huddlestons are her relations, so this has given a high view of Mrs Skully's nobility!"[3] A letter of 29 April from Mary Scully to her mother implies that she had been presented at the Viceregal court. Another of 12 June refers to attending a private dinner in Phoenix Park, at

[1] Lest Scully should be suspected of ulterior motives, it may be mentioned that negotiations for the marriage preceded Lord Hardwicke's appointment to Ireland (see MacDermot, *The Catholic Question* p.49).

[2] See the Huddleston Papers, particularly C2/84, C3/HR16 and C1/MH54.

[3] *The Jerningham Letters*, ed. Egerton Castle.

which Lord Hardwicke said many fine things about Richard, and adds that her husband was all prepared to go to the last levee when his law business prevented him. Finally, in March 1803 she wrote of the preceding winter's gaiety in Dublin, with its many balls and concerts at the Castle. If we hear no more of her Castle life it is probably because her declining health curtailed both her correspondence and her social activities.[1] On her husband's side the overwhelmingly Protestant complexion of the Viceregal court offered no warm welcome to a young, Catholic and untitled barrister, but from the circumstance that Scully kept up with Lord Hardwicke after the latter's retirement it may be inferred that they were on a not unfriendly personal footing.

In submitting an offer by his father to raise a regiment in July 1803 and in intervening a year later to get his brother Edmund out of a scrape Scully dealt direct with the Lord Lieutenant or his secretary.[2] There is no evidence to show that he made any contact with the Civil Department at Dublin Castle, which dealt with Catholic affairs and to which McKenna reported, but by 1804 he was on terms of intimacy with an official who was now on the periphery of the administration but had formerly been at the centre of things as the private secretary of Lord Castlereagh—his neighbour in Baggot Street, Robert Marshall, Inspector General of Exports and Imports. How he and Scully became acquainted we do not know, but in 1805 Mary Scully's cousins, Betsy and Fanny Huddleston, who had visited her in Dublin, went to Harrogate with him; and in a letter of 1 August 1805 her sister Jane described him as "a great friend of Mr Scully . . . one of the most amiable men I ever knew."[3]

To Scully's social connection with the Lord Lieutenant and his friendship with Marshall we must add a third ingredient which alone made it possible for him to embark on the intrigue that forms a sub-plot to the main story of the 1805 petition: the presence in Dublin Castle of a Chief Secretary who by temperament and previous experience was cut out to play the secretive role required of him. As an Undersecretary at the Home Office, where he had mystified John Keogh in the curious episode mentioned above, Sir Evan Nepean had been in charge of the police department and during his ten years at the Admiralty he had had the handling of foreign intelligence that included reports on the continental activities of the disaffected, among whom there would have been many United Irishmen. Indeed, on his appointment to Ireland Henry Addington had recommended him to Lord Hardwicke specifically on the ground that he was "acquainted with the names, the system and the projects of the disaffected, in the development of which he was at one time peculiarly useful."[4] At his own level he enjoyed a sort of private friendship

[1] See her letters in *The Catholic Question*, pp 55-115 *passim.*

[2] See *The Catholic Question*, pp.67,74.

[3] Huddleston Papers,C1/MH42,58.

[4] See his biography in *The History of Parliament: The House of Commons,* 1790-1820.

with Pitt (in a way that Lord Hardwicke did not) and he may been allowed or even instructed by Pitt to report directly to him if he should see see fit.[1] When he rose to a higher sphere in 1802 and became a baronet with a seat in parliament he could bask in the reputation of having been one of the leading civil servants of his day. However, although he was at first very favourably impressed by his new Chief Secretary's conduct of business at Dublin Castle, Lord Hardwicke was soon deploring in him a lack of judgement, a tendency to act on his own and a vanity which made him attach greater weight to his own discoveries than to reports received by often better informed colleagues. In Scully, at first indirectly through Robert Marshall but later in person, he was now to find himself, whether intentionally or not, the accomplice of a lawyer "who could not take his tea without a stratagem"[2] and drawn by him into a manoeuvre which, if it failed in its primary object of establishing direct contact between the Catholic body and Pitt, helped to foil his own and the Lord Lieutenant's efforts to get the petition postponed to that ever elusive day when it might be presented with a better prospect of success.

[1] In a letter of 28 July 1805 William Cobbett wrote to Windham that Lord Hardwicke complained of "the powers with which Sir Evan Nepean was vested to treat with the Catholics &c &c independent of the Lord Lieutenant. This, you know, is assez à la manière of Mr. Pitt" (Calendar of Windham Papers).

[2] A line adapted by Thomas Wyse from the poet Edward Young and applied by him to Scully in the sketch he drew of him in his *History of the late Catholic Association* published in 1829.

I

THE CATHOLIC COMMITTEE OF 1804

James Ryan to the Freeman's Journal

[Extract] Marlborough Street, 4 August 1810

. . . . .

It is unnecessary for me to particularize the unfortunate transactions which took place in July, 1803. It is not my purpose to advert to them for any other purpose than to point out their natural effects upon the public mind, and to bring to recollection, the strong measures which the Government subsequently adopted, armed as it was, by the suspension of the Habeas Corpus Act, and the enaction of Martial Law, and instigated to those measures by the general imputation of its inactivity previous to the 23rd of July.[1] Such proceedings could not have failed to create a considerable reluctance upon the part of the people of this Country, to assemble upon any political subject.

In the summer of 1804 Lord King, a nobleman of distinguished rank and talents in England, feeling for the degraded situation in which our body were placed, intimated to my friend Mr. Wm. Parnell, of Avondale, his intention of moving in the succeeding session of Parliament, for the entire abolition of the Penal Code. After some correspondence between these personages and, (as I was informed) Lord King having consulted Mr Fox, relative to the step he mediated [*sic*], it was conceived no motion in Parliament would be productive of beneficial consequences, unless there was a previous application on the part of the Catholics, to both Houses, by way of petition. In such an event, Mr Fox expressed strong hopes of success, believing it would be impossible for Mr Pitt to refuse his support to the prayer of our application when it was so well understood, through the declarations of his friends, *that he never would return to power*, unless he was privileged by a certain authority to propose and support the Catholic claims. Those considerations determined Lord King to relinquish his laudable and patriotic intentions. Mr. Parnell, and my friend George Evans of Portrane, called upon me, communicated the facts I have just stated, and urged me to endeavour to procure the desired Petitions. I was sensible of the difficulties I would have to encounter, but hoping that substantial advantages would result from the effort, and encouraged in that hope, by the high authority who, it was reported to me, recommended it, I conceived it would have been pusillanimous and cowardly to have shrunk from the attempt. I accordingly undertook it, and as it may throw some light on the subject

[1] The Irish administration had been castigated for letting the Emmet rising of that day take it by surprise.

I have in view, I shall state some communications I had with a *few* Catholics, previously to my venturing to call upon any number of them to assemble, and *their* subsequent conduct.

Being at this period in habits of intimacy with Mr. Keogh, of Mount Jerome, and knowing his previous experience in Catholic affairs, I called upon and imparted to him the object I had in view; I solicited his advice and councel, and urged him much to attend the first meeting which would take place. Mr. Keogh approved of the undertaking, and said, if I would have the meeting at Kimmage, (a place where my family were for the summer months, and further in the country, by two miles, than Mount Jerome), he would attend it.[1] I replied, I conceived it would be improper to have it there, as Government might attribute *other* motives to us, than those which would actually occasion our meeting, and that I was convinced if the Catholics would assemble, it should be as publicly as they might wish, and as free from disguise and concealment as possible; this point being disposed of Mr. Keogh favoured me with his advice as to the men I should commence an association with, which he said he gave as the result of long experience. He commenced by recommending me not to have anything to do with Lord Fingall, or any of those of his rank or connections, because of their obligation to obey the mandates of the Castle; also not to embarrass my efforts and proceedings, by having named on any Committee which should be appointed, Mr. McDonnell, because, said he, he is always *wavering* and *never decided*; not to trouble myself about Mr. James Connolly, for he cared not for anything but *money-making*; not to encumber myself with Mr. Denis Thomas O'Brien, for he would be afraid of his own *shadow*; not to have Mr. Weldon of Dame Street, for he was what he deemed an *Orange Catholic*; but, said Mr. Keogh, form a committee of such men as the O'Brien's of High Street,[2] and you will be sure of carrying every measure you may desire, without the vexatious embarrassments which the men of the other description will inevitably throw in your way. On this point we also differed, as I declared my resolution to guard as much as possible against divisions and jealousies amongst the Catholic Body, and that Lord Fingall and his friends should have the opportunity (if they possessed the will) *for the first time in their lives*, to co-operate with their suffering brethren, in an application for their Emancipation. I had myself next introduced to Sir Thomas French, to whom I also imparted the objects I had in view, and it would be injustice on my part not to acknowledge, that to his exertions I was considerably indebted fur the final success of my undertaking, although I shall hereafter have to mention his name, *not* with similar feelings of approbation. Sir Thomas approved of the endeavour to unite all descriptions in the intended application, and confident of his support, I commenced my labours.

[1] Keogh's house lay in what is now the Mount Jerome cemetery; Kimmage about a mile and a half to the south-west. Both are now part of Dublin.

[2] Richard and Michael O'Brien, wholesale woollen drapers.

From the causes I have already stated, I was obliged to begin by making personal applications at the houses of such Catholics as I considered would be least likely to be awed into inactivity, by the fear of offending Lord Hardwicke's administration, which it was known had been formed by Mr. Addington (now Lord Sidmouth), who came into power upon the avowed principle of resisting the concessions, which it was generally understood his predecessor, Mr. Pitt, had determined to recommend the granting of to our Body. After visiting every house where I had the hope of success and which took me above three weeks to perform, no more than fourteen gentlemen attended the first meeting, which was convened at my house, and when met they seemed to think it prudent to separate, without entertaining the consideration of the question for which they had been assembled. At this meeting, of which Lord Fingal was Chairman,[1] Counsellor Scully attended and proposed a resolution of thanks to me, for having had the boldness to permit Catholics to assemble in my house; I resisted the proffered compliment, and we separated, having only come to the determination of meeting at the end of a fortnight. The result of this meeting I communicated to Mr. Keogh, and solicited him without effect to attend our adjourned meeting. During this interval I was employed in giving every publicity which I could to our intended meeting, being restrained by a positive stipulation at the meeting I have alluded to, from an insertion of it in the public papers . . . .

Source: Freeman's Journal, 11 August 1810.

Theobald McKenna to Sir Evan Nepean

Copy Grove Lodge, Stillorgan, 18 October 1804

Sir,

On the best enquiries I have been able to make, I cannot find that any motion has reached Dublin relative to the matter on which you did me the honour to speak with me. I have for some time disused very much my communication with the distant counties, but I do think that your informant took the prevailing sentiment manifested in conversation for an overt act. I think it not uninteresting to government to observe that upon this subject there has never existed so much eagerness as at present. I attribute this to a wish in men who are satisfied with their own acquisitions to open new prospects to the rising generation. This would be got over but for the irritation occasioned by the spirit manifested on the part of many

[1] A slip of memory: Lord Fingall first attended on 27 October.

Protestants since July 1803, and this perhaps may be resolved into a wish to monopolize the emoluments of the yeomanry.

I observe some compliments paid to Mr Grattan at Kilkenny. This strikes me as the people there are not in habits of political action; the impulse was new, it will not stop there, and whatever is set on foot will find a ready and immediate correspondence in Waterford. There it may stop, as the people in the adjoining counties are too much dispersed to be brought together without greater pains than are likely to be taken. I think I can trace the originating cause in the Kilkenny affair, altho' I only know of it from the newspapers. I think it highly probable that a communication, utterly independent of Dublin, or its vicinity, may be set up from the counties I have named with political characters in England.

I trust you will excuse me troubling you with these details [rest missing].

Source: HO 100/123 f.112.

Sir Evan Nepean to John King

Secret. Dublin Castle 24 October 1804

Dear Sir,

Mr Parnell, one of the sons of the late Sir John Parnell, came to Dublin a few days ago from the county of Wicklow, his general place of residence, and called on me at the Castle yesterday afternoon, and, in the course of the conversation which took place between us, he stated that a meeting of the principal Roman Catholicks of Dublin, meaning merchants and men of property, is to take place to day for the purpose of considering an application to Parliament for the repeal of the several acts, by which persons of that religion are subject to certain disqualifications.

On his mentioning this circumstance, I asked him whether it was intended to be a public, or a private meeting? what the particular points he adverted to were? and who were the persons who were most active in bringing forward the application? He told me that they were the Byrnes, McDonnel, the Ryans and many others, all men however of consequence in point of property, and that the meeting would not be publickly notified—That the principal objects they had in view, were the repeal of the disqualifications in respect to the filling certain publick offices, and to the sitting in Parliament—That those and other restraints had been severely felt by the Roman Catholicks, and had disinclined many of that religious persuasion from endeavouring to exert any influence they may now possess over the lower orders of the people, who, under an impression that their superiors possess no influence with government, did not look up to them as much as they had formerly been accustomed to do—That it was the opinion of the promoters of the petition, if any attention should be paid by Parliament to their application, that the lower orders of people would begin to think their situation not so desperate as they now felt it, that the distinctions between them and the Protestants were likely to be discontinued, that they would then be likely to listen to the advice of the upper classes, and that a stop would thereby be put to any intercourse or connexion with France.

I could clearly discover that he (Mr. Parnell) was actively engaged in bringing forward the petition, and that he wished to draw from me an approbation of the measure, and an assurance of promoting the objects of this petition. He told me that the Committee intended to send the petition in the first instance to Mr. Pitt, and that in the event of his discouraging their application, that it was their intention to put the petition into the hands of Mr. Fox or some other person connected with his party—That the Roman Catholics had no wish to make it a matter of opposition, but that the placing it in such hands would naturally render it so; that he knew that party (meaning the opposition) were disposed to promote the objects of the petition, and that the Prince of Wales had also expressed an intention of using His Royal Highness's influence with his friends in its favour.

I told Mr. Parnell that I conceived the bringing forward any petition of that description in the present state of the country would be very injudicious; that the public mind was already a good deal agitated, and that the stirring questions of that importance in the present moment would operate as a further interruption to the tranquillity of the country—he told me that he and his friends thought differently, and that the compliance with the prayer of the petition would be the only effectual means of tranquillizing the minds of people, and of inducing them to become good subjects, which they were not in the present moment.

I asked him what was the intention of the Roman Catholics in respect to the clergy? He said that he did not believe any one member of the Catholic Church was at that moment in the secret; that they did not mean to interfere about them; that they cared very little whether they had salaries or not; that they did not mean to say a word upon the subject of the tythes, considering that as any other tax in the country, to be disposed of by the government to whatever description of clergy it pleased to favour.

I found from Mr. Parnell in a very early stage of our conversation that the plan had been completely arranged, and that nothing I could say on the subject would be likely to produce the smallest effect, even for the delaying the petition, if I had been disposed to express any wishes of that sort. I therefore refrained from giving him any further opinion, than what I have already stated, upon the measure.

On Mr. Parnell's leaving me he told me that he would call on me again on Friday, when he would tell me what had been done, and the substance of the petition, and in what way it may be determined to dispose of it.

I did not learn from Mr. Parnell's conversation that he had had any communication with the Roman Catholic gentlemen of Roscommon, but he rather wished me to understand that the measure had very recently been determined upon.

I think it right upon this occasion to inform you that about ten days ago an intimation was given to me by Mr. French, one of the representatives of the county of Roscommon, that the Roman Catholics had some project, of the description I have mentioned, in contemplation, and that on receiving this information, I availed myself of every proper opportunity that offered of enquiring, particularly of Mr. McKenna (a gentleman of the Roman Catholic persuasion who has been in habits of communicating confidentially with government) what had transpired on the subject. I found that neither of the persons with whom I communicated had been consulted, and that no credit was then given to the report. I have however since learnt that Mr. McKenna has lost the confidence of the Catholicks, in consequence of a supposed correspondence between him, and a gentleman, employed in one of the State Departments in England.[1].

The Lord Lieutenant has directed me to communicate these circumstances to you, for Lord Hawkesbury's information, and to acquaint you that you will from time to time be apprized of the further proceedings of the Committee.

Source: HO 100/123 f.104.

Sir Evan Nepean to John King

Secret. Dublin Castle, 25 October 1804

Dear Sir,

After I had closed my letter to you of yesterday's date, I heard that Lord Fingall had arrived in town and had expressed an intention of calling upon me. I therefore thought it right to delay the sending of my letter to you untill I had had an opportunity of seeing his Lordship. He soon after paid me a visit, and, after discussing the business which had led to this interview, I asked his Lordship, confidentially, whether any information had reached him of the intended meeting of the Roman Catholics? He told me that he had not then heard of it, and did not believe any such meeting could be likely to take place; that he would however make some enquiries, and let me know.

His Lordship has since called upon me, and informed me that the meeting is to take place Saturday next, for the purpose of discussing the different objects, and for

[1] Identified below as Edward Cooke.

preparing a petition to Parliament, and that the person with whom he communicated had apprized him that he would be desired to attend it.

His Lordship endeavoured to impress on my mind a belief that he had not been previously consulted on the propriety of the intended meeting, and that if he had been so apprized he should certainly have communicated the circumstance to me. He stated that he did not then know what communication had taken place with the gentlemen of the Roman Catholic persuasion distant from the metropolis, and that he was undecided as to the part he should take at the meeting, but that he had so far however made up his mind, that if he found it to be the general opinion of the respectable Catholics of the country that the petition should be presented, he should certainly become a party to it. That his view of the question might be different from mine in one respect; but that I might be assured if he had not felt the pressing necessity of further concessions being made to the Catholics he should not have acquiesced in any petition, particularly in the present moment, and that no man in the country was less disposed than he was to join in any step that might be embarrassing or even inconvenient to government.

With these assurances his Lordship left me, and if any thing further should transpire before the meeting of Saturday it will of course be communicated to you for Lord Hawkesbury's information.

Source: HO 100/123 f.114.

Sir Evan Nepean to John King

Private. Dublin Castle, 25 October 1804

Dear King,

You will receive by the express two letters on the subject of the intended petition of the Roman Catholics, which will explain to you nearly all I know of the purport of the petition.

It has been mentioned to me, and I believe some credence may be given to the report, that Lord King is likely to have had some hand in bringing forward the Catholic petition—his Lordship is known to be in the most intimate habits of acquaintance with Mr. Parnell and has at times resided months together with him in his house in Wicklow, indeed Mr. Parnell hinted to me that he knew his Lordship would, if called upon, be ready to bring forward the Catholic petition in the House of Lords. I have also had occasion to know, from more circumstances than one, that Mr. Parnell is very much connected with Mr. Grattan, resides within a very short distance from him in the county, and is constantly in habits of intercourse with him, and I should not be surprized if it should hereafter turn out, that he has also been one of the promoters of the petition.

You will see by Mr. McKenna's private letter to me, what he thinks of the opinion of the country in respect to the Catholics—he is an intelligent man, tho' not, as you will see by his own account, so much in the confidence of his countrymen as he has formerly been.

When I last saw Mr. McKenna he told me he was then engaged in a work[1] which would shortly be sent to the press on subjects connected with the situation of the Catholics in this country, which will furnish matter well worthy of notice in respect to the clergy. I shall endeavour to prevail on him to let me see the manuscript, as I understand it contains a return of all the Catholic ecclesiastics with their rank and distribution.

No accurate account of that sort have I yet been able to get, though I was desired by Mr. Pitt to procure it, if I found I could do so without creating a suspicion of my having some object in view by that enquiry, beyond the satisfying my curiosity.

Dr. Troy told me a few days ago that the Catholic clergy some years since amounted to no less than 2000 persons, but that since the war and the difficulties that had presented themselves in the education of their priests in foreign countries, the number had been considerably diminished, and in the present moment did not, in his opinion, exceed fourteen or fifteen hundred—this information however I have since been told by the Lord Chancellor[2] is entirely fallacious, as from a variety of accounts which have reached his Lordship, it appears that the number, instead of being diminished, has of late years been increased.

In discussing this subject with his Lordship he told me he had understood that the measure of giving salaries to the Roman Catholic clergy was considered in England as a measure nearly, if not quite decided upon. I am however disposed to think that his Lordship's informant may be mistaken, as I was told by the Lord Lieutenant no longer ago than yesterday, that his Excellency's opinion had not even been consulted on the subject, and what the more inclines me to entertain doubts of any determination on that head is, that I perfectly well recollect, during one of my last conversations with Mr. Pitt, that he told me some consideration would be likely to be had of the measure when my report of their rank and numbers should be communicated to him. If I am not misinformed, a return of the Roman Catholic clergy was made during Lord Cornwallis' residence in this country, which can of course be found in your correspondence.[3]

In case Lord Fingall returns from the funeral of the Duke of Leinster this evening, it is probable I shall see his Lordship in the course of tomorrow, and I shall then be likely to have some further information from him. I rather believe that I forgot to

[1] *Thoughts on the civil condition and relations of the Roman Catholic Clergy, Religion and people in Ireland*, J. Budd, London, 1805.

[2] John Mitford, first Baron Redesdale.

[3] HO 100/99 & 100/128 f.153; Castlereagh, *Correspondence*, IV p 97.

mention to you in either of my former letters that his Lordship observed in the course of our conversation yesterday, that, if the management of the business had been left to him he should have felt his ground before he should have advised the presenting the petition and that he did not much confide in the prudence of Mr. Parnell or of the friends with whom he believed he had communicated, evidently alluding to Lord King as one of them.

[PS]

Mr. McKenna's correspondent in England, to which I have alluded as a person employed in one of the State Departments, is Mr. Cooke.

Source: HO 100/123, f.108.

Sir Evan Nepean to John King

Private Dublin Castle, 3 p.m. 27 October 1804

My dear King,

A private friend of mine has just called on me and informed me that several Roman Catholic gentlemen are now at the house of a Mr. Ryan, discussing the different heads of the intended petition, and are likely to sit for some time. I understand that Ryan and others are extremely violent, and that some difficulty will be felt by the well disposed in stemming the torrent and keeping things quiet.

You will perhaps ask me what has occasioned this violence on the part of Mr. Ryan? to this I can only answer that it is stated by him to have arisen from a want of common attention to the Catholics—the continuance of the Ld. Chancellor in his office, and a variety of other matters which I shall tell you when we next meet, an event which I suppose will very shortly happen.

Lord Fingall, who I believe, is now at Mr. Ryan's, dines with me today, as does Mr. Parnell, but it so happens that there are a dozen other people of the party, so that it is hardly probable that I shall be able to have any conversation with his Lordship, or that Mr. Parnell will say anything to me on the subject this evening.

11 p.m.

I have just learnt from Mr. Parnell that not less than fifty persons met today and that a debate took place on the propriety of presenting the petition in the present moment, and it having been decided in favour of bringing it forward a committee has been appointed to meet on Saturday next, to prepare the petition.

Source: HO 100/123, f.122.

Proceedings of a meeting of the Catholics at the house of James Ryan Esq.in Marlborough Street, Dublin

27 October 1804

Present: Lord Fingall, Sir Thos. French, banker, Mr T.D. O'Brien, R. McDonnell, John Byrne (son of E. Byrne), Jas. Conolly, merchants, Dr. Tuomy M.D., James Ryan, McLoughlin, Thos. Dillon, Edwd. Moore, Val O'Connor Junr., David Finchley merchts., Dens. Sculley, Barrister, Mr Cabally Esq. of Meath, worth abt. £12,000 p.an., and others in all abt. 35.

The meeting was convened by private notices. One o'clock p.m.

Lord Fingall showed much irresolution and much unwillingness to take the chair, on learning that a Petition to Parliament was the matter to be proposed by Mr. Ryan; he was however much pressed to do so by Mr. McDonell and Sir Thos. French and Mr. Ryan intimated that he should be under the necessity if Lord F. persevered of moving that Sir Thos. French should take the chair. Those gentlemen took much pains to convince Lord Fingall, that by taking the chair he would not be committed to any measure that might be adopted and that the disapprobation which his Lordship expressed of a Petition to Parliament at this juncture was perfectly consistent with his being in the chair and putting the question on it at the present meeting. After half an hour's conversation of this nature Lord Fingall took the chair.

Mr. Ryan addressed the meeting for upwards of an hour and concluded by moving the following resolution:

> "That it is the sense of this meeting that the present time is proper for a petition to Parliament for a repeal of the entire of the Penal Code effecting [*sic*] the Catholics".

In his speech he went much at large into the state of the Catholics at and since the union, the stipulations made with them, Mr. Pitt's resignation, and return to office; and stated the reasons why he considered this the most proper time for the petition. He came with the intention of moving for a committee this day to frame a petition and he brought in his pocket some papers which he produced as the outlines of such petition and also some resolutions for vindicating the Catholic character from some recent imputations, disavowing solemnly any intention of disturbing the present arrangement of property in this country or the present possession of the confiscated estates, and denying as false the notion that Catholics cannot be good subjects of a Protestant government—he read the petition which was warm and strongly coloured, and pretty long. There was another petition, but shorter, to the Lords; however as it seemed better to refer them to a future meeting he did not now mean to go further than the Resolution which he moved.

Mr. Randall McDonnell, Mr. Dens. Thos. O'Brien and Sir Thomas French warmly supported him.

Mr. Scully opposed, in a speech of about half an hour, recommending due precaution to be taken and much deliberation and enquiry before they would resolve to petition. He pressed that a communication should first take place with government, and especially with Mr. Pitt, since it does not appear that he has yet been applied to on the subject—he wished to avoid all public meetings and particularly many and long resolutions unless absolutely necessary—he wished also to avoid alarming the fears or jealousies however idle of his Protestant countrymen whom he had professionally daily opportunities of knowing to be generally inclined towards religious liberty, if not alarmed or irritated. He thought that much depended upon their conciliating and deserving the support of Mr Pitt in whose power it was to do everything for them and without whom they could do nothing. The influence of his great name over the public mind in England was so eminent and extensive that it could not be secured by too much assiduity or too marked a respect. The reputation of Mr. Pitt's character gave a weight to his opinions which had litterally proved of great weight to the Catholic cause and however differently some persons may judge of some parts of his public character still a person placed in so delicate a post should in his judgement considering the difficulties which he must have to encounter be viewed with infinite indulgence. The Catholics particularly owing respect for his enlarged and manly conceptions of the necessity of relieving them and the dignified energy with which he publickly expressed those conceptions.

Mr. Scully thought that in reason and common calculation they might reckon upon his good will and support as far as circumstances perhaps beyond his control would enable him to bestow it; he therefore pressed it as a previous step that the noble Chairman and one or two persons to be associated with him should be authorised to express the sense of this meeting which appears to be unanimously in favour of an application of some kind, altho' he with the noble Chairman and perhaps some others had not yet made up their minds that such application should be directed to Parliament as the motion suggests—he thought it was going too far for a first step, a kind of short cut that might lead them into perplexity and error unprepared as they were and unprovided with the necessary means of information—he likened it to the case of bills of a private or local nature: the persons solliciting such bills always applied themselves to such members of the legislature and such means of influence, explanation and argument as should enforce their claims and smooth such diffs. as they could foresee. They found it necessary always to augment the means of success and to avert or soften any intended opposition; how much more necessary are such steps in so important a measure as the present the failure of which may involve the quiet and happiness of many thousands and the peace of families and the repose of the Empire. In bills of a public nature also it was an ordinary courtesy to communicate beforehand with those persons who have the direction of public affairs, and to take the like pains in recommending the measure sought for—why should not this courtesy be observed towards Mr. Pitt's administration from whom we have so much occasion to augur favourably.

He was sorry that the motion coming in this sudden way went as far as it did, for altho' he did not know but that this might be a proper time for petitioning, yet neither would he venture to say according to the dictates of his conscience and best consideration, that it absolutely is now a proper measure. His object was, previous enquiry and information; that they should not commit themselves rashly by plunging into resolutions which would urge them to proceed without leaving it open to them to halt or retreat—he saw no other method fit to be pursued save that which he recommended and he could wish that an adjournment of two months could be agreed on in order to give time for procuring the necessary information—This motion however he would not now wish to put, but if the gentleman would not consent to substitute some palatable motion instead of that which he had made, he should be under the necessity either of making his motion or putting a flat negative upon the resolution proposed.

Mr. Ryan said, that as it appeared to be the sense of the meeting as well as he could observe that his resolution met with their unanimous concurrence with the single exception of Mr. Scully, he had only to move that the question now be put, but he would first remove some of his objections & answer some of his observations—in this he occupied about a quarter of an hour.

Mr. Scully spoke for some time to explain that he did not mean as the gentleman understood, that the Catholics were to wait merely to ask Mr. Pitt's leave or advice but that they should hold communication with him, which he had already recommended, by way of representation of the earnest and general feeling which pervades the Catholic mind upon this subject, the necessity of the measure for the good of the state and to give Mr. Pitt a true idea of the state of this country as connected with this important subject—He did not see any want of dignity in this proceeding as objected to—the present meeting cannot be called as has been said the Representatives of the Cathcs. of Ireland, or even of Dublin. They represented only themselves. That kind of delegation which the gentleman supposed this meeting to possess is prohibited by the law of the land[1] and even the present meeting of 30 or 40 gentn. would be attended with some risque under another act if it had not been sanctioned by the magistrates now present.[2] Therefore he rejected the idea of its being beneath the dignity of this meeting as representing the Catholics of Ireland to adopt the measure he proposed, nor could he bring himself to act contrary to the dictates of his conscience in this matter for the empty purpose of displaying a false dignity.

[1] The Convention Act of 1793 (*33 Geo.III, Ch.29*).

[2] Some Catholics, e.g. Randal MacDonnell and Nicholas Mahon, were Conservators of the Peace in Dublin.

Mr. R. McDonnell again in support of the resolution. Dr. Tuomy observed that the past experience showed that Mr. Scully's proposal of treating with min[iste]rs was a measure of no good promise.

Mr. Scully in answer entered at length into the history of the different repeals to show that they have proceeded in most if not all cases from ministry, but always with their perfect concurrence. He cited proceedings of the Scottish Catholics in 1778, of the English Catholics in 1779 and 1780, and 1791—of the Irish in 1773, 1778, 1782, 1792 and even in 1793, which last act he observed would have been more complete had Ministry been with us in the beginning; even in 1803 he observed that a little act of no great importance indeed, but relieving the English Catholics from a mere legal diff[icult]y about the oaths to be taken, had emanated solely from min[iste]rs and been conducted by the Master of the Rolls.[1]

Sir Thomas French seemed to wonder at Mr. Scully's moderation in approving the resolution considering that he was in his profession and by the landed property of his family, one of the most aggrieved men in the country by the penal laws. He adverted to the refusal of the offer made last year to Govt. of raising a regt. (by Mr. Scully or his father) free of expence. This was refused because the command could not be given to a Cathc., altho' Mr. Scully left the appointment of officers to the crown.[2] Sir Thos. enlarged upon Mr. Pitt's duplicity, said he could not trust him etc.

Mr. Corbally on the same side as Mr. Scully spoke shortly and well. Mr Byrne on the same side with Mr. Scully, thought the resolution went too far, and moved an adjournment of a week,

Mr. Scully, (who had suggested the motion to Mr. Byrne) seconded it, but wished that Mr. Byrne had made it for a month at least. There appeared now to be a rising disposition rather against Mr. Ryan's motion—probably a fourth part would have divided against it.

Mr. McDonnell rose—lamented the differences and hoped the meeting would not break up without coming to a resolution of some kind. Still unanimity was necessary especially of the talent and consequence of the meeting in whatever should be adopted. He proposed therefore a middle line which would leave the question of a petition still open and moved:

> "That it is the sense of this meeting that this is a proper time for an application for relief from the penal laws"

Mr. McDonnell hoped that Mr. Ryan would withdraw his motion and Mr. McDonnell's was unanimously carried.

[1] For these acts see the Chronological Table in Appendix I.
[2] See *The Catholic Question*, p.57.

The gentlemen were now retiring; but just as there were ten or twelve left about ½ past 4, it was moved that the words "and that this meeting do adjourn to this day week" [be added] to which there was no opposition. R.M.

Source: HO 100/99 f.163.

Sir Evan Nepean to John King

Private Dublin Castle, Sunday, 28 October 1804

My dear King,

By my letter of yesterday you will be informed that a meeting was held on that day at Mr. Ryan's, and that the gentlemen who attended it came to a resolution to meet again on Saturday next for the purpose of preparing a petition to Parliament. I have just learnt that Lord Fingall was in the chair and that several Roman Catholic gentlemen of considerable property attended when they came to the following resolution, viz.

> "That it is the sense of this meeting that this is a proper time for an application for relief from the Penal Laws, and that this meeting do adjourn to this day week"

I understand that there is not any disposition in the leaders to look up with much confidence to Lord Fingall, nor to any of his family, who, they say, are under the influence of, and have received favours from government. Mr. McKenna who I also mentioned to you in a former letter is not more in the confidence of the Catholics than Lord Fingall.

Source: HO 100/123 f.124.

Sir Evan Nepean to John King

Sunday morning, 4 November 1804

My dear King,

I wish you would send the enclosed to Mr. Pitt. It contains the proceedings of the Catholics at their last meeting—he will tell you why it has not been sent to you. You will hear from me on the subject in the course of the next twentyfour hours.

Source: HO 100/123 f.140

Sir Evan Nepean to John King

Private. Dublin Castle, 4 November 1804

In my letter to you of the 27th ultimo I had the honour of apprizing you, by command of the Lord Lieutenant, for the information of Lord Hawkesbury, that the Roman Catholics who had met on the preceding day, for the purpose of considering a petition, had adjourned their meeting to Saturday the 3rd instant. The meeting accordingly took place yesterday and was attended by the Lords Fingall, Gormanstown and Southwell, Sir E. Bellew, Sir Thos. French and between sixty or seventy other persons. The business of the meeting commenced with an important conversation on the choice of a chairman, after which it was decided that Lord Fingall should take the chair—Mr. Ryan then moved that a petition from the persons now present be presented to Parliament for a repeal of the Penal Laws. He was seconded by Sir Thos. French and opposed by Mr. Byrne, and still more forcibly by Mr. Scully, who conceived such a petition to be contrary to the 33rd of the King, an act prepared by Lord Clare for the express purpose of preventing Catholic meetings.

The point upon which there seemed to be the greatest difference of opinion was, whether the Peers and Baronets then present should themselves constitute a committee or whether a certain number of Dublin merchants should be added to them—the number of persons proposed to be joined with them to consist of eight or ten.

The chief advocates for the Dublin merchants were Mr. Ryan, one of the body, and Sir Thos. French, who has lately set up a bank here.

The chief opponent, Mr. Scully, contended that all the merchants of the kingdom had as great pretensions as those of Dublin, and that the landed interest was perhaps to be considered before either of them.

After much desultory conversation and some wrangle, a Mr. Nangle moved, as he said, for the sake of unanimity, that Mr. Ryan and the other gentlemen present should before the next meeting consider of the most beneficial measures for the common interest and inform themselves of the necessary dispositions in certain quarters, and to cooperate, if required, with the titled persons already mentioned. This proposition was warmly and unanimously adopted, and the meeting accordingly adjourned to Saturday the 17th instant.

It is necessary that I should inform you that late in the afternoon of Friday I received a visit from Mr. Ryan and Mr. McDonnell, two of the active promoters of the petition. Their object appeared to me to be for the purpose of apprizing me, that notwithstanding a great number of Roman Catholics were to meet on the following day, I might be assured that there was not the least probability that any degree of disorder would arise, that the persons to compose the meeting were gentlemen of character, and intended to conduct their proceedings with the utmost regularity.

It was evident from their manner that some intimation had been given to them of apprehensions being entertained by Government that, from the number of people likely to be collected, some disorder would arise, and that in the event of its taking place, it had been determined that some of the leaders should be taken into custody. I told these gentlemen that I did not entertain any such apprehensions, and that I had not either directly or indirectly authorized any person to hold any language which could lead to such a conclusion as had been drawn.

They then explained to me that the object of the intended meeting went no further than to consider whether, under the present circumstances, it would be advisable to bring the present situation of the Roman Catholics before Parliament and that if it should be decided, to present a petition, the purpose of it would, they conceived, be confined to the repeal of the remaining penal laws, and that it occurred to them that no time could be more favourable for that purpose than the present moment, that the Catholics were dissatisfied and expected that something should be done for them, and that the compliance with the prayer of the petition would convince them that their case was not desperate; and that instead of looking, as was imagined by some people, to foreign assistance, they would become good subjects.

I then stated to them that with every good disposition on the part of Mr. Pitt, it might possibly happen that their petition might be rejected; that by such a decision their cause would certainly be injured; and that I wished to know if they were prepared to say whether such a determination might not be the means of throwing the country into confusion.

They answered me that they had no apprehensions that such a decision would be productive of the consequences I had entertained.

I then told them that I found it impossible to agree with them; that a time when the country is threatened with invasion and a very unpleasant spirit existing in different parts of it, could not be a proper moment for their presenting their petition; and that if such consequences, as I had alluded to, were produced, the promoters of the petition would have a lot to answer for. That supposing the petition to be confined to the objects they had stated, I did not see what very material benefit would be derived by the lower orders.

They said that they supposed Mr. Pitt to be friendly to their petition and that the time might come, as it had done before, when he might be removed from the government, and would then be unable to render them the assistance he could now do.

I argued that if they believed what they said to me, and confided in Mr. Pitt's zeal for their cause, they ought to leave it to him to bring forward their case whenever he might conceive the period to be favourable for so doing; that by a proceeding so ill timed as this appeared to me, I could not help submitting to their consideration, whether it might not expose his political situation to some degree of danger? that I conceived many persons who were not of their religious persuasion had been very active in bringing about this question; and that I knew the object of these people could be nothing more than to embarrass his administration, and to make them the tools of it.

They declared they knew nothing of such an interference and that if they thought any views of the persons in opposition to government had been mixed with the question they would not attend any further meetings.

A great deal more passed though not of much importance, but before they left me they expressed an intention of communicating to me the result of their meetings, which, as yet, they have not yet done.

Lord Fingall called upon me yesterday morning, previously to the meeting, and informed me of his intention of attending it. And after entering into nearly the same arguments with him as I had done with Mr. Ryan and Mr. McDonnell, he told me that he should do what he could to keep things quiet, and prevent any precipitate mode of proceeding; but that at that moment he could not at all see what might be the result of the meeting, that no one could be better disposed than he was to keep the country quiet, and that he hoped it would still be so.

I took occasion in the course of our conversation to endeavour to learn from his Lordship the different points to which the petition would be likely to be directed, and was given to understand that it was meant to be confined, as far as he could discover, to the repeal of the remaining disqualifications.

I asked him whether anything had been proposed by their meeting in respect to the Roman Catholic clergy? He said, nothing—that they seemed to care very little about them. I said that this appeared odd, as it was not generally believed that they were negligent of the interests of their clergy; and that I could wish to know from his Lordship whether the Catholics meant to stop, supposing the points contained in their intended petition were conceded? as if otherwise there could be no end to petitioning.

He said he could say nothing about that subject further than that it would be a good thing if something could be done for the clergy.

I did not wish to bring his Lordship to any further explanation on this point, especially as the time of the meeting approached. A circumstance however struck me in the course of the conversation which I cannot help mentioning to you, that the first notice which had reached his Lordship of the intention of petitioning Parliament at this time was communicated to him by me. This circumstance will convince you that his Lordship is not very much in the confidence of the most active promoters of the petition.

Source: HO 100/123 f.134.

Lord Hardwicke to Lord Hawkesbury

[Copy]
Private

Dublin Castle, 11 November 1804

My dear Lord,

I have not hitherto written to your Lordship on the subject of the intention, which has lately manifested itself among the principal Roman Catholics of Dublin, to present a petition to Parlt., because Sir Evan Nepean, having had a direct communication with more than one of the gentlemen, who were present at the meeting which was held on Saturday sen'night at Mr. Ryan's house, has been better qualified to convey to you, in his letters to Mr. King, a statement of what had passed, according to the reports which he received. Having however had an opportunity of conversing upon the subject with Lord Fingall, of whose fair and honourable intentions I have the best opinion, I think it right to state to your Lordship the subject of our conversation.

Lord Fingall assured me, that he had no knowledge of any intention to bring forward the question, till a very few days before the meeting took place. That he did not understand it to have originated in any opposition to Government, but believed it to have proceeded principally, if not entirely, from the Roman Catholic merchants of Dublin. That his own opinion was decidedly against any agitation of the question at the present moment, because he was convinced it would be very unfavorable to a temperate and impartial discussion of those claims, in which, for the sake of his family, if not for his own, he certainly felt a considerable interest. That consequently he had objected to the measure of bringing forward a petition at this time, but he was obliged to confess that neither his influence nor that of other gentlemen, who thought as he did, was sufficient to prevent the petition being presented to Parlt. The mercantile interest among the Roman Catholics had increased so much of late years in wealth and importance, that the weight formerly enjoyed by the nobility and gentry of that persuasion had considerably diminished. That he still flattered himself however, that he might have sufficient influence to prevent the introduction of any intemperate or improper language: and that at all events he could be of more use by maintaining his connexion with the party, than by suffering himself to be detached from it by any difference of opinion as to the expediency of urging their claims at the present moment.

Lord Fingall told me that a committee has been appointed to consider of the question, and to obtain further information, with a view to an ultimate decision at their next meeting which is fixed for Saturday the 17th inst. I did not understand that the committee was to make any report in writing, but rather that the individuals comprising it, viz. Lord Fingall, & four other gentlemen were to endeavour to collect the opinions of those, who were favorable to the question. It is supposed that several gentlemen from the southern counties and from Connaught will be present at the next meeting, whose opinions are similar to those of Lord Fingall: but he repeatedly said that he considered it almost certain, that the final determination of the meeting would be to present a petition to Parlt.

I have endeavoured to state to your Lordship the substance of what I collected from Lord Fingall, in consequence of different observations which I made to him in the course of our conversation. Amongst other things, I observed to Lord F., that the measure was generally supposed to have originated with the opposition in England, and that it was brought forward rather in the view of embarrassing Mr. Pitt, than in the hope & expectation of success. That if I were as hostile to those claims, which must necessarily be interesting to his Lordship and the Roman Catholic gentlemen of Ireland, as many persons were, I should be far from wishing that the measure should be postponed. That I certainly wished it for the sake of public tranquillity, and because no party could derive advantage or gratification from it, but the enemies of the country & of the King's Government. That it was highly probable that in the discussion of the measure many aggravating circumstances would be stated by its opponents; that at any rate the attention of the public would be drawn to every part of the question, and that such a Protestant feeling might be excited as would greatly diminish the chance of success, whenever the question can be discussed under more favorable circumstances in a period of peace. That the very circumstance of bringing forward the question at this time, would excite a prejudice against it in the minds of many moderate and independent members of Parlt. who would not submit to the appearance of intimidation. That in fact the state of the country would not warrant any person in being influenced by such a motive; for tho' the discussion and failure of the question might produce irritation, it would not be attended with much internal danger, or add many to the ranks of rebellion in the event of invasion.

Lord Fingall stated in one part of the conversation, that there were many amongst the Catholics, who were originally against the Union, and that others were made dissatisfied at finding, that it had not produced the advantages which they expected to derive from it. That those, who are in favor of bringing forward the question at the present moment, support their opinion by considering Mr. Pitt as favorable to their cause, if in a situation to support it with effect. Upon this I could not help observing, that if they considered Mr. Pitt as favorable to their cause, it would have been better to have left to him the choice of the time; that after all that had been done for the Roman Catholic body in the course of the present reign the few remaining disqualifications, which by no means affect the mass of the people. could not be considered as a pressing grievance, that required immediate redress without any consideration of the circumstances of the times, and that in Mr. Pitt's speech upon the Union, which has been very correctly printed, no specific expectation was given upon the Roman Catholic claims, nor any other observation upon the subject, than that the question would be discussed, whenever it should be brought forward, with greater safety in an united than in a local Parlt., and that the claims themselves might be conceded with less danger.

Lord Fingall was perfectly ready to agree to every thing that could be urged against the expediency of bringing forward the question at present, and further admitted that it might fairly be objected to upon this ground, that it did not contain the whole of what would be required by the Roman Catholics, the clergy having been entirely left out of the consideration by those, who had suggested the measure.

Lord Fingall told me that he had written to Lord Kenmare, whose sentiments he had no doubt would coincide with his own.

I understand Mr. Scully, the barrister, was one of the principal opponents of the measure of petitioning at the present time; and as he is a sincere Roman Catholic I have no doubt that he considers it highly impolitic with a view to their own interests. Having some knowledge of Mr. Scully and having lately rendered some service to his brother, who is an officer in Lord Mathew's Legion in the county of Tipperary, by putting an end to a quarrel which had arisen from party and religious animosity,[1] I should have endeavoured to obtain from him some particular information upon the subject, if I did not fear that by sending for him to the Castle at this particular moment, I might in fact prevent his effecting the good, which he possibly still may, upon the present occasion.

Lord Fingall called upon me for another purpose, to inform me of Major Plunkett's arrival in London,[2] but he appeared desirous of communicating his opinion upon the subject of the petition, and satisfied that the opportunity had occurred.

Source: Hardwicke Papers, Add.MSS. 35,709, f.159.

Lord Hawkesbury to Lord Hardwicke

Private Whitehall, 15 November 1805

My dear Lord,

I have received your letter on the subject of the meetings of the Irish Catholicks. Nothing can be more proper than the sentiments you expressed to Lord Fingall on this most important and delicate question. It is very material that the Catholics

[1] Arising from the wearing of Orange badges by the Monaghan Militia in Co. Tipperary (see *The Catholic Question*, p.74).

[2] Backed by Hardwicke and the Home Secretary Lord Fingall's brother, of the Austrian service, had arrived from Prague hoping to raise a battalion under his command (Hardwicke Papers, Add.MSS.35,709, f.144).

should be apprized that whatever his opinion may be on the merits of the question it will be impossible for Mr. Pitt under the present circumstances to take any other line than that of resisting it to the utmost of his power, that any expectation of carrying the question at this time will be completely disappointed, that it is little short of insanity for the Catholicks to think of pressing their claims at present, for the consequence will infallibly be that many persons will be committed against them who under other circumstances might come to a different conclusion, but who having once taken their line upon the question, may be disposed afterwards to adhere to it. The agitation of the question at this time may influence the opinions of many likewise on the merits of the question itself. It will impress them with the conviction of the *malus animus* of those who bring it forward, as the removal of the existing disabilities would not practically benefit ten persons in the whole country, and that the object must therefore be either to embarrass government by the agitation of the question at a most unreasonable time, or to make their measure the foundation of further claims and pretensions of the most alarming nature to all who are attached to the existing constitution in Church and State. I have taken the liberty of throwing these ideas for your consideration, that you may make whatever use you may think proper of them in your further communications with any members of the Catholic body.

Source: Hardwicke Papers, Add.MSS. 35,709, f.165.

Lord Hardwicke to Charles Yorke

Private and confidential — Phoenix Park, 15 November 1804

My dear Charles,

. . . . Sir Evan Nepean has certainly not answered the expectations formed of him. He seems to me never to have taken a liberal view of any subject, to dwell upon trifles, and to suffer the weight and character of the office to be diminished, is disposed rather to listen to every tale bearer under the idea of judging for himself than to consult with those in whom he might safely confide and to whom he might give just as much or just as little credit as he pleased. . . . he some time ago took all the criminal business of his office out of Marsden's hands, discharged several State and other prisoners the former had taken up and detained under his own warrant, and discharged some very improperly. Added to this his injudicious acceptance of a seat on the Board of Admiralty, has given the general idea that he came only for a short time, and has inconceivably diminished any weight he might otherwise have possessed . . . . Sir Evan Nepean and myself have gone on perfectly well and I mean to do so, *usque ad finem* . . . .

Source: Hardwicke Papers, Add.MSS. 35,706, f.104.

Sir Evan Nepean to Mr. Pitt

Private 18 November 1804

Dear Sir,

I send you the minutes of the last meeting as taken by Mr. Marshall from Mr. Scully's report to him. I have been obliged to be very cautious in respect of my intercourse with Mr. Scully because a knowledge of his communication with me would not only destroy his influence with the Catholics, but occasion a jealousy on the part of Lord Fingall, who, though an excellent man, is rather too apt to receive impressions of that nature.

[Enclosure]

Saturday 17 November 1804

Proceedings of a meeting[1] of the Catholics at Mr. James Ryan's in Marlborough St. Dublin, consisting of the persons who were present at the last general meeting; and of Mr. Keogh and about 20 gentlemen from various parts of the country—in all upwards of 80 persons.

Before the meeting took place a previous conference was had between about a dozen gentlemen; in which, for the sake of unanimity, it was agreed to propose this day "that a select committee should be requested to prepare an application for the total repeal of the penal laws; and to consider of the mode and time of presenting the same; and that they should report their proceedings and opinions to the next general meeting to be held on the 14th Decr. next, at Lord Fingall's house". This resolution was accordingly proposed to the meeting and was unanimously adopted.

During the previous conference above mentioned, Mr. Keogh rated Lord Fingall with great severity for seceding on a former occasion, attributing to his Lordship in that respect all the miseries since endured by the Catholics.* Mr. Keogh was the person fixed on at the conference for stating the result of it to the meeting at large.

The resolution gave general satisfaction, and the meeting broke up in the greatest good humour. It must be observed, however, that the wish and impatience for repeal were strongly manifested; tempered however by a wish to avoid giving offence or alarm to others; and universally, an earnest desire to conciliate Mr. Pitt and obtain his support.

Whatever tended to throw light upon Mr. Pitt's intentions was sought for and received with avidity, and no other cooperation was hinted at. At the same time this feeling produced an equally strong anxiety and somewhat of uneasiness at the want

[1] Inserted, seemingly in Scully's hand, "the 3rd general meeting".

of explanation on this head. Very many persons at the meeting, Mr. Scully amongst the rest, have drawn this impression from Mr. Pitt's silence—that he is favourably disposed, but in some way, to them unknown, not in a situation in which he can freely act, nor even perhaps at liberty to explain to the most discreet of the Catholic body the reasons and circumstances which at the moment influence him with respect to them—yet these persons seemed to think that a confidential (and by him authorized) communication on this subject to one or two select persons of the independent Catholics would at this crisis be of the highest consequence and [coul]d be made with safety, whatever the nature of it.

There was nothing further from the views of the leading Catholics than the idea of alienating, far less that of embarrassing or opposing him, considering him as they did to be friendly to their claims, and to have powerfully served them by his past avowal upon the subject—they would feel pain at the idea of his being embarrassed by others, or of his political influence being shaken especially by the Addingtons and that party.

R. Marshall

[P.S.]

The committee chosen were, Lord[s] Fingall, Southwell, Gormanstown; Sir[s] E. Bellew. Thos. French, Thos. Burke; Mr. Scully, O'Connell, Lynch, Bellew, barristers; Dr. Drumgoole; Mr. R. McDonnell, J. Byrne, Keogh, Ryan, Conolly. The others were country gentlemen and merchts. R.M.

* [Marginal note] Lord Fingall and his own particular friends had shewed a disposition to withdraw if the plan of petitioning was not given up altogether, which led to the attack made upon him by Keogh.

Source: HO 100/99, f.173; 100/123, f.176.

Sir Evan Nepean to John King

Confidential. Dublin Castle, 18 November 1804

Dear King,

By the express which arrived yesterday afternoon, I was favoured with your letter of the 15 instant marked private.

. . . . The letter you mention from Lord Hawkesbury to the Lord Lieutenant on the Roman Catholic question was received by the same express, and if Lord Fingall could have been found, his Excellency would have had an immediate interview with him on the subject, although he could have done no more than to repeat to his Lordship from authority, what he endeavoured to impress on his mind must be the natural feelings of the King's ministers in respect to their proceedings, with this addition, that Mr. Pitt had determined to oppose the petition if now brought forward—his Lordship was however not at home when I sent to him, but on his return late in the evening he sent me word that he should call at the Castle this forenoon.

After waiting some time in expectation of his Lordship, I received the inclosed letter,[1] by which it appears that he is so much indisposed as to be unable to come out, and is not (I am informed) in a situation to communicate either with his Excellency or with me—the cause, Mr. Cadell tells me, is that his Lordship has been so agitated during the last week by the frequent discussions he has had with the promoters of the petition, that he has brought on a feverish complaint, and requires to be kept quiet for a few days.

Since Tuesday last [13th] two private meetings have been held at Lord Fingall's house, where several of the best informed and most respectable of the Roman Catholics attended, and a draft was afterwards prepared of certain resolutions which his Lordship intended to submit to the consideration of the meeting yesterday, but from the temper in which the majority of the persons then present appeared to be, he found that it would have been difficult, if not impossible, to have carried them.

Under those circumstances it was judged adviseable to adopt the inclosed resolutions,[2] by which you will perceive that the meeting is adjourned to the 14th of next month, and is to take place at Lord Fingall's house instead of Mr. Ryan's. In the list of persons composing the Committee there are five or six persons who are considered by Lord Fingall and his friends to be objectionable, particularly Mr. Keogh, who, you may remember, was one of the committee sent with the petition to England in the latter part of the year 1792; but means will be resorted to for the purpose of excluding them, if possible, from any confidential communications, if it should be determined to continue the Committee after the next meeting and their names should not be omitted—this measure will however [have] to be managed with much delicacy, as Mr. Keogh has no inconsiderable influence over a certain class of the Roman Catholics—I mean of the worst description, and is a man of considerable property and talents.

The general outline of Lord Fingall's resolutions is, a determination on the part of the Catholics to take any means in their power to obtain a repeal of all the remaining disqualifications, which measure they conceive to be essential to the happiness and tranquillity of the country; but not to bring forward their application until the time should arrive when it can be done without embarrassment to the King's government.

[1] A short note signed by R. Caddell from Harbourstown, Drogheda.

[2] Not found: probably a list of resolutions including the one cited on p.24.

They contain professions of strong attachment to His Majesty and the Royal Family, and a declaration not to connect themselves with any person in opposition for the purpose of effecting the objects they have in view.

If, as it is hoped will be the case, between this and the time of the next meeting, the majority of the Catholics should manifest a disposition to act with more temper and moderation, it is (I understand) Lord Fingall's intention to bring forward the resolutions I have mentioned, and I think it not improbable that he will be able to carry them, though, as I have before observed to you, it is evident that his Lordship's influence has diminished in the same proportion as the consequence of the mercantile interest has increased. Within the course of a few years many persons engaged in commercial pursuits have arrived at a pitch of great opulence, and have obtained a considerable degree of influence over the clergy by personal attention and their constant habits of intercourse with them.

I do not hear that more than ten or a dozen gentlemen have arrived from the country to attend the meetings.

Source: HO 100/123, f.168.

Lord Hardwicke to Lord Hawkesbury

Private and confidential

Dublin Castle, 20 November 1804

My dear Lord,

I had this day a conversation with Lord Fingall, of which I will endeavour to give your Lordship the substance, at least so much of it as may go to new points or tend to illustrate those which I detailed to you in my former letter. His Lordship told me that the meeting of Saturday the 17th was very short and that the Committee was appointed for the purpose of preparing an application proper to be laid before Parliament if they should ultimately determine to present it; and of considering of the best mode of conveying the application to Mr. Pitt. I then stated to Lord F. the substance of your Lordship's letter of the 15th inst; and without in any degree weakening the terms in which you authorised me to represent Mr. Pitt's sentiments, I told him that if it should be ultimately determined to bring forward the question at the present moment, that it would be impossible for Mr. Pitt, whatever his sentiments might be upon the general merits of the question, to take any other line than that of resisting it to the utmost of his power. I then stated, in conformity to the sentiments expressed in your letter, such reasons as occurred to me, to show, not only that there was no chance of the question being carried, but that the circumstance of its being brought forward and canvassed both in Parliament and out of doors at so unseasonal a time, would probably remove to a great distance the gratification of the wishes of the Roman Catholicks, and at the risque of producing in the meantime considerable irritation and great publick inconvenience.

As Lord F. had stated the intention of applying to Mr. Pitt before any petition should be presented to Parliament I thought it necessary to ask his Lordship whether it was intended to make such application by letter or by deputation; and whether it was proposed to ask his opinion merely for the sake of knowing it, or because they intended to follow it. He replied that he rather believed it was intended to send over a deputation consisting of some of the principal persons who had attended the meetings; and that as he (Lord F.) had conceded the point of making an application to Parliament, when he found it impossible to resist it with effect, he concluded they could not pass him by in any such deputation to England. In regard to the other point, he did not feel able to answer it distinctly, but replied that he was very apprehensive that even the knowledge of Mr. Pitt's opinion would not prevent the question being brought forward. He was not however prepared to say in whose hands it might be placed, and he believed that point had not yet been a subject of consideration. Lord F. added that it was intended to publish either a pamphlet or a short tract to be delivered to members of Parliament, for the purpose of doing away an unfavourable impression which exists against the Roman Catholicks of Ireland upon two different points; first in regard to their supposed claims upon the forfeited estates and the dangers to the landed proprietors of the country, and secondly, as to the supposed facility of dispensing with oaths. The latter point Lord F. observed was one upon which many respectable Roman Catholics who had taken the oath of allegiance prescribed for them by law felt extremely hurt in consequence of insinuations which had been thrown out at different periods, and they were consequently anxious to clear themselves in the opinion of their countrymen. Lord Fingall appears evidently mortified at not having been able to prevent the agitation of the question, but he dares not choose to separate from the Roman Catholick body, though he disapproves of the conduct of those whose influence has proved superior to his upon the present occasion. He told me that amongst other arguments which he had used at the meeting and in private conversation, he had urged the present situation of the Pope; his evident dependence upon the French Government which was now to be demonstrated to all the world by his forced journey to Paris.[1] To this it was replied, that they did not regard the situation of the Pope and that he had nothing to do with the measure proposed for the removal of Roman Catholick disabilities; that it was a mere ecclesiastical question, and one that could not be fairly connected with the subject. In the course of the conversation Lord F. stated that the state of the Roman Catholick clergy had never been mentioned at any of the meetings, and that in discussing it privately with different gentlemen, he found that

[1] For the coronation of Napoleon (on 2 December).

a very great difference of opinion prevailed upon the propriety of asking or accepting any payment from the State. That some thought it would give the government too great an influence, and that others thought it would render the priests less attentive to their religious duties; that at any rate the question which regarded the laity was that which they considered the most important and the most likely, if granted, to ensure the satisfaction and tranquillity of the country. Lord Fingall is strongly impressed with the necessity of bringing forward the question, whenever it is discussed, with a view to a final adjustment; and is aware that the interests of the Roman Catholicks must suffer by the agitation of it, without a prospect of its being set at rest. In answer to an observation which I made, that I conceived the Roman Catholicks would not willingly lose the credit and advantage of his co-operation, and that they would probably soon return to him notwithstanding any difference which might actually arise upon the expediency of making an application to Parliament at the present moment; he said that so far from that having been the case after the similar disagreement which took place in the year 1792, when his father and the late Lord Kenmare separated from the rest of the body, he had been himself personally very ill received at the first publick meeting which he attended in the county of Meath after his father's death from the recollection of that very disagreement. That Mr. Keogh and the others who had succeeded in their mission to England notwithstanding the disagreement and secession to which he referred, were now likely to be considered as successful agents in the concerns of the the Roman Catholicks, and that it appeared to him, that they derived great encouragement from the result of their proceedings in 1792, when the measure of the elective franchise and other concessions were urged, shortly after the battle of Jemappe,[1] and immediately before the commencement of the French war. He describes Mr. Keogh as a man of considerable ability and influence, and likely from his having been one of the five who presented the address at the King's Levee on the 3rd of January 1793, to be included in any deputation which may now be appointed. In a paper which I sent to your Lordship a few days since he is stated to be a person suspected of disaffection. Though he is very zealous in the Catholick cause, and would probably go to great lengths, I do not believe there is any reason to suspect him of being connected with any scheme of disaffection at present. He was intimately connected with [T.A.] Emmet, McNevin and other rebel leaders in 1797, and before the Rebellion, but left the country before it broke out and went to England. After the insurrection of 23rd July, his papers were seized by some yeomen who were sent to his house, among others, to search for arms, and although he professed to be not very well pleased at the compliment which had been paid him, yet he explained himself frankly and candidly as to his situation and opinions. He then stated that he had settled three of his sons in different pursuits in England and Ireland, that he was possessed of considerable

[1] Where the French defeated the Austrians on 6 November 1792.

property, and that he was one of the last men to join in any plan of rebellion. I mention this because it is possible that the idea entertained of him, and the dislike expressed by Lord Fingall of his being a member of the committee appointed to meet previously to the next meeting of the 14th of December, may arise from a knowledge of his former practices and connections. Lord Fingall is to have some further conversation with the members of the committee upon Sunday next and has promised to call upon me the next day to communicate the result.

[Pencilled minute]

I do not believe this Mr. Keogh is disaffected in the way alluded to, i.e. as connected with the rebels, but I should think no R.C. more likely to have in mind the aggrandizement of the civil power of the papists, or more likely to take measures for that purpose. Mr. Pitt will recollect his conduct in '92.[1]

J[ohn] K[ing]

Source: HO 100/123, f.182.

Lord Hardwicke to Lord Hawkesbury

Private. Dublin Castle, 26 November 1804

My Dear Lord,

Lord Fingall called on me this morning in order to communicate what had passed at the meeting of yesterday. About eighteen gentlemen met at his house, and in addition to those who were members of the Committee, he had invited some others who had not attended any of the previous meetings. Of these he particularly mentioned Mr. Roche of Limerick, Mr. Bagot who has property in the Co. of Dublin, and Mr. McKenna, a lawyer, who wrote one of the best pamphlets in favour of the union, but does not appear to have been hitherto in the confidence of those who have been the most active in reviving the discussion of this question. The conversation yesterday appears to have turned principally upon the propriety of presenting a memorial to Mr. Pitt independently of any consideration of the petition to Parliament, but neither of these points will finally be determined till the meeting of the 14 of December, though from the circumstance of the Committee being so numerous, and consisting of the principal persons who attended the former meetings, Lord F. thinks that whatever opinion they may form will probably be conclusive. I understand that Mr. Keogh is the person who suggested at some of the

[1] King was no doubt thinking rather of the Catholic Convention and Keogh's reputation as an agitator than of his visit to London at the end of the year as a member of an Irish Catholic deputation.

former meetings an application to Mr. Pitt; and advised that a petition to Parliament should be prepared without deciding on the proper time of presenting it. I collected however from Lord Fingall, that though in the discussion of this subject, the desirability of postponing the introduction of such a petition for a certain time had been fully admitted; and particularly of doing so at a moment when apprehensions might be entertained of an invasion of Ireland, that this argument would afford no ground for postponing it to any distant period, that in March or April, the probability of invasion would be considerably less from the season of the year, and that such an argument against bringing forward the question could not apply with equal force. Lord Fingall who had availed himself of the communication which I made to him of Mr. Pitt's sentiments, as expressed in your Lordship's letter of the 15th inst., contended that such a knowledge of his opinion ought to be fully sufficient with those who meant to be guided by it; and that he did not conceive that an application such as that as was proposed could be attended with any advantage, unless it was meant to embarrass. I did not collect that anything was stated in answer to this argument, except that no direct communication having been made to Mr. Pitt from the Roman Catholicks, the knowledge they had of his sentiments could not so far as they were concerned be considered as official. Lord Fingall suggested that at any rate there would be no necessity of sending a deputation to London, as Lord Kenmare and Lord Trimlestown were at present in England; but he apprehends that those who have taken the lead in the question here, will not be satisfied without having some person to represent the mercantile interest; and thinks it probable that Mr. Keogh will be selected for that purpose. His opinion is however that the deputation will not exceed three.

It is to be observed from this statement, that though the application to Parliament may not be made immediately by the Roman Catholicks themselves, it is scarcely to be hoped that that they will be induced to postpone it for any considerable period. I desired Lord F. to explain the degree of impatience which had begun to shew itself for the agitation of this question, when no particular grievances were stated, and when no irritation existed in the country. He attributes it to the increased wealth and consequence which many of the Roman Catholicks have derived from trade, and to the desire they feel of not being excluded by their religion from those objects of pursuit which are open to the rest of their countrymen. Formerly the Irish Brigade in France, the Spanish and particularly the Austrian service, opened a wide field for the younger sons of Roman Catholick families; that in the year 1779 there were upwards of 600 Irish officers in the Austrian army; that at present there is scarcely one third of that number, and of those many are not Irishmen by birth. That notwithstanding the Irish Act of 1793, which permits Roman Catholics to have commissions in the Army, there are very few in his Majesty's service, in which they cannot be employed in any higher rank than that of Colonel; that the lawyers complain that they cannot be King's Counsel; and that though Roman Catholic gentlemen may serve on Grand Juries, yet it depends on the courtesy of the Sheriff, who must be a Protestant. So much do some of the Roman Catholic merchants feel the exclusions to which they are liable that Mr. McDonnel lately told Lord Fingall, that if he did not believe there was an early prospect of the disabilities being removed he would leave the country and return with his family to Spain. It is not however to be supposed that many would reason in the same manner, but that they would rather speculate on their descendants conforming to the established religion.

Lord Fingall says that the clergy have lost much of their influence over the common people whom they could formerly entirely govern, and that this influence is falling into the hands of the merchants and others who are above the lower class. He considers the College at Maynooth as having actually kept up the Roman Catholic religion in Ireland, and as being its great support now; for that at the time of its establishment, there was upon the continent only one place of education, in Portugal, where a supply of priests could have been obtained. Lord Kenmare disapproves of the agitation of the question at present as well as Lord Fingall; but I do not believe that either of them will refuse to sign their names to the application to Parliament; as they think it would weaken the general cause, and furnish an argument to their opponents that there was a difference of opinion as to the measure itself. Lord F. appears to think that there is no person whose opinion has so much weight as Mr. Keogh, and thinks that if a communication were had with him through Mr. Marsden to whom he is known, that possibly some change might be made in his opinion, as to the final decision of the meeting of the 14th of December. As it is certainly an important object to prevent the agitation of the question or at least the agitation of it with the concurrence of the Roman Catholics, I shall consider of the propriety of opening such an intercourse with Mr. K. for the purpose of communicating to him directly the opinion so strongly entertained by Mr. Pitt, and the great improbability of the question being supported by any considerable numbers if it should be brought forward at the present time.

Source: HO 100/123, f.188.

Lord Hardwicke to Lord Hawkesbury

Private — Dublin Castle, 28 November 1804

My Dear Lord,

I understand the Mr. McDonnel who is mentioned in some of my former letters as one of the leading men amongst the Roman Catholick merchants of Dublin, expresses himself with much less anxiety on the subject of the application to Parliament. He told Mr. Marsden yesterday that he did not believe the Roman

Catholicks would give any trouble at present, and as he has considerable weight and influence over the body, and was amongst the most eager for a petition to Parliament, at the present moment, I think it not impossible that the opinion of the next meeting will be different from that which I have been brought to expect from my communications with Lord Fingall. I shall therefore postpone for the moment any communication with any of the other persons mentioned in my last letter, and I should be very happy if the opinions of the leading merchants of Dublin should so far change, from whatever motive, as to induce them to lay aside their intention of making an early application to Parliament. If that should be the case, as it certainly originated here, there would be no danger of the question being taken up in any other part of the country.

Source: HO 100/123, f.192.

Lord Hardwicke to Sir Evan Nepean

[Copy]
Private

Phoenix Park, 1 December 1804

My dear Sir,

The enclosed letter which I wrote to Lord Hawkesbury a few days since, contains a full statement of my conversation upon Monday last [26 November]. At that time you will see, that so far from objecting to communications through other channels, he was rather more desirous, on account of the influence which he supposed Keogh to possess, that Mr, Marsden should have a communication with him. I wrote to Lord Hawkesbury on Wednesday to say that as I understood there was a disposition to give up the petition to Parliament, I should not encourage any communications with Mr. Keogh, and that as for myself, I should confine them to Lord Fingall. His, Lord F.'s, idea however was, that every endeavour should be used, likely to effect the object of keeping back the question and that tho' I knew he would not wish me to communicate directly with Mr. Scully, or possibly any other person, yet I can have no idea of his being hurt at communications being made of the opinion entertained of the government in England, to all those persons who possess the greatest influence in Dublin. As to Mr. Lynch I think he should have the £300 per annum, till his engagement can be satisfied His engagement was made to him on account of his influence in Galway, where his services may still be useful[1] for the reason abovementioned, and his connexion with Sir Thomas French, I think it will

[1] For his support of the Union M. F. Lynch had been promised a chairmanship of Ouarter Sessions and in October 1803 he had warded off a petition in Galway.

be proper to let him have it and I have therefore desired Marsden to tell him so tomorrow morning.

I think giving up the petition to Parliament will not be of much use, unless they can also be persuaded to abandon the idea of making a statement of their case, or of sending a deputation with a memorial to Pitt.

Source: Hardwicke Papers, Add.MSS. 35,754, f.5.

Proceedings of the 2nd meeting of the Select Committee at Lord Fingall's

Sunday, 2 December 1804

Mr. McDonnell proposed that for the present the Committee shd. content themselves with a mere statement of grievances. Mr. Keogh supported him; but he took occasion to inform the committee that he had just recd. an acct. by the Irish Mail that His Majesty was again indisposed.

Mr. Bellew said that if the committee came to any resolution of the kind, it might as well be in the shape of a mere statement of facts, as in the shape of a petition. Mr. Scully said, that since that was the opinion of Mr. Bellew and his friends, he (Mr. Scully) should prefer a petition—he spoke for a great length of time and in strong language for a petition. And he stated the grievances of the Catholics, the late subjects of irritation such as the Chancellor's letters,[1] Mr. Wickham's map[2] tracing out their property perhaps for confiscation, Lord Hardwicke etc.

The meeting seemed to be almost unanimous for it.

Mr. Keogh gave up his statement and said he would vote for a petn.; and, in the end, so did Mr. McDonnell.

The original motion was amended by leaving out the whole of it except the word "that" and substituting words to the effect that "a petition be presented to both Houses", and the amended motion passed unanimously.

Mr. McDonnell, Mr. Scully, Mr. Taafe, Mr. O'Connell and Mr. Lynch were appointed to draw up the petition agst Sunday next, to which day the meeting adjourned.

R. Marshall

Source: HO 100/99, f. 177.

[1] To Lord Fingall (see Castlereagh's *Correspondence* IV, p.298).

[2] No other reference to this map has been found.

James Ryan to the Freeman's Journal
(continued)

A third meeting was fixed upon in order to appoint a committee to deliberate on what would be most prudent to do. At this meeting Mr. Keogh (I believe at the particular request of Mr. McDonnell) attended, and contributed much to the determination of appointing a Committee, of which he was made, with his own consent, a member; it was then agreed the meetings of the Committee should be held at Lord Fingall's, and the general meetings at my house. The Committee had several meetings, when Mr. McDonnell because [? became] solicitous that Mr. Keogh should attend his duty on it, and it was agreed that Counsellors O'Connell and Scully, Mr. McDonnell and myself, should wait upon Mr. Keogh to request his attendance—We did so, and although he did not give us any *distinct promise*, he did attend, but at a very late hour. The Committee met at Two o'Clock, but he did not arrive until nearly four. As Mr. MacDonnell had previously intimated that Mr. Keogh would make a specific proposition to the Committee; no business was entered into until he made his appearance, he immediately commenced a long speech upon the danger of the times, the folly of exasperating the Administration, and concluded by proposing as the most adviseable and *dignified* step, that the Catholic Body should *memorial* Mr. Pitt; this proposition was received with merited indignation, and Counsellor Bellew, the reputed organ of Lord Fingal, and his friends, declared that hostile as he was to Petition *at that time*, he would sooner agree to it than *degrade* the Catholic Body, by supplicating the Minister for that relief they had a right to demand, as an act of justice, from the legislature. Mr. Keogh, finding his proposition was not very kindly received, he retired; and on the following day, addressed a letter to Lord Fingal, requesting his name should be erazed from the list of the Committee, without assigning any other reason than he did not find himself able to attend their future meetings; the request was complied with, and Mr. Keogh ceased to interfere further in our deliberations. . . .

Source: Freeman's Journal, 11 August 1810.

Lord Hawkesbury to Lord Hardwicke

Private. Whitehall, 3 December 1804

My dear Lord

By accident I did not keep a copy of the letter I wrote to Your Excellency in which I stated to you Mr. Pitt's determination on the subject of the Catholick question. As Mr. Pitt may receive some communications from the Catholic body on this subject and as he is desirous of making his answer as nearly conformable to the sentiments contained in my letter as possible, I shall be much obliged to you, if you would direct your Private Secretary to make a copy of that letter and enclose it to me. I have great satisfaction in perceiving by both your last letters but particularly that of the 28 ult. that some of the Catholicks are becoming more cool and reasonable on the subject, and that hopes may be entertained of inducing them to forego their first determination. If this can be accomplished without holding out to them any expectations for the future, I think (as it would tend to preserve the internal tranquillity of the country) it cannot fail to produce very beneficial effects. I am persuaded the more I think on the subject, that nothing could be more contrary to the interests of the Catholicks than the agitation of the question at the present moment and that if it was not for the apprehensions that might be entertained of the effects of the agitation on the peace of the country the decided enemies to the Catholick pretensions are the only persons who could reasonably desire the discussion of it under the existing circumstances.

Source: Hardwicke Papers, Add.MSS. 35,709, f.184.

Lord Hardwicke to Lord Hawkesbury

Private and confidential Dublin Castle, 3 December 1804

My dear Lord,

I understand that at the meeting which was held yesterday at Lord Fingall's. a committee of five was appointed to prepare a statement of the case of the Roman Catholicks, and their present disabilities, to be submitted to the general meeting on the 15th inst., and to be adopted either as a petition to Parliament or as the ground of some other proceeding, as may be judged expedient at the time. The committee of five consists of Mr. McDonnel, Mr. Lynch, Mr. Scully, Mr. [O']Connell, and another, and the two former, as well as Lord Fingall informed Mr. Marsden this day, that the general disposition of the meeting was against a petition. . . .

Source: HO 100/123, f.198.

Sir Evan Nepean to John King

Confidential Dublin Castle, 8 December 1804

My dear King,

I have obtained a copy of the report of the Sub-Committee of the Catholics intended to be made to the Committee (which will meet at Lord Fingall's) tomorrow, and have sent it to Mr. Pitt. I have been obliged to do so by the parties from whom I obtained it, under an impression they have taken that if a trace of it were to be left in this office, it would operate very prejudicially to their future interests.

I will explain to you when we meet all the circumstances which have given rise to this. It is now near one in the morning and I have a confounded pain in my head, which I have had almost without interruption for near a fortnight past. I hope to see you soon, and if ever they catch me in Ireland again I will give them leave to hang me.

Source: HO 100/123, f.202.

Report of the Subcommittee

Private and Confidential Sunday, 9 December 1804

Report of the Sub Committee appointed by the General Committee of the Catholics

> to draw up in the form of a petition to Parlt. a statement of the Penal Laws still existing against the Catholics, and their effect as prejudicial to that body and to the Empire at large, and to report the same or the progress they shall have made therein.

To the Right Honble. and Honble. the members of
the General Committee of Catholics

Your Sub Committee have diligently applied themselves to the execution of the task imposed upon them, and have had frequent meetings for that purpose. They have employed much time in reviewing and investigating the various restrictions and inconveniences by law inflicted upon the Catholics. They have carefully attended to and examined the multiform and oppressive operation of the laws against the Catholics in every walk of life, and particularly as they affect the administration of justice, the spirit of the constituted authorities, and the general temper of civil society in public and in private life. They have found that by copiously detailing these laws, and by expressing their consequences to the Catholics and the Empire at large, they should necessarily frame a very serious and afflicting statement of grievances, and originate the enumeration and discussion of complaints against abuses of authority and of public duty in this country which would, perhaps, strongly affect the passions of various descriptions of their fellow subjects.

They apprehend from such a statement, consequences to the Catholics and the Empire at large, which they cannot contemplate, even remotely, without feelings of great doubt and delicacy, and they acknowledge that they have been embarrassed and materially retarded by these considerations, in their progress and preparations.

Your Sub Committee have therefore, after much and frequent deliberation, deemed it finally to be most prudent and advantageous, considering all the circumstances, to act upon your resolution, as a resolution purporting, in its spirit and intent, that they should prepare a petition to Parlt. upon the subject of your instructions, containing such statements, observations and materials as shall appear to them to be most eligible and expedient.

They are engaged in preparing a petition to Parlt. upon the latter view of your resolution (the propriety of which view they beg leave to submit to your consideration) and they have the satisfaction to state, that a rough draft of a petition is in a state of some forwardness, and nearly prepared.

Your Sub Committee hope and expect, that on Wednesday next they will be able to lay before you such a draft of a petition as they shall deem likely to be honored by your adoption and to be found suited to the various circumstances of time, feeling and interests, which have fallen under their consideration:

(signed) 1 J.Taafe
2 M.B.[*recte* M.F.] Lynch
3 Denys Scully
4 Danl. O'Connell
5

Note. The other member of the Sub Committee, Mr. R. McDonnell, has been prevented from attending it (except on the first day) by a complaint in his eyes.

Source: HO 100/99, f.179.

Lord Hardwicke to Lord Hawkesbury

Private and confidential

Dublin Castle, 10 December 1804

. . . . at a meeting of the Sub-Committee which was held yesterday at Lord Fingall's, it was determined to prepare a petition, expressing in temperate language and in general terms the desire of the Roman Catholicks to be relieved from the remaining disqualifications and relying upon the wisdom and justice of Parliament. Lord Fingall says that this mode has been adopted in preference to a statement of their case, because such a statement must have been accompanied by comment and illustration, which extending to greater length might have excited a degree of feeling and irritation which they profess to desire to avoid as much as possible. The sub committee is to meet upon Thursday next in order to settle the draft of the petition, and Lord Fingall is in hopes that the general meeting of Saturday the 15th inst. will agree to postpone further consideration of it, as Mr. Bellew intends to move an adjournment to the second Sunday of February. If this motion should be agreed by the meeting on Saturday next, it is possible that the question may be kept back for the present session, but I understand that an opinion still prevails amongst many of the Roman Catholick gentlemen, that no inconvenience will arise either to the publick or the cause itself from an early discussion of the question.

Lord Fingall appears to be now convinced of what he was at first unwilling to believe, that the idea of bringing forward the R. Catholick subject at the present moment, originated with the opposition in England. He told me that he had lately seen a letter from Mr. Fox in which he strongly recommends an application to Parliament, which he says will be supported by himself and all his friends, and which Mr. Pitt cannot with consistency oppose. He further urges it, for what Lord Fingall called the following extraordinary reason, that it is called for in order to satisfy the conscience of the Roman Catholicks, who cannot give a stronger proof of their loyalty and attachment to the government of Great Britain, or disclaim in a more decided manner any expectation of aid from France, than by shewing that they rely entirely on the British Legislature. Letters have also been received from several members of the opposition, and amongst others from Lord Henry Petty, who strongly urges the propriety of an application to Parliament. Lord Fingall hopes that if the meeting of Saturday next shall agree to Mr. Bellew's motion, and adjourn the further consideration of the subject to the middle of February, that it will not be difficult at that time to carry the further postponement of the question to a more distant period. He observed however that upon this, as upon many other occasions, those who were for the more moderate opinion were less inclined to come forward and support it, than those who were more eager and violent. It is clear that a very considerable change has taken place in the opinions of many since the first meetings, and Lord Fingall says that nothing has so much contributed to produce it, as the decided manner in which Mr. Pitt's determination to resist it, if brought forward under present circumstances, is expressed in your Lordship's letter of the 15th of November.

Source: HO 100/123, f.20.

Lord Hardwicke to Lord Hawkesbury

Private Dublin Castle, 15 December 1804

My dear Lord,
at the general meeting of the Roman Catholics which was held this day the form of a petition was presented by the committee, accompanied by a resolution which was agreed to for postponing the further consideration of it till the 2nd of February. It is understood that no meeting will be held till that time, when I hope the majority of them will be convinced of the inexpediency of bringing the subject before Parliament at present. Lord Fingall says that the discussion was very temperate. and that two gentlemen, one from the county of Kerry, and the other from Clare, who were rather disposed to be violent were very ill received.

Source: HO 100/123, f.210.

Unsigned to John King

[draft/copy] [Dublin] 16 December 1804

Sir,

I am commanded by the Lord Lieutenant to acquaint you for the information of Lord Hawkesbury that the committee of Roman Catholics met yesterday at Lord Fingall's, when the sub-committee, which had at a former meeting been directed to prepare the intended Petition to Parliament, reported their proceedings and presented the draft of the Petition.

The meeting did not consist of more than 100 persons. The draft was read and unanimously approved and the General Meeting adjourned to Saturday the 2nd of

February next. Previously to the adjournment of the General Meeting it was proposed that the persons who comprised the Select Committee, with six others making in all thirty-one, should be a committee for the purpose of superintending the conduct of the petition and of transacting all other affairs which should be deemed for the advantage of the Catholics.[1]

The Select Committee then appointed a Sub-Committee consisting of the five persons[2] who prepared the Petition and four others, with authority to procure the signatures to the Petition, and to assemble the Committee of 31 as often as should appear to be requisite. The names of the persons added were Mr. Nangle, Mr. James Ryan mercht., Mr. Chas. Ryan, Dr. Drumgoole. Under the general powers given to the Committee of 31 they are considered to be at liberty to have the petition presented thro' whatever channel and at whatever time they may think fit. It is understood that the prayer of the Petition is in effect, that all Roman Catholic laymen may be relieved of every disability, excepting that of succeeding to the Crown. These disabilities may nearly be summarized under the following heads:

To sitting and voting in Parliament
To be appointed Sheriffs and Sub-sheriffs
To hold dignified offices in the Law
To be allowed to vote in vestries
To be eligible for admission into the Bank direction
and other Corporations
To fill the higher ranks in the army.

The Petition is said to be written in very temperate language, declaring the willingness of the Catholic Body to accede to such measures as can be suggested for the further security of the constitution in Church and State, and that it is no part of their plan to aggrandize the Bishops of their own communion, nor to seek to etc, etc as in the Coronation Oath.[3]

Source: Hardwicke Papers, Add.MSS. 35,754, f.167.

[1] The six are named in the margin as: Sir Fr. Gould; Honble. W. Blake; Mr. Php. Roche; Mr. Dowall O'Reilly; Mr. Chas Ryan, formerly a surgeon; Mr. Edward Moore, a merchant.

[2] For the names of the five see p.38.

[3] A reference to paragraph 15 of the petition (see Appendix D), upholding the privileges of the established church.

John Keogh to Owen O'Conor

Mount Jerome, 3 January 1805

Dear Sir,

. . . .

There are few who are so ill qualified to give you a reply to the subject of your inquiry—the present proceedings of those who are acting in the name of the Catholics. I did not attend any of their several meetings, except the third, at which I had the pleasure to see you, and a private one at Lord Fingal's. I then caused my name to be erased from the list of the committee. When the late revived committee[1] conducted the claims of the Cathcs, the least part of their labours was that of preparing a petition. A vast number of previous measures were adopted, to pave the way for the success of their petition. They consulted with their brethren, not only in Dublin, but in all the distant counties; they conciliated the liberal Protestants in and out of Parliament; they applied to and convinced His Majesties ministers that Cathc emancipation would be for the interest of the throne and the empire (and all these were previous to any aggregate meetings), and by such conduct they triumphed over a violent and formidable opposition from grand juries, corporations, and county meetings, and finally obtained the privileges which are now enjoyed.

When I heard of an aggregate meeting—and in all such meetings consultation or consideration is not possible; men may exhibit themselves by speeches, but cannot consider or reflect—and that no previous meeting of Cathcs had been consulted in either city or country, or any men of understanding sanctioned the measure or approved the meeting—it was a new mode—I naturally wished the mover success; but I lamented that in a business wherein every Cathc and his posterity was deeply interested, that this meeting should be forced forward without any previous consultation, that I could hear of, with any one of the whole body. The two first meetings produced great divisions—the third was expected to break into hostilities. I was prevailed upon by Dr.[*sic*] Randal M'Donnell to attend the third, and to try and prevent such disgrace by reconciling the parties. This was accomplished. Men advanced in years are attached to methods which they knew to succeed, and so I feel myself influenced. I could not reconcile it to myself to take any share of the responsibility (however small my share) of measures so opposite to those pursued by the late Catholic Committee, which had been sanctioned by the Cathc Convention, by the Parliaments of Ireland and England, by the Ministers, and finally by His Majesty.

[1] That of 1792, which organised the Catholic Convention and sent a deputation to London, where it was received by the King on 2 January 1793.

I have thus opened myself and answered your letter, but in the private confidence of a friend and of a gentleman, and not to be made any public use of, for I sincerely hope that my apprehensions may be ill-founded and occasioned by the caution and timidity so usual to old age.

Source: John O'Donovan: *The O'Conors of Connaught*, p.324.

Alexander Marsden to Lord Hardwicke

17 January 1805

My Lord

I have had two or three interviews with Mr. McDonnell of whose consequence among the Catholic body your Excellency is sufficiently informed, & I wish to detail what passed, as some of it is material.

I have latterly thought it right to pay this gentleman some additional attentions, as every day made it more manifest that his influence which acted on what may be called the opposition of the Catholics was extending with the moderate of that party, and on the other hand, Lord Fingal who, with his Lordship's friends, were in the first instances most properly looked to by Your Excellency as those who formerly represented, & for the most part swayed the Catholic body, were in the progress of the discussions which have lately taken place likely to be left in a minority.

I have always been on familiar terms with Mr. McD., and as I have generally considered that I could get hold of him by his vanity (for Your Excellency has few direct modes of influencing the Catholics in this country) I have talked to him about his consequence & influence more than I should otherwise be disposed to do. He, as might be supposed, continued to affect that he was carried on by others, not they by him.

As a sort of compliment to me on his part he came to me three days ago, and informed me under injunctions of confidence greater than the circumstance seem to require, that Sir E. Nepean had desired to have a copy of the Catholic Petition, and that it was intended to send it to him that night. He intimated that as I might consider that certain persons here, better entitled to have a copy of the Petition, were passed by in sending it to Sir E.N. I might have a copy of it if I chose.

The proposal I conceived might be made as well by design, as from good will to me, & therefore I answered that it did not hurt me in the least that the petition should be sent to Sir E. N.; on the contrary that as I entirely disapproved of bringing forward the petition, I would much prefer not seeing it at all—that the contents of the petition were wholly immaterial to me, as I knew what they must be, and I took the opportunity of again urging Mr. McD. to give all his consideration to the real interests of the Body, and to add his weight to the party of Lord Fingal, instead of aiding those whose intentions & respectability could not be rated with his Lordship's.

Your Excellency knows that two days ago I received a letter from Lord Cornwallis, in which is a paragraph containing excellent good sense on the subject of the Catholic proceedings in this country. For every reason I thought it right to let Mr. McD. see this letter (which I have also communicated to Lord Fingal} and I sent it with a note to him. He called upon me this day in consequence, and I have had again a good deal of talk with him, the result of which is the most material part of what I have to state to Your Excellency.

Suppose, says he, that the Catholics were to prepare a statement of their case, not in the form of a Petition, & were desirous of presenting it to the Lord Lieutenant, would it be received?—(He wished me to understand that the question was merely asked by himself)—I asked him would, in such a case, other modes of proceeding be dropped?—Yes, he meant so—Would they expect an answer—No, not further than that His Excellency should say he would transmit it—Lord Pelham, he said, had refused in a similar case.[1]

I told him that I should consider this idea as merely his own. & not mention (as he required) his name to any Catholic as suggesting what he had done, the proposition should be duly considered. It occurred to me to mention that at the meeting which is to be held on Saturday next some measure might be resolved upon which might interfere with any new arrangement—he said he would take care it should not—that the business on that day would be confined to the question of the day upon which the General meeting first appointed for the 2d of Feby. should be held—That he was certain it would not be changed from that day unless its being a Holy day with the Catholics should make them fix the day before, or the day after. . . .

Source: HO 100/128, f.11.

Lord Hardwicke to Lord Hawkesbury

Private — Dublin Castle, 20 January 1805

My dear Lord

From a circumstance which has recently occurred, I am inclined to believe that there is at present a disposition amongst the Roman Catholicks who have taken the

[1] In July/August 1803: see Chronological Table (Appendix I).

lead at the late meetings, to lay aside the intention of petitioning Parliament if any mode can be found by which the subject, so far as they are concerned, may be dropped for the present, without exposing them to the imputation of having proceeded a certain length without coming to a conclusion. It is only upon this principle that I can account for Mr. McDonnel having proposed to Mr. Marsden that I should transmit a statement of their case to His Majesty's Ministers, and that he had reason to believe that if that course were taken that the business would drop. As the subject is of considerable delicacy and importance, I wish to avoid giving any answer that may either commit myself or embarrass H. Majesty's Ministers; and therefore I request your Lordship will inform me as soon as you conveniently can, and in time for a private communication with Mr. McDonnel before the meeting of the 2d of february, how far it is considered adviseable to prevent a Petition from the Roman Catholicks by receiving a representation of their case in the manner suggested.

If the proposal had been so made as to require an immediate answer, I should not have thought myself justified, since the Representation will probably contain nothing in itself improper, in refusing to transmit it, at the desire of the most respectable part of the Roman Catholicks, reserving however the power of acting upon it as I might afterwards think right upon a full consideration of its contents. As Mr. Marsden has by my desire stated in writing the substance of what passed with Mr. McDonnel, I enclose his letter for your Lordship's information; and if it should be thought more adviseable to prevent the Petition from being presented to Parliament, than to leave the Roman Catholicks to pursue their own course, I think it most probable that Mr. McDonnel's influence added to that of the moderate party whose opinion has been already expressed against it, will effect the object.

I have had no opportunity of conversing with Lord Fingall since Mr. McDonnel's overture; but as he has always appeared extremely desirous to prevent a Petition, and even advised some weeks ago that Mr. Marsden should have a communication with Mr. Keogh for that purpose (as I mentioned to your Lordship in a former letter)[1] I have no apprehension that he will feel in any degree hurt at the communication with Mr. McDonnel; more especially as the result supposing it to end in a relinquishment of the measure of petitioning will be consistent with the line which Lord F. himself has recommended from the beginning.

Source: HO 100/128, f.9.

[1] See p.32.

Lord Hardwicke to Lord Hawkesbury

Private Dublin Castle, 23 January 1805

. . . .I had an opportunity of conversing with Lord Fingall yesterday, upon the subject of the idea suggested by Mr. McDonnel, and have the satisfaction to find that he will most readily concur in any measure, or with any party for the purpose of preventing a Petition to Parliament. I shall give no answer to Mr. M. till I know your Lordship's sentiments and those of the King's ministers. . . .

Source: HO 100/128, f. 19.

Lord Hawkesbury to Lord Hardwicke

Private. Whitehall, 26 January 1805

My dear Lord,

I have communicated to Mr. Pitt your letter of the 20th instant together with the enclosure from Mr. Marsden on the subject of what had passed between him and Mr. McDonnel respecting the Catholick Petition. We are both of opinion that no inconvenience could arise from Your Excellency's transmitting a Representation of the case of the Catholicks to His Majesty's Government in this country, provided the Representation was drawn out in decent and respectful terms, and no expectation was thereby held out that the application could receive the countenance or support of the King's Govt. It is certainly of importance for the peace of Ireland that the agitation of the question should be prevented at the present moment if possible, but I will confess to you that it is my individual opinion that it would be better even that the question should be discussed and decided, than that the minds of men should be kept in a feverish state respecting it. The policy of the Catholicks in pressing the question at this moment is to me unintelligible. It never can be combated with greater advantage by those who are hostile to their pretensions, and many who may be in a state of doubt will be decided by the consideration of the expediency of doing anything at present. It is now quite certain that every encouragement has been given to the idea of a petition by the opposition in this country and that they will feel themselves most sincerely disappointed if the question is not by some means or other forced on during the present session.

Source: Hardwicke Papers, Add. MSS. 35,709, f.234.

Lord Hardwicke to Lord Hawkesbury

Private Dublin Castle, 28 January 1805

My dear Lord

I have just been informed by Lord Fingall that at a meeting of the Roman Catholick Committee which was held yesterday, Mr. McDonnel proposed that it should be recommended to the general meeting of the 2d of february to lay aside the intention of petitioning Parliament and to adopt some other course. He suggested two modes by which this object, which upon full consideration notwithstanding his former opinions, he thought important to the interests of the Roman Catholick body, might easily be effected; either by communicating through the medium of the Irish Government to the King's Ministers a statement of their case, or by sending over one or two gentlemen to communicate with Mr. Pitt. Mr. McDonnel was supported by Mr. [D.T.] O'Brien, a Roman Catholick merchant of Dublin of considerable weight and responsibility, who, having seconded the motion for a petition at the first meeting at Mr. Ryan's, felt it necessary to state the reasons which had induced him to alter his opinion; & to consider [it] desirable & expedient to postpone this application to Parliament. Among the reasons assigned by both these gentlemen for their change of opinion, they stated their conviction of the injury the cause would receive by being brought forward as a Party question which they could not avoid apprehending from what had passed in both Houses of Parliament since the opening of the session.[1] Mr. Lynch also supported Mr. McDonnel's proposition in a speech, which in Lord Fingal's opinion did credit to his ability & moderation. There was a considerable difference of opinion upon Mr. M.'s proposal, which received less support & had less effect upon the meeting than Lord F. had expected from the influence which he supposed him to possess. A very long discussion took place which was carried on with some warmth; & the meeting which consisted only of twenty persons, ended by an adjournment to Wednesday next the 30th inst., on which day the Committee will determine what course of proceeding they are to recommend to the general meeting of the 2d of february. Those who support the measure of petitioning, contend that no inconvenience whatever can arise from a discussion in Parliament at this time of the Roman Catholick claims; and that the probability of the question being brought forward at all events, affords an additional reason for presenting a Petition. Upon the whole I collect from Lord Fingall's

[1] In the debates on the Address after the opening of the new session on 15 January the Duke of Norfolk (in the House of Lords) and Fox (in the Commons) had affected surprise and concern at the omission in the King's Speech of any reference to Ireland and the Catholic question (*Hansard* III, 21, 32).

conversation, that a Petition will in all probability be presented to both Houses of Parliament; some of those who urged it having gone so far as to declare that they will certainly present one though there should be only ten signatures besides their own.

Lord Fingall informed me about a week ago that in consequence of Sir Evan Nepean having applied for a copy of the Petition, he had been desired by the meeting at which the circumstance had been mentioned to communicate a copy of it to me, in order to avoid all appearance of a want of personal attention. Having some doubts how far it might be proper to receive a copy of such a paper on the part of the meeting, I told Lord F. that I felt some objection to commit myself in any degree upon a subject of so much delicacy; that being perfectly acquainted with the points to which any Petition or Statement must necessarily refer, & being convinced it would be expressed in proper language, I could easily form an idea of the nature of such a paper, & could have no wish to see it as a matter of curiosity; but that I desired [it] to be understood, if it were considered as a mere private communication from his Lordship that I was by no means disposed to reject what was intended as a mere personal attention in consequence of the Petition having been transmitted to Sir Evan Nepean so long since as the 16th or 17th inst. though if I [had] been informed of his intention to make such an application through any channel whatever I should have thought it right to object to it. After what has passed, if I learn from your Lordship before the next meeting on Wednesday, that it is the wish of H. Majesty's Ministers that I should receive a Statement or Representation for the purpose of being transmitted I shall think it right to communicate it without loss of time; as a knowledge that such a paper will be received & transmitted, may possibly have some effect in preventing the Petition from being presented to Parliament, which I think on every account extremely desireable.

P.S.

Sunday 9 0'clock.

I open my letter to acknowledge the receipt of your letter of the 26th inst. by express; from which I am happy to learn that your Lordship and Mr. Pitt are of opinion that no inconvenience can arise from my consenting to transmit a Representation of the case of the Roman Catholicks to His Majesty's Ministers, as I think it not improbable that it may have some effect in preventing the petition from going forward.

Source: HO 100/128, f. 29.

Alexander Marsden to John King

Secret — Dublin Castle, 30 January 1805

My Dear Sir

I wrote to you by an express this morning which I fear has not got off owing to the strong Easterly winds. . . .

The Catholic Committee met to day, and I have not yet fully ascertained what was done by them, and I am obliged on account of the tide to send this to the Waterside at an early hour—I have just got a note from Lord Fingal of which I make a copy which you will submit to Lord Hawkesbury as a private communication—Lord F. does not encourage us to think that much can be done, and indeed, however he may thin the ranks of the opposition among the Catholics, & gain over those of real weight, there will still be some left who from personal vanity, will be disposed to be active & mischievous, but whose consequence, as representing the Catholic body, may be represented as contemptible.

[Enclosure]

Jany 30th 1805

"Though we did not decide, but separated rather in disorder, every thing I could see leads me to conclude there will be a Petition. All do not approve of it, but a great many will be found to sign—middle measures were but badly received. We some of us agreed to meet at ½ past eleven on Friday morning, previous to the Genl. Meeting on Saturday. I deplore the business in every way I consider it—it is only just now we have broken up our meeting or I should have waited upon you."

Source: HO 100/128, f.37.

Lord Hardwicke to Sir Evan Nepean

Dublin Castle, [3] February 1805

. . . . I wish I could conclude without adverting to the correspondence which you have privately carried on, and the communications which have consequently taken place, with members of the Roman Catholick Committee, without dwelling upon the impropriety of such a correspondence in your situation, and upon a subject of so much delicacy and importance it is sufficient to say that it has had the effect of discrediting the authenticity of the declaration which I was authorized by Lord Hawkesbury's letter of the 15th of November to make to Lord Fingall of Mr. Pitt's opinion and intentions and of weakening the influence which his Lordship and his friends had been exerting to prevent the petition from being presented in Parliament.

From these and other considerations I am compelled to desire that our correspondence upon publick business may now close, and to declare that I no longer consider myself responsible for any of your acts, nor bound by any of your engagements.

Source: Hardwicke Papers, Add. MSS. 35,706, f.177.

Lord Hardwicke to Lord Hawkesbury

Private. Dublin Castle, 3 February 1805

My dear Lord,

I think it necessary to enclose for your Lordship's information a copy of a letter, which I have felt myself under the necessity of writing to Sir Evan Nepean. Your Lordship knows my opinion of the inconvenience which has arisen from his continuing so long in a situation which it was evident he was only intended to hold till a proper arrangement could be made. You are also aware of the endeavours I have used to give effect to the wishes expressed by government to keep back the Roman Catholick Petition, and to support the exertions and influence of Lord Fingall; and I had the satisfaction of learning that there was a prospect of that influence being encreased by the accession of some of the most respectable of the Dublin merchants. I need not under these circumstance express to your Lordship the surprise as well as concern which I have felt at finding that a private correspondence, carried on by Sir Evan Nepean, has tended to give an idea that the declaration which I made in consequence of your letter of the 15th of November of Mr. Pitt's determination to resist the question if brought forward in the present state of affairs, was not his real opinion, but the result of a cabinet decision to which he was committed, though not entirely concurring in it. I do not say that anything to this effect has ever been stated in the secret correspondence to which I allude, but I understand from Lord Fingall himself and from other authority equally to be relied upon, that the idea of the determination of government not being correctly known originated from the application of Sir Evan Nepean for a copy of the Petition in order to shew it to Mr. Pitt, from a report that some communications had passed between Sir Evan's correspondents and some of the Committee, and from the continuance of the same correspondence and communication upon the same subject unknown and unauthorised here, and manifesting a more authentic and direct communication between the Roman Catholicks and the government in England than any that had passed through my channel. Convinced as I am that this course cannot be approved of, I have been obliged to close my correspondence with Sir Evan by a private letter, not choosing to take the strong step of notifying the General Post Office that he is no longer the Chief Secretary.

The meeting of this day adjourned for a fortnight, but I understand the Petition was read and at the next meeting the time of presenting it will be determined.

Source: Hardwicke Papers, Add.MSS. 35,710, f.7.

Lord Hardwicke to William Pitt

Private

Dublin Castle, 3 February 1805

My dear Sir,

[After reproaching Pitt for his failure to answer his letters and iginoring his offer to send the Attorney General to London to discuss the situation in Ireland Lord Hardwicke continues]

In my letter of the 14th of November I stated very strongly, though not more than the occasion required, the great inconvenience which had arisen from the unsettled state in which the important office of Chief Secretary had been suffered to remain, the appointment of Sir Evan Nepean to the Admiralty at the time of his return to Ireland at the end of August having given the idea that he merely held the office till some more proper and official arrangement could be made. . . .

The recent conduct of Sir Evan Nepean has made it absolutely necessary that I should bring our official intercourse and correspondence to a close. My object has been in all communications which I have had with Lord Fingall to confirm him in the opinion which he appeared to have originally formed concerning the inexpediency of bringing forward the question at the present time and under the present circumstances of the country. . . . Lord Fingall has told me more than once that whatever change had taken place in the minds of those who were at first disposed to be violent, was produced by the declaration which I was authorised to make by Lord Hawkesbury in respect to your determination to resist the question to the utmost of your power. . . . This effect however has been counteracted by the return which has been given to a private, unauthorised and unjustifiable correspondence which Sir Evan Nepean has been carrying on since his departure;

and by the communications which have in consequence been made to some of the Roman Catholick Committee. . . .

If therefore the present state of things is suffered to continue for another month, or to express myself more distinctly, if a person proper to fill the office of Chief Secretary is not recommended and approved by the beginning of March I shall feel myself under the necessity of exercising the power which is vested in me by His Majesty's patent and commission, of appointing Lords Justices and returning to England.

Source: Hardwicke Papers, Add. MSS. 35,710, f.9.

Lord Sligo to Lord Hardwicke

7 February 1805

My dear Lord,

. . . .

As to the Catholic question we have nothing but mischief to expect from it. Mr. Pitt most positively asserts he gave no authority for any encouragement being given to present the petition, nor even to ask for a copy . . . . Sir Evan Nepean avows it all to have been his own and with great deference I wish he had more head or we less of him, and Mr. Pitt seems of that mind.

Source: Hardwicke Papers, Add.MSS. 35,756, f.60.

Robert Marshall to Lord Hardwicke

Private. Bagot Street, 10 February 1805

My Lord,

I return your Excellency many thanks for your kind and condescending willingness to comply with my request for an audience, but upon more mature consideration, I entertain doubts whether I ought to give your Excellency the trouble of it, as from the decisiveness of the step you have been pleased to take against Sir Evan Nepean, I rather apprehend, that the means I possess of entirely satisfying Your Excellency's mind with regard to the incorrectness of the information which led to that step, cannot now be employed, with any effect useful to Your Excellency. I regret the circumstance the more, from the cordial desire I feel at all times of testifying my best wishes for your Excellency's service.

Source: Hardwicke Papers, Add.MSS. 35,756, f.101.

Alexander Marsden to John King

Dublin Castle, 14 February 1805

. . . .

I cannot yet pronounce what will be the determination of the Catholics on the 17th [*sic*] inst—I saw Lord Fingal to day, and others—If it be determined to proceed with the Petition I am satisfied that it will be the act of that portion of the Catholic body which is now beginning to be denominated the Opposition; & I think that Lord F. and others who perceive this are becoming averse in a greater degree to this measure, and less disposed to yield to the clamour of others—I cannot however be certain of this.

Source: HO 100/128, f. 62.

Lord Hardwicke to Lord Hawkesbury

Private Dublin Castle, 20 February 1805

My dear Lord,

. . . .

Mr. Scully, who is one of the deputation, also called upon me yesterday, by way of apologies for the communications which he has had with Sir Evan Nepean, both personally, & through the Inspector General of Imports and Exports, Mr. Marshall, conceiving that those communications were entirely with my concurrence, and that he felt it was the same thing as holding them with myself. He said that Sir Evan Nepean had applied for a copy of the petition in order to shew it to Mr. Pitt, and Mr. Marshall had had some communication with him as to the contents of it, and the mode of rendering it more agreeable to Government in point of form & exposition. He admitted that Sir Evan Nepean had advised him strongly to postpone the measure of petitioning, but that he had given the less weight to his opinion from finding him entirely ignorant of the subject & of the history of what had passed upon it of late years in this country. When I explained my surprise at a question having been raised upon the authenticity of the declaration which I had been authorised to make to Lord Fingall of Mr. Pitt's determination to resist the question if brought forward under present circumstances, he said that the authenticity of the declaration had not been questioned, but that it had nevertheless been suggested that the application might be made to Mr. Pitt himself, and that this idea had been strengthened by the application which the Chief Secretary had made for a copy of the petition, as it was supposed by his express desire. . . . Lord Fingall appears to have been extremely hurt at the proceeding which has been adopted and will endeavour to prevent the gentlemen who go to England with a petition from associating as a Deputation with any persons who may be desirous of considering them as objects of party. I understand . . . that the petition will not be sent out of Dublin for signatures.

Source: HO 100/128, f. 67.

Sir George Hill to Alexander Marsden

[Extract] 21 February 1805

There is much anxiety on the Catholic Petition. It is said that Lord H[ardwicke] has dismissed N[epean] for communicating & tampering with the Catholic body without acquainting His Exc. of his doing so. N. avows this, assigning as his excuse that exclusive of his having promised the Catholics not to disclose to H. Exc. (by whom & Mr. A Marsden they have been ill used) what passed, he had a feeling of his own to keep the communication with them a secret from Lord H. as he was certain it would have been imparted by H. Exc. to Mr. A Marsden, whom he (N) did not think a fit person to know anything of the matter. Mr. Pitt not approving of his thus passing by Lord H. he of course quits the Chief Secretaryship.[1]

Source: Hardwicke Papers, Add. MSS. 35,756, f.323.

[1] The extract is in Lord Hardwicke's hand and reads as if it came from a report from a third party which Sir George Hill sent to Marsden.

Sir Evan Nepean to Lord Hardwicke

Admiralty, 5 March 1805

My Lord,

Your Excellency's letter of the 3rd of last month reached me on the 9th, the contents of which are of such a nature that I confess I have been under a considerable degree of difficulty in deciding what line to take upon it.

My first duty however to myself, to my friends and the public is to prove by a plain statement of the facts that I am capable of repelling the charges your Excellency has thought fit to bring against me.

[There follow paragraphs about two minor charges].

The point however of most importance is the charge of my having held a secret intercourse with the Roman Catholics, and thereby counteracting the measure which your Excellency had adopted for the purpose of preventing the Petition to Parliament—and I have been informed that your Excellency has gone so far as to authorize your Private Secretary publicly to avow that my proceedings in this business have been of such a nature as to preclude the possibility of your holding any further correspondence with me.

That I had a secret intercourse with a person in Ireland connected with the Roman Catholics[1] is most certain, and I have the satisfaction of finding that he is ready to come forward, and to contradict in the most positive and unqualified terms the imputations implied in your Excellency's letter.

By his testimony, as well as that of Lord Fingall and every other person with whom I communicated, I can if necessary establish beyond question the fact that so far from discrediting, I have given every weight and authority to the official communication announcing Mr. Pitt's intended line of conduct, and otherwise distinctly discountenanced the measure of a petition.

But in the situation in which I was placed I did most undoubtedly think it my duty to collect every information in my power of the views and proceedings of the Roman Catholics and to communicate it to Mr. Pitt, and if I could obtain this information for him only upon a most positive stipulation of withholding all knowledge of the particulars from your Excellency and from every other person connected with the Castle, I certainly did not hesitate, nor should I hesitate again if placed in similar circumstances, to receive on those terms information which I conceived to be so important to the public service.

[1] Probably Robert Marshall (see p.52). According to an entry for 5 March in his Diary Scully assured Nepean that he and other members of the committee would, if desired, come forward to clear him.

And I mention, not as apology to your Excellency, but merely that I may state the whole case, in refutation of a partial or mistaken statement of it, the circumstance of my having given your Excellency such advantage from my intelligence, as I felt to be consistent with my engagements to those to whom I was indebted for it, by more than once pointing out to your Excellency the inaccuracy of the information you had obtained thro' other channels, and I recollect one instance particularly during the absence of Lord Fingall from Dublin on a point which had relation to the powers which had been vested in the Select Committee.

As to the cessation of our official intercourse Your Excellency will know that nothing you have said, or can say, has or can have had any effect whatever in producing the step on which I had long determined, and which I have only waited Mr. Pitt's convenience to carry into effect, and I have now the satisfaction of learning from him that such measures have been taken as will lead to the immediate nomination of my successor.

Source: Hardwicke Papers, Add. MSS. 35,715, f.215.

William Pitt to Lord Hardwicke

Downing Street, 9 March 1805

My dear Lord,

. . . .

It is a matter of great concern to me that you should have received so unfavourable an impression of Sir Evan Nepean's conduct, but I wish rather to abstain from dwelling on that subject, being persuaded that if you are satisfied with the person proposed as his successor you cannot be desirous of indulging any retrospect, or of terminating his mission in any manner unnecessarily painful to himself or his friends. I think it is only necessary to say, on the subject of the Catholic petition, that he has given here the strongest assurance of his conduct having been very different from what appears to have been represented to you, and that he did everything in his power to discourage its being brought forward. I have not yet seen the Catholic deputies, but probably shall on Monday.

Source: Hardwicke Papers, Add. MSS. 35,710, f.40.

Lord Hardwicke to Lord Redesdale

[Copy] Dublin Castle, 11 March 1805

My dear Lord,

I send you for perusal a letter from Mr. Pitt which I received this morning by an express of Saturday. From the latter part, in which he refers to Sir E. N.'s exculpation of his conduct in respect to the Roman Catholic Petition, it is evident that he has forgotten the ground of the complaint, which was not that he had encouraged the Roman Catholics to present a petition, but that by communicating through Mr. Scully both directly and through Mr. Marshall, he had given an idea to persons ready enough to adopt it, that the communication made to the meeting by Lord Fingall was not a correct statement of Mr. Pitt's sentiments. Mr. Lynch, a Barrister & nephew of Sir Thomas French, asserts that when Lord F, made the declaration of Mr. Pitt's intention to resist the petition that Mr. Scully denied it to be the true statement of Mr. Pitt's intentions, & referred to a conversation which Lord F. himself had had with Sir Evan Nepean, as a ground for his expressing the doubt. I have also understood, what was by no means unnatural when people are disposed to catch at any thing, that Scully's connection with a Cambridgeshire family and acquaintance with me from that circumstance, gave a greater degree of weight to what he alledged in regard to Mr. Pitt's real sentiments. It is also well known that Scully was against the petition at the present time, at the first two meetings, and that it was not till after his communication with Sir Evan Nepean that he became so violently in favour of it. . . .

Source: Hardwicke Papers, Add. MSS. 35,778, f.98.

Lord Hawkesbury to Lord Hardwicke

Whitehall, 17 March 1805

My dear Lord,

The Catholic deputies have had their interview with Mr. Pitt. It passed off as well as could be wished and Mr. Pitt was led to believe that they would not put the petition in the hands of any person in opposition and that they would authorise the person who presented it to declare that it was not their wish to press for any decision on the question at the present moment. We have since however learnt that they have been tampered with by some of the members of opposition, and that it is not unlikely that the business will at last be devolved upon them. However this may be it is certainly desireable to keep ourselves in the right as long as possible and it is therefore very much to be deprecated that in the present state of things counter addresses should be presented or counter resolutions voted by the Grand Juries and other publick bodies. . . .

Source: Hardwicke Papers, Add. MSS. 35,710, f.42.

Lord Hardwicke to Lord Hawkesbury

Private
[Draft/copy] Dublin Castle, 23 March 1805

My dear Lord.

Your letter of the 17th was received by the express the day before yesterday. . . .

Your Lordship may be sure that I will use my best endeavours to prevent the expression of any Protestant feeling in consequence of the measures of the Roman Catholicks. I flatter myself however that no disposition will appear on the part of the gentlemen of the country to present Counter Addresses, or to promote representations from the Grand Juries at the Assizes. It is a matter of considerable delicacy and I should be apprehensive that in some places the measure itself might be suggested by the desire to avoid it. In consequence however of the opinion expressed in your letter, in which I most entirely concur, I have already spoken to different persons whose discretion I can rely on, and who are likely to attend the Asizes . . . I will also take care to let it be understood in places where such a feeling may possibly be excited, that it is the anxious wish of Government to avoid any measure that may tend to provoke discussion or produce irritation, and to confine the consideration of the question, if it is to be brought forward, to the two Houses of Parliament.[1]

Source: Hardwicke Papers, Add. MSS. 35,710, f.50.

[1] There follow three pages, struck out by a line drawn down the middle, in which Lord Hardwicke voices his fears about the *Dublin Journal*. It is wrongly supposed, he says, that nothing in it is printed without first being approved by the government. Although Giffard, the editor, and his son were generally inclined to support Government and had derived considerable emoluments from the way in which they had been favoured, there were three subjects on which they claimed a degree of independence, one of them being the Catholic question. It might be expedient, he suggests, to take steps to ensure that the character of the government did not suffer from their rashness and violence.

II

DENYS SCULLY'S LONDON DIARY

INSTRUCTIONS TO THE DEPUTATION

At a numerous meeting of Roman Catholic Noblemen, gentlemen and merchants held by adjournment in Dublin on Saturday the 16th February 1805

RESOLVED UNANIMOUSLY

1st That Lord Fingall, Honble. Sir Thomas French, Sir Edwd. Bellew, Counsellor Denys Scully and Mr. Ryan be appointed as a deputation to carry into effect the under-mentioned Instructions, and that the other Roman Catholic peers (of whom Lords Trimlestown and Southwell are now present) be requested to accede to the deputation.

2nd That the petition prepared by the Catholic Committee and reported by Lord Fingall to this meeting, be now signed by Lord Fingall and the other Roman Catholic gentlemen, and that the above mentioned deputies do present it to Mr. Pitt, with a request that he will bring it into Parliament—they being authorized to state to him that if he shall feel himself precluded by strong reasons from supporting the petition at this moment, the petitioning Catholics authorize him to state that they do not press the immediate adoption of the measure prayed for—And if Mr. Pitt shall decline introducing the petition under such circumstances, that then they shall procure its introduction by such other Member as shall seem most eligible, with authority to such Member to make the like declaration in the like case of his Majesty's ministers declaring themselves precluded from affording their support at this moment.

Tuesday, 26 February 1805

I prepared for a journey to London as one of a deputation of 5 persons appointed at a meeting of R. Cathc. gentlemen on the 16th inst. to cause the Catholic petition, to be presented to Parliament. The other deputies being Lord Fingall, Honl. Sir Thomas French, Sir E. Bellew, Mr. Jams. Ryan, & such other Cathc. peers as shall accede to the Deputation.

I embarked this evening for Holyhead in the *Uxbridge* Packet, Capt. Jones, and found among the passengers, Lds. Fingall & Southwell, Honl. Col. Plunket, & Mr. Jas. Ryan.

Wednesday, 27 February

Arrived at Holyhead about noon after a passage of 14 hours & took a place in the Mail Coach for London tomorrow.

Examined my letters of introduction to London, & found letters,

from Mr. George Ponsonby	to the Honl. Charles Grey
	to the Hon. C. J. Fox
	to Major Ponsonby
from Richd. Kirwan Esq.	to Lord Trimleston
from Wm. Fletcher Esq.	to Dens. Bowes Daly Esq.
from W. McMahon	to Col. McMahon
from Robt. Marshall	to Lord Castlereagh
	to Lord Chichester
	to Edward Cooke Esq.
	to John Foster Esq.
	to Genl. Dalrymple
	to Ld. Hutchinson
	to Dens. Browne Esq.

Also a letter

from Mr. McKenna	to Capt. Dardis
from R. Marshall	to Sir George Shee Bart.
	to Earl of Dorchester

Thursday, 28 February

Left Holyhead in a mail coach for London.

Saturday, 2 March 1805

Arrived in London at 7 this morning & drove to Mrs. Bostock's, in Thayer Street. Found there a note from Mr. Chas. Butler of Lincoln's Inn, requesting me particularly to let him know of my arrival, as soon as I should come to town.

At eleven, called upon the Revd. Mr. Underhill of Lincoln's Inn Fields chapel, found him at home, and conversed with him more than half an hour, chiefly upon the Cathc. subject.

At 12, called upon Mr. Chas. Butler of Lincoln's Inn, found him at home. He said he wished much to see me that he might know the real intention of the Irish Catholics, and our objects as Deputies, as Mr. Fox etc were quite displeased with what had been rumoured to be their object—I explained the matter and he seemed satisfied—especially in finding that the Caths. intend to petition annually. He suggested that they ought to employ Counsel to state their case at the bar of Parliament & strongly recommended Mr. Curran for that purpose. He praised Mr. Fox highly—He thinks the Prince of Wales' sentiments upon the subject very uncertain—that he talks both ways—that he inwardly does not like Caths.—which is the case of all the royal family—but the Prince has said to him (Butler) when he was introduced to him by Mr. Sheridan, that he agreed with him in all his sentiments about Ireland, and that every thing must be done for Ireland—that the Prince paid him (Butler) some personal compliments. On the whole, that the Prince is unsteady, & has adopted the line of forbidding his particular members, McMahon & Tyrwhit, from supporting it in Parlt., but that his great friends, Lord Moira etc, are to support it.

Mr. Butler proposed going with me to introduce me to Mr. Fox, and talk with him immediately upon the subject, to which I acceded—and we went immediately, and called upon Mr. Fox in Arlington Street, but he was not at home. We then called upon Mr. Sheridan in George's Street Hanover Square, but he was also out—Mr. Butler then parted from me with great expressions of civility & regard, repeating his wish that I should again call upon Mr. Fox this very day.

About 2 o'clock I called upon Ld. Castlereagh in Upper Brook Street No.12. He was at home. I sent Marshall's letter up to him, & was shown upstairs into his study. He received me with great civility, considering his general coldness of manner. He led me to the Catholic subject, and affected great concern that we should have come forward to petition—that the time is very unfavourable etc—that the public mind is unprepared—that the ministry with all their strength, at this moment, could not carry it—that the coronation oath is still considered an insuperable obstacle—tho' he is not of that opinion—that the Test Laws are also considered necessary to be inviolably adhered to—that for his part he is personally favourable to our measure in every point of view, but that he sees no chance of any success at present. He wished, at any rate and above all things, that we should avoid all discussion of it in Parlt. He desired not to be understood as speaking the opinion of Mr. Pitt, for that he will give his own opinion at the proper time—and he wished to know how soon we should desire to have an interview with Mr. Pitt—He gave me to understand that Mr. Pitt is perfectly willing to give it.

When I mentioned my own idea of a Declaratory Vote of Parlt. in our favour upon the principle, as a mode of gratifying the Caths. which would not infringe the coronation oath, and when I added, that, if such a vote were procured, I should for my part be content for the present session, he objected to it as an impracticable object. He stated a variety of objections to it, but, upon discussion, waved the greater number of them, and at length seemed to entertain the project—so that it evidently made some impression upon him.

He listened, with pleasure & attention, to my expression of the leaning of Caths. of property towards Mr. Pitt, & generally seemed to give consideration to the different facts & opinions which I communicated, tending to impress Government favourably towards the Caths.—in which I took all the pains in my power, explaining fully the circumstances & reasons which have impelled them now to come forward.—When I left he seemed quite uncertain about the course to be taken—He appears to be the person entrusted by Mr. Pitt with the management of the business. Our conversation lasted more than an hour.

I went again to Mr. Fox's and left Mr. Ponsonby's letter for him. He was gone to Carleton House, and not expected home till late, & to go the country in the morning for a few days. I left my card and a message that I would call upon him at ½ p.9 in the morning.

I called at half past four at Colonel McMahon's house in Charles Street and left his brother William's letter for him, & a note to say, that I would call again at eleven tomorrow morning.

Sunday, 3 March 1805

At half after nine called upon Mr. Fox, found him at home, and conversed an hour with him upon the Cathc. subject.

He much disapproved of the measure they proposed to take—said, that it lays them at the feet of Mr. Pitt—that it discredits their cause, and weakens the zeal of their friends—that they will lose much in point of parliamentary strength by it—and that it would be better to have had no petition than one under such a restriction as this. He had seen letters from even some of the Catholic committee stating the grounds supposed to be taken, especially one from Lord Fingall—and that he took his impressions from these—for no other letters or mention of the subject have appeared here save from those persons—He had even heard that we had made an express instruction, not to receive the aid of the opposition. He thinks that our making a declaration against pressing the adoption of the measure now, has the effect of declaring against it during the king's reign—that he censured such an idea—it points odium against the king—He said that we appear to have acted as Charles 2d did—to court our enemies and neglect our friends—He added (ironically) that we have been too great politicians in the business.

He has heard that the king, within these few days, has applauded Pitt for having managed & played us off so well for him. On the whole, he considers us to be in a very bad situation.

When I ment[ione]d the idea of pressing Mr. Pitt to a Declaratory Vote of both Houses upon the principle, he approved of it—said that alone could get us out of the scrape—and advised, that if we feel ourselves authorized, we should get that point carried—There is no doubt, he said, but the prince will, immediately upon coming to the throne, carry the measure—this is beyond question—a thing perfectly settled and certain—no doubt also, but Mr. Pitt could, if he chose, carry it now thro' both Houses by an immense majority—The minority could not, in the Commons, amount to 70, if the House should count 450—in the Lords the minority might be now strong, but still he could certainly carry it for us—he listened, but rather impatiently, to my explanation of the real intentions of the proposed proceedings—he read the paper containing our instructions—and agreed in my interpretation of them—but said that the general understanding would be, that we ourselves have given an opinion against the discussion—however, towards the close of the conversation, he seemed to be more inclined to make allowances for the situation of the Caths. and to understand their proceedings as we could wish—He desired to see me again on his return to town in a couple of days.

He was in a plain woollen dressing gown, and without his cravat.

At half p.10 I called at Lord Moira's, but he had left town last night for Leicestershire, & his return was uncertain,[1]

I then called at the Marquis of Buckingham's, and left the letter of Mr. McKenna for Captn. Dardis, but he had gone into the country, and was ill. His return also uncertain.

At eleven I called upon Colonel McMahon at his house, 16 Charles Street, found him at home, and conversed for upwards of an hour with him.

He is certain that the Prince will be our friend, and that he is now most warmly interested for our success—but he has lately formed a resolution (by Mr. Fox's.advice) to avoid exposing himself to slander and obloquy, which would attend his taking a public part in it—he will therefore not vote himself for it, nor suffer his few confidential members to vote—but all his friends in Parlt. (who are not actually in his service as McMahon, Tyrwhit etc) will support us. He, McMahon, disapproves of this, and suggests my endeavouring to change Mr. Fox's opinion upon it, and to get it to come to the Prince from him rather than from McMahon.

He offered to present me to the Prince—but we agreed to defer it until after we should have seen Mr. Pitt—he thinks Mr. Pitt our most powerful support, if he will

[1] See p.86. Scully had for several years enjoyed the friendship of Lady Moira but there is no evidence that he knew her son, who may have wanted to avoid him.

come forward—and advised my seeing him. He thinks the best channel will be thro' Sir E. Nepean, and that no time should be lost. He thinks it very doubtful what Pitt will do—whether to propose the measure to the King and carry it, or to make his departure from Ministry upon it, & keep us in his hands, or refuse us altogether. He does not think that the King has used any such expression, as Mr. Fox mentd. to me, for he knows that within the last 8 days the King was wholly ignorant that there was to be any petition—and he does not believe that Mr. Fox has any channel of information of what the King may have said since—but he would not wonder if the King took it perfectly easy, for he believes him to be wholly insensible, & not much anxious on any subject—that the common idea, that such a thing would derange his mind etc, seemed very erroneous in this respect, & is contradicted by frequent experience—for he has latterly heard many things of that kind, without being disturbed—He appeared rather surprised at learning that Lord Moira left town last night, for he had dined at Lord Grenville's. He advised my calling upon Chas. Grey by all means, as he can influence Mr. Fox's mind, and explain to him what is necessary—He was going to Carleton House, would see the Prince, and desired to see me again tomorrow at eleven.

At half p.12, I called upon Sir E. Nepean at the Admiralty Office, found that he was gone to Mr. Pitt for half an hour—I left my card & address, & said I would call at 12 tomorrow.

At one, called upon Mr. Charles Grey at his house 7 Portugal Street, Park Lane—He was not at home. I left Mr. G. Ponsonby's letter for him and a message that I would call at 9 tomorrow morning.

I then called upon Mr. Edw. Cooke at his house, North Row, Park Lane and (he being out) left Marshall's letter for him and my card—there is no certain hour of seeing him.

Afterwards I called on Lord Hutchinson at his house, 71 Park Street, and (he being out) left Marshall's letter for him, and my card for him and his brother Christopher.[1]

Dined at Mrs. Bostock's in Thayer Street in company with Henry Huddleston. He told me his friend Mr. Green, a Catholic Attorney of Gray's Inn Square, is one of the proprietors of the *Morning Post*, and requested him to communicate to me his willingness to insert from time to time such articles as might be useful—I wrote immediately an article of some length which I gave to H. Huddleston for that purpose.

At seven received an extremely polite note from Sir E. Nepean. It was dated ½ past two, & desired my company to dine with him today at 6—I wrote in answer that I recd. his note too late for that purpose, but would wait upon him at the Admiralty at one tomorrow.

[1] Christopher Hely Hutchinson.

Monday, 4 March 1805

At nine called upon Mr. Chas Grey, but he was not up, nor expected to be up for an hour yet—The best hour for seeing him is eleven.

Afterwards took lodgings at Willis', an attorney, 7 Great Rider Street, St. James's.

At ten went to the St. James's Coffee House, and saw in the *Morning Post* the article[1] which I wrote last night. At eleven called on Colonel McMahon's, but found a note there from him, saying he had been called out unexpectedly by indispensable business & desiring me to appoint either tomorrow or Wednesday morning. I left a note for him giving my own address at Great Rider St. & leaving it to himself to make the next appointment.

A little before 12 I called upon Sir E. Nepean at the Admiralty, but he was confined in the Board Room and could receive no message until two.

Called at Byfield, the newsvendor & sent the *Morning Post* thro' him to Mrs. S[cully] in Bagot Street—& wrote to her this post.

Called upon Lord Fingall & Col[one]l[2] Plunket at Nr. 5 George St. Hanover Square, but they were out.

Called on Lord Southwell at Fladong's Hotel, and found him at breakfast (at one) with Lord Fingall & his brother & Mr. Dom[inic]k O'Reilly—found that they had come last night only to town—made an appointment to meet them at breakfast at 9 tomorrow morning—Ld. F. etc in great spirits at the paragraph in the *Morning Post.*

Called in Thayer St. and removed my luggage etc in a coach to my new lodgings in Great Rider St.

A little after 2 called upon Sir E. Nepean at the Admiralty, but he was still confined in the Board Room—I found that Mr. Corry was waiting above stairs to see him & I met the Abp. of Dublin's[3] coach at the Admiralty door, & himself going in—he past me quite close & went up stairs rather surlily—I sent up my card to Sir Evan, & he sent me down a note which he had written in the morning, appointing a meeting in Thayer St. at half past ten tomorrow morning.

Afterwards called upon Mr. James Ryan, my colleague, 34 Clarges Street, but he was not at home.

Left Mr. Geo. Ponsonby's letter and my card at Mr. John Ponsonby's house 31 Curzon St.—he being not at home—and also left Marshall's letter and my card at Sir George Shee's house, 9 Berkeley Square—He and his family are staying at Nottinghill House, Kensington Gravel Pits—but he comes to town every day.

Called at Mrs. Bostock's in Thayer St. to apprize her of Sir Evan Nepean's

[1] See Appendix C.

[2] See p.22, n.2. On leaving Prague Lord Fingall's brother had been promoted to the rank of Colonel

[3] Charles Agar, Viscount Somerton, formerly Archbishop of Cashel, where Scully may have known him at least by sight.

intention of calling upon me tomorrow—and to get the keys of my trunks, which I had forgotten.

Returned to Great Rider Street & found that Mr. Chr. H. Hutchinson had called upon me.

Mr. Jas. Ryan also called, and proposed my going with him to Mr. John Ponsonby's, Curzon Street—and accordingly we went and called there at 5 o'clock, but he was not at home. He then proposed my going with him & his friend Mr. Evans to dine at the Piazza C[offee] House, to which I consented. We accordingly dined there—I saw Sir M. Somerville and old John Beresford there at separate tables—Also Lds. Fingall, Southwell & Colonel Plunket passed by the C. room after having dined in a private room in the house

At half past eight called at Ginger's, Piccadilly & agreed to take books from him for what he has sold of my pamphlets.[1]

He says that Mr. McKenna's late pamphlet[2] does not sell yet—but that Mr. Bellew,[3] who wrote the *Trinodia Necessitas*, has praised it very highly to him—there is no recent publication very interesting or much in demand from the booksellers

Tuesday, 5 March 1805.

Breakfasted at Lord Fingall's lodging at Nr.3 George's Street Hanover Square, in company with Lord Southwell, Colonel Plunket & Mr. Ryan.

We talked over our business, but no interesting information appeared. Ld. Fingall rather inclined to ask Mr. Pitt for as much for the Catholics as can be had—Lord Southwell doubtful whether we can at all hope for any thing—Mr. Ryan, decided that we should ask, & doubtful whether we ought to execute the authority invested in us to declare etc to Mr. Pitt

At ten went to Mrs. Bostock's where at half past ten Edward Cooke called, and conversed with me upon the subject, stated the objections about the Test Laws, but expatiated much upon the great advantages to the Empire from granting our claims—He admitted all this, but confined himself to the objection resulting from the King's scruples. He talked much upon the present state of Ireland, the number of Catholics in the south and west, and hoped much for their advantage—He was extremely civil—but seemed to have a guard over his conversation, and stopped himself two or three times as if he was on the point of saying something beyond what was prudent.

[1] *An Irish Catholic's Advice to his brethren* and (with McKenna) *The Address of the Roman Catholics of Dublin*, both published in 1803, the former being followed in 1804 by a second edition in which Scully replied to his critics.[2] On the *Civil condition of the clergy* (see p.10). The London edition, printed for J.Budd, is dated February, but was still unpublished as late as 4 April.[3] Robert Bellew, whose *Hibernica Trinodia Necessitas* was published in 1803. The three necessities were a regulation of tithes, a provision for the clergy and Catholic Emancipation.

At eleven, and just as Mr. Cooke was going away, Sir Evan Nepean called—We talked upon the Cathc. subject—He did not seem to think so badly of our chance as Cooke or Lord Castlereagh—He said that we might depend upon the utmost civility from Mr. Pitt—that it was not by any means as yet resolved to reject us—that it would be submitted by Mr. P. to his Majesty's confidential servants—that there would, of course, be some differences amongst them upon such a subject, but the result is uncertain—At all events, no persons could be more agreeable as deputies to Government, than we are, especially as it is understood that Mr. Ryan is only deputed as from the commercial body, & was so proposed by Mr. R. McDonnell—that our reception should be most kind. He said (as did Mr. Cooke) that upon the main subject there are many considerations both ways—and he added that they were very weighty on both sides and would take time to adjust and decide upon—He said that, as for the report that his Majesty's mind is of late become more favourable towards us, he has not ascertained the fact, and does not know how the matter stands—He appeared to be seriously attentive to the several observations which I urged in favour of Ministry granting at this time what we desire, and upon the improbability of their ever finding another opportunity so favourable, or having to treat with deputies of this description.

We then talked upon his recent difference with Lord Hardwicke, & he was gratified by my statement of the facts upon that occasion—and my assurance that I, and the others of the committee, would be ready to come forward, whenever he pleased, to clear him, Sir Evan.[1] He said he felt as perfect a contempt for Lord H. as Lord H. perhaps did for him—that he was as independent & as perfectly respectable in the world as Lord. H. and felt superior to his attempts—that he had signified to Lord H. his sentiments pretty strongly—and that, after what had passed, he could not think of going back to take office under Lord H.—but that no successor is yet named.

He invited me to dine with him on Friday at his house at Fulham and will take me out in his carriage.

After I had staid about 2 hours at Mrs. Bostock's, I went to Lord Trimleston's No.17 Portland Place, and delivered the letter to him from Mr. Richard Kirwan of Dublin & my card. He was at home and I had about three quarters of an hour's conversation with him—It was loose, but generally relating to the Cathc. subject. He is for the petition, if we have Ministry with us, but against it, if Ministry oppose us—He will put his name to it and join in our proceedings—He talked about old times, the state of Ireland etc., etc. I then called on Mr. Ryan according to appointment, but he was not at home—tho' it was past one. I then called upon Mr. Fox, and left my card; then went back to my lodgings. Afterwards went to Ginger's in Piccadilly & ordered home some writing paper.

[1] See Nepean's letter of this day to Lord Hardwicke (p.55).

Delivered Marshall's letter at Mr. Denis Browne's, 23 Dover St. & left my card, he being out.

Called at Lord Llandaff's in Grafton Street, & left my card, he being in Cheltenham & not expected back for 10 days.

Called at Lord Mathew's, 23 Albermarle Street, & left my card—he leaves town very shortly for Ireland.

Delivered Marshall's letter at Mr. Foster's Lower Brook Street, & left my card, he being out.

Called again upon Mr. Chas. Grey, found him at home, & talked upwards of an hour with him. He appeared very reasonable, moderate & perfectly a man of business. He thought that it would be gaining a point, if Mr. Pitt would lay our petition upon the table of the House, with a declaration in favour of its principle, and did not agree with Mr. Fox, that it would weaken our claims. He read our Instructions & desired a copy, which I promised to give. He spoke of proposing a meeting to Mr. Fox, Lord Grenville etc to consider what is to be done, & what they would advise us to do, but he professed that he would abide by whatever Fox should think upon it. He asked whether I had seen Lord Grenville, and said that he and Fox were most interested for us. Upon reading our Instructions he seemed to think that Fox's construction is the natural and ordinary one, and that a special pleading upon it will not be admitted—that Mr. Pitt will make the greatest possible advantage of it—and that it would be very awkward to force a discussion with such a declaration against it—that the division in our favour would be a very small one—less by a hundred than otherwise. He proposes to talk about it with Mr. Fox, and arrange some plan with him.

He inquired very particularly about the present state of Ireland—and asked earnestly my opinion, whether I thought that (even upon the now existing penal laws) a new government in Ireland, liberally composed of fair popular men, acting justly by the people, preventing all violence and injustice and making no distinction between persons on account of their religion, would not be a government that might conciliate the people for the present and attach them to the common cause. He added that such a government should give equal employment to Caths. as well as Prots.; and shew and profess a disposition to grant all that remains to be granted when it would be in their power. I answered that I thought such a government would answer well, provided the people could consider it a stable one, and could see that it had a good footing and support in the English cabinet. He seemed much satisfied with this. He was generally very civil, and seems altogether a very superior man, and particularly clear, rational, manly and unaffected.

Returned to my lodgings & about four Mr. Richd. Martin of Galway called upon me, and professed much good will to our mission. He said that a friend of his, a Mr. Johnstone of Hanover Square (M.P.) would call upon me and ask me to dine—He asked many questions about what we had done and would do etc—said that Lord Mathew will support us, but Bagwell not—the Knight of Kerry [Maurice Fitzgerald] also supports us. He pressed me to go and take a beefsteak with him and a friend, but this I declined as I must stay at home the evening.

Whilst he was with me, Mr. Denis Browne came to return my visit of this morning, and seemed quite warm against our petition, tho' he will vote for us—said that he thinks, and will declare in the House, that tho' he votes for it, he thinks it imprudent and highly mischievous in us now to come forward—the Empire being distressed, the same obstacles remaining, Mr. Pitt unsettled in his place etc,—that he knew the whole was set on by opposition—that they boasted at the end of the last session that they would put Pitt to the wall with the Catholic question—and Lord King has since put up Ryan to the agitation of it—that the whole is the work of a few ambitious men, eager to embarrass the Minister—that to his certain knowledge we are ruining the measure, and making eventual success for ever impossible. He used many arguments of this nature very fully and at length, but begging my pardon, as he proceeded in his discourse. He had it from Mr. Pitt's own lips very lately (when he asked him his opinion on our petition) that nothing could be more improper and injurious to the public, by throwing fresh obstacles in the way of success. There was much conversation & explanation upon this subject, between him and Mr. Martin (who opposed him)—I heard him very quietly, and when he was done, I explained to him a few points, as to the origin and progress of this measure not entering into the main argument with him at present—which softened him greatly.

He said, however, that if the discussion came forward, which he thinks inevitable, the greatest mischief to the cause will ensue. Numbers of members, having the Court at their back, will declaim most violently & publish their speeches—many are now primed and prepared to inveigh against us. Out of doors also a great noise will be made. They will write pamphlets, paragraphs in newspapers, preach in pulpits against us, and thus an outcry from one end of the kingdom to the other—We shall have anew the Protestant mob and zeal, and all the old fury revived. He is sure that at all events the opposition are determined to force a discussion, whether the Caths. please it or not—for they have boasted that they would. He paid some high compliments, however, to the character of the deputies (except Ryan) and said much of compliment to me particularly—he said that Marshall in his letter requested him to introduce me to the Marquis of Sligo—The Marquis is not able (from illness) to come out, or he would wait upon me—but, if I will meet him there at eleven tomorrow, he will introduce me to the Marquis. After all he said against our mission, he went away in good humour, as if he had been relieved by venting his displeasure.

Mr. Martin ou[t] staid Mr. D. Browne, and, after a little conversation in which he repeated his desire to take a beefsteak with me today & offered his services generally and gave me a frank for Sawston,[1] he left me.

Lord Mathew called & left his card.

[1] Seat of Scully's father-in-law near Cambridge.

I sent a note to Chas. Butler (in answer to one from him) promising to go on Thursday to Mrs. Butler's music party, and thanking him for his communications.

Wrote to Lord Fingall for the petition, which he sent to me in return by his servant, with a note, desiring to see me to meet Sir Edward Bellew at eleven tomorrow, to which I sent a note in answer, that I would call at half p. ten, being engaged to Lord Sligo's at eleven.

Wednesday, 6 March 1805

At half past nine, called at Mr. Grey's, and, he not being up, left the copy of our Instructions as I promised, including it in a note enjoining his holding it as a confidential communication from me.

At ten called at Mrs. Bostock's.

At half p. ten called at Lord Fingall's, & found him at home with his brother and a Major Burke of the German service.[1] Mr. Ryan called in, & afterwards Mr. Edward Hay. We talked upon Catholic subjects. At eleven I called at the Marquis of Sligo's upon Mr. Denis Browne. He was at home and introduced me to the Marquis. He and the Marchioness were at breakfast. I staid there almost an hour. We talked about Ireland generally, its population, the recent disturbances, their causes and nature, the state of trade etc. And he said he wished to be prepared upon those subjects for the debate expected this week in the House of Lords upon the Habeas Corpus Suspension Bill—The Marquis did not talk upon the Catholic subject—but his brother Denis Browne talked with me about it in a separate room, but evidently in a less peremptory tone against it than he used yesterday—The Marquis seems a good hearted jolly plain man, corpulent and infirm—his brother Denis seems a bustling empty freshcoloured Irish squire, quite calculated for the old local Parlt. of Ireland, having no idea of public good or difference from the Minister.

At half p.12 called at Mr. Fox's, but he was out.

At one, came to Lord Fingall's by appointment, and found him with Lord Southwell, Coll. Plunket. Sir Edwd. Bellew, Sir Hugh O'Reilly and Mr. White of Leixlip. Mr. Ryan came soon afterwards—and we held a meeting of an hour. composed of Lords F. and S., Sir E. Bellew, Mr. Ryan and myself. Discussed some points, but came to no final resolution, Sir T. French not being come yet—agreed to wait till Friday for him—and to dine together tomorrow at Fladong's in Oxford Street at 5 o'clock. Returned to my lodgings at a little before 3—and afterwards went out, and met Lord Mathew, who goes tomorrow to Ireland for a fortnight, & requested me to write to him at New Geneva Barracks, Waterford, in case we should want him, as he is at our command, and obeying the orders of the Committee.

Called at Mr. Richard Martin's, at Beall's hotel, Jervis, & left my card. Called upon Mr. John Joseph Dillon, No. 2 Lincoln's Inn, New Square, found him at

[1] Unidentified. *The Times* of 23 May reported the departure of an Irish contingent for Prussia.

home, and talked half an hour with him on the Cathc. subject & his pamphlets—He is going to publish a new edition of his former pamphlet in favour of Caths. sitting in Parliament.[1]

He inveighed much against Charles Butler, and says he does not speak with him—that he is a deceitful undermining & envious man, especially against young barristers—and that he appears lately to have acted scandalously in Lord Arundel's business.

At 5 called upon Mr. H. Huddleston at Gray's Inn Sq., but he was not at home. I called again in half an hour & found him & agreed to meet him in an hour at the Gray's Inn Coffee house.

At six dined at the Gray's Inn Coffee house, and in half an hour Mr. Huddleston joined me, whilst I was writing a paragraph to give him for his friend Mr. Green of the *Morning Post*. I finished the paragraph & gave it to him to send this night.[2] We then talked upwards of an hour together, and he agreed to call on me next Friday at half past ten o'clock to introduce me to Mr. John Huddleston, the India Director who is in Parliament, and has lodgings in Duke Street, St. James.

At half past nine I returned to my lodgings.

Thursday, 7 March 1805

At half p. nine called upon Mr. Fox—but he was not up, having come home late from the House of Commons.

At ten breakfasted at the York C. house, St. James's Street.

At nearly eleven left the case of Mrs. Scully's health at Dr. Baillie's, 72 Grosvenor Street, for his opinion, with 2 g[uinea]s fee—& that I shall call for the answer of the Doctr. on Monday morning next between 9 & 10, which is his only time for seeing visitors.

At eleven called upon the Earl of Dorchester at his house, Tilney Street, Mayfair, & sent in Marshall's letter to him—I was shown in to him and found him sitting in an arm chair, unable to use his feet, but perfectly well (as he said) and in excellent spirits in all other respects. He spoke very kindly of my father[3] & quite decidedly upon supporting the Catholic petition. I explained to him that it came forward principally from the Catholics who supported the Union. He said he sent two hogsheads of strong beer 14 months ago to Poole in Dorsetshire to a Mr. Jeffries, which have been lying there ever since, and one of them was to be forwarded to my father. He said that my father is one of the strongest minded, most acute and honest men he ever knew, & that (he knows not how) in 3 or 4 days they became quite intimate. He talked much of the state of Ireland and in favour of our claims—and desired to see me any morning before 12, or about 2 o'clock.

[1] No new edition of his 1801 pamphlet has been found.

[2] See Appendix C.

[3] James Scully was one of the Earl's tenants in Co. Tipperary.

At half p.12 I called upon Lord Shrewsbury, Stanhope Street, Mayfair—found him at home with his lady & Mrs. Selby. He feels very spiritedly upon the Catholic subject—and inclined to press a discussion. He & his lady talked about the stage, singers, actors, and Betty, the young Roscius.[1] They also enquired a good deal about our Catholic business and seemed very much interested in its favour.

At 12, I called upon the Marquis of Sligo according to appointment—found him alone. He entered much at large into our Cathc. subject—spoke with much feeling & apparent sincerity on the justice of our claims—he is almost wedded to it, & will support us, but that discussion must now be very prejudicial, as success is hopeless, & it will only injure & alienate Mr. Pitt to force it upon him—He spoke very sensibly and impressively upon this subject and seems a very fair honest man—said he had it from Mr. Pitt's own mouth within this week, that our coming forward is imprudent & injurious—recommended our putting it in as good a train for avoiding discussion as we can—offered to procure an interview with Mr. Pitt, & that he would now write a note to him for the purpose, but this I waved in order to avoid jealously or suspicion of my colleagues, as I told him I would not only keep my hands clean, but avoid being doubted for a moment. He listened with patience & attention to every thing I observed upon the subject, and desired to see me again at one tomorrow.

Our conversation lasted for an hour and a half. He asked me to take a beefstake today with him or his brother, or to come tomorrow, but I was engaged for both days. He said that he knew that the King is personally estranged from Mr. Pitt on account of this subject.

At a quarter past two, called at Mrs. Bostock's—and at two returned to my lodgings and found cards from Mr. Ryan, Mr. McDonnell,[2] Mr. Hay, Mr. Whyte, & Mr. Butler of Lincoln's Inn.

Mr. Roger Scully called and staid some time. He lodges in 2 Macclesfield Street, Soho Square.

Lord Hutchinson called and staid an hour and a half and whilst he was here, Colonel McMahon & Mr. Richd. Martin called, and as they were going away, Colonel Bagwell called and sate half an hour.

Called upon Mr. Martin at Beall's Hotel, got a frank for Mrs. Scully, & sent off the letter. We conversed a good deal about the Prince of Wales' probable line of conduct. He said he is to be presented to the Prince tomorrow—and will mention my opinions to him.

Called upon Lord Fingall & Colonel Plunket at five—found them at home & staid a few minutes.

Went to dine with Lord Southwell at Fladong's hotel—did not get dinner until past six—it was very badly served and the evening was heavy and dull. There were

[1] W. H. W. Betty, named after an ancient Roman actor.
[2] M. I. McDonnell, of Lime Street Square.

Ld. Fingall & his brother Colonel Plunket, Mr. Cruise of Lincoln's Inn, Mr. Whyte, O'Reilly, Ryan, Wogan Browne, Colonel Plunkett (Lord Dunsany's brother), Sir Edwd. Bellew.

Returned to my lodgings, dressed and went to Mrs. Charles Butler's music party, 44 Great Ormond Street. Found there a good deal of company—many women,—none handsome, except Lady Shrewsbury, who was with Mrs. Selby—talked principally with her, Mrs. Selby, Mr. Butler, Mr. Martin, Lds. Fingall & Southwell & Mrs. Butler. Mr. Butler introduced me to Mr. R. B. Sheridan, who talked apart some time with me upon the Prince's middle line of conduct—I gave him freely my opinion, that the middle line of policy will not please etc, etc—Lord Fingall introduced me to Sir J. Throgmorton, and we talked a long time upon the state of the Irish and English Catholics. He appointed to call upon me at twelve on Saturday. Was invited stay supper which was given at about one in the morning. I sat between Sir J. Throgmorton & Mr. Thos. Sheridan. There were besides, Mr. R. B. Sheridan, Mr. Throgmorton, Sheldon, R. Curran, R. Martin, & 2 other gentlemen—Mrs. & 2 Miss Butlers and Miss Cormack—also Mr. Dignum. The supper was very poor and bad & the port abominable. There was much singing of Mr. Dignum, Mr. T. Sheridan, & Mr. C. Butler. Mr T. Sheridan sings sea songs etc uncommonly well & with taste. His father seems uncommonly fond of him & occupied about him. He was dull and exhausted after the long debate of last night, in which he delivered 2 brilliant speeches.

Came home with Mr. Martin at half p.4 this morning.

Friday, 8 March 1805

Rose at half p. nine.

Mr. H. Huddleston called, and we went to call upon Mr. John Huddleston M.P. at 33 Duke Street St. James—he was not at home and I left my card.

Breakfasted at 11 at the York C. house & called afterwards upon Mrs. Bostock's, where I found letters from my father & Mrs. Scully.

(N.B. Roger Scully had called upon me at nine this morning before I was up).

At one called upon Lord Sligo, found him at home & staid an hour—he spoke again about my having an interview with Mr. Pitt, but we agreed to defer it until the first general interview with the deputies.

At two, went to Lord Fingall's, to the meeting of the deputation, where he, Lords Kenmare, Southwell, Trimlestown, Sir Edwd. Bellew & Mr. Ryan attended.

Conferred together until half past four. Lord Fingall said in the course of the conversation that he had heretofore conceded very far in the business, & will not now concede any more, which seemed rather a peremptory declaration.

Returned to my lodgings at half past four, and found the card of Lord Lismore, who is at Batt's hotel, Jermyn Street.

At a quarter past five Sir E. Nepean called, & took me in his carriage out to his country house near Fulham, on the Thames side, about 4½ miles off—There was only his lady (a sensible notable-looking woman) his daughter about 16 years old & 3 sons from 11 years down to 5 years old.

An excellent plain dinner on silver—good wine, and he gave an uncommonly good bottle of claret—I slept there.

Saturday, 9 March 1805

Breakfasted at Sir E. Nepean's country house at half past ten—and he brought me back to town in his carriage—I arrived at about half past eleven.

Our conversation, of which there was a great deal, was mostly upon the state of Ireland, some of the principal persons in both islands, his neighbours, Ldy. Lonsdale, Sir Wm. Guise, Mr. Ellis etc—He was not communicative upon the Catholic subject, said he did not know what would be done—but his private opinion is that Mr. P. will hold a cabinet council and have the matter decided then. I told him, that we sent the letter yesterday to Mr. P. in Lord Fingall's name, desiring to know, when he can receive the Catholic deputation—He said, we should soon have his answer—and that he thought it would be a very decided one, either to adopt our cause altogether and carry the measure, or else to refuse the petition & have nothing to do with it—but that he will not take a middle line, or one clogged with any restrictions.

When I returned at half past eleven - I found the cards of Mr. Addis 13 New Boswell Court, Lincoln's Inn, and Mr. Flanagan of 15 Henrietta Street, with a note from H. Huddleston to introduce him, Mr. Addis. Also another note from H. Huddleston to say that Mr. Joseph Shee invited him and me to dine with him on Tuesday next, & to know whether I would. I wrote (by the P[enny] Post) to him & to Shee that I could not.

At 12, Sir John & his brother Mr. Throgmorton called and staid half an hour. I shewed him our petition, which he read and much approved of.

Afterwards called upon Mr. R. Martin, whom I saw—also upon Mr. Wogan Browne, 3 Bury Street, to return his visit, and returned the visits of Colonel Bagwell, Lord Lismore and Mr. Whyte 9 Bury Street.

Delivered W. Fletcher's letter to D. Bowes Daly at Batt's Hotel—and sate with him half an hour—a Captain O'Beirne was with him for a while.

At 2 attended the meeting of the deputation—the same members being present as yesterday—and conferred till 5 o'clock. No answer to yesterday's note to Mr. Pitt—Settled the outlines of the conversation intended to be had—Lord Fingall has heard that Mr. Pitt had determined to refuse us—but not on very good authority.

Returned home at 5 o'clock & found the cards of Mr. Foster, 32 Lower Brook Street, and Mr. George Evans, Ibbetson's Hotel, Vere Street—and Mr. Richd. Curran.

N. B. Heard today that Sir Thomas French was sufficiently recovered to be expected to sail from Dublin as on Wednesday last—this said by Wogan Browne, who has it from Mr. Redington, Sir Thomas's father in law.

N. B Lord Kenmare has a very silly manner—looks as if he was henpecked and frightened—he said, amongst other things, when asked his opinion, that the opinion of Ld. Fingall should be his, that he pinned himself upon Ld. F. and took every thing according to what he would say.

N. B. Sir John Throgmorton and his brother seem to be very spirited men, & of a manly rational cast of mind—the former is acute and feeling—and he comprehends quickly—has a very good plain manner and is exceedingly prepossessing in his appearance.

N. B. Dens. Bowes Daly ment[ione]d to me what passed last winter (concerning the Prince's sentiments) between him, Col. McMahon, Mr. Fox and Lord Fingall—& said that Mr. Fox told him last night, that the Prince does not care if his decided partiality to the Catholic cause was told about every street in town.

N. B. Sir E. Nepean's eldest son Molyneux is at Trin. Coll. Cambridge[1] under Tavell—his children at home are fine and promising & he seems to enjoy much domestic happiness—he bought (for £25000) an estate,near Bridport, now underlet at £1900 a year. It is upwards of 3000 acres, and will be worth £4000 a year, when the leases fall in. He told me that Lord Hardwicke has actually recommended W. B. Scully[2] for the Ensigncy & pointed him out particularly in a list of 7 so recommended—He said he would take care to have a strong command sent over immediately to Dublin against *Faulkner's Journal*, on account of its recent attack upon us—Lord Sligo told me he would have the same done, and he would join in a Protestant prosecution of the paper.—Sir E. Nepean told me that in & about London, persons associate very much in political knots together—this forms a bond of connection—Mr. Pitt comes in often late to dine at Sir E.'s[3]—takes a chair in a corner & lays aside state and gravity—He gambols and plays with the boys etc, etc. Sir E. in 1776 (then 22 years old) was Secretary to Sir Henry Clinton in America, when Lord Moira was aid-de-camp to him—He was afterwards 13 years Under Secretary to the Home Secretary of State—and Lady N. says he has not had a leisure-day for 23 years—always at work or in an office. Sir E. said that the two cleverest young men lately come into political life are Lord H. Petty, and Mr. Smith,[4] who is now in the Secretary of State's Office.

N. B Lord Hutchinson said of Fox & his friends, that in fact they only want to make tools of the Catholics & care nothing about the main object, provided they embarrass Mr. Pitt.

[1] Scully had been at Trinity ten years earlier.

[2] A second cousin, for whom Scully's father had applied for a commission in July 1804 (see *The Catholic Question* p.80).

[3] Nepean had quarters in the Admiralty.

[4] John Henry Smyth, who lost his post in 1806.

Dined at home—and at half p.6 went to Mrs. Bostock's, drank tea there & returned and finished the correction of the petition. Then wrote letters to Mrs. S. & my father—& answered Mr. McDonnell's invitation to dine on Thursday, and Mr. Addis' offer of his services as our Secretary, transcriber etc, saying that I will lay his offer before the other deputies and inform him of the answer.

Sunday, 10 March 1805

At half p. ten— went to Lord Fingall's with the petition fully corrected—& breakfasted with him.

Went to Mass in South Street with him and D. W. O'Reilly—after having left cards at Lord Shrewsbury's, Sir John Throgmorton's, Mr. William Throckmorton's. and Mr. W. B. Ponsonby's. Met at South Street (one o'clock Mass) Mr. Throgmorton, Mr. Edwd. Jerningham, & Mr. Wm. Cruise, who invited me to dine on Tuesday next with the Cisalpine Club.

Walked a good deal with Mr. E. Jerningham towards Portman Square etc—& he promised to call upon me tomorrow at half p. eleven to introduce me to Lord Carlisle. He was inclined towards a petition of the Engh. Catholics, & said they would consider it—but hitherto they thought we meant it merely as an Irish business & not to admit them—which I undeceived him in.

At two went to the meeting at Lord Fingall's—All attended save Mr. Ryan. It was agreed to accept Mr. Addis's offer of service and employ him, where necessary—which I wrote him word of in the evening by H. Huddleston—no answer yet from Mr. Pitt nor any account from Sir Thomas French.

At a quarter past 3 returning home met John. J. Dillon & walked home with him—I found the cards of Lt. Colonel Bagwell 45 Pall Mall, Mr. Colclough 39 Pulteney Street, Mr. Cruise of Lincoln's Inn, Mr. Guthrie Hatchett's hotel Piccadilly, Mr. Dillon[1] 3 York St. York Place, Portman Square.

At half p. 3 went with John J. Dillon towards Thayer Street, & met Colonel Bagwell in Piccadilly, who told us that a Cabinet Council is now sitting, probably upon our subject—he would not say whether he would vote for or against us, that he has not made up his mind, & that it would be a happy measure if coming forward favourable to Government, but injurious if not favoured by them—Whilst we were talking, Prince William of Gloucester,[2] passing by quite near, saluted him respectfully—I observed the Prince—he has a soft washy face, goodnatured but vapid—pale and thin—being only recovering from illness—his gait of walking is very drawling & ungraceful—I parted from Dillon in Thayer Street. He told me that some years ago, upon a reference to the then Atty. & Solicitor General (Scott & Mitford)[3]) for their opinion to the Crown, whether the King could, without injury to

[1] Henry Augustus Dillon.

[2] Third son of George III and future William IV.

[3] Now respectively Lords Eldon and Redesdale.

the Test Laws, appoint Catholics to offices, of which by law they are capable, they gave an opinion in the negative, which has governed the King since, and much injures the Catholics. If true, this is a most serious fact: he recommends our requesting from Mr. Pitt a revision of that opinion by the present Atty. & Solicitor General, as the result would be favourable to us.

Dined at 4 at Mrs. Bostock's. H. Huddleston was there—I gave him the letter to deliver to his friend Mr. Addis, appointing him to call upon me tomorrow or Tuesday, at eleven o'clock.

A little after this returned home.

Monday, [11] March 1805

At nine breakfasted at home.

At half p. nine went to Dr. Baillie's for his answer in Mrs. S's case. Found him at home, and conversed with him some time upon it—he was very frank and satisfactory, and gave me good hopes of her recovering full health, which filled me with the greatest opinion of him & put me in high spirits. He gave me his written opinion—and I returned home. On my way I put into the Twopenny Post my answer to Mr. MacDonnell of the City, Lime Street Square, saying that I would dine with him on Tuesday—and hoping he will excuse my not having returned his visit, which is owing to my being quite engrossed by the Cathc. business.

At twelve Mr. Edwd. Jerningham called upon me—and we went to Lord Carlisle's in Grosvenor place behind the Queen's house in the park. Lord C. was at home, but denied to us, being engaged deeply with his agent about particular business. Jerningham says, that Lord C. is very shy, nervous and fearful of entering deeply into conversation with a stranger. We left our cards. Jerningham is very entertaining and very much interested in the Cathc. business. He said that Sir E. Knatchbull's election at Canterbury was not lost by the cry of " o Popery" on account of his having married Miss Hawkins, as was said—that Sir E. himself does not think so—and that he would have lost his election at any rate—that he actually proved at the election, by the parson, that his child was baptised in the Protest[an]t faith.

Jerningham said that Dr. Rennell's sermons or lectures against Popery at the Temple were disregarded and rather ridiculed by the lawyers etc & by all who attended—and that this shews how hard it is to interest people now against Popery—that it would be impossible now to raise a cry in Engld. agst. Popery—that the lower English knew nothing about it, nor would they take the pains to enquire or listen to the matter. He wished much to promote the identity of the Irish with the Engh. Catholics.

Returned to my lodgings at one. Mr. Grey & Mr. John Ponsonby called—Mr. Grey said he had seen Mr. Fox, & they had agreed that, if Mr. Pitt brings in the petition, no further debate can arise than merely the observation of members on his not carrying the measure, & that they will make full and copious speeches upon the motion, that the petition do lie upon the table—but that no division could be risked—that if Mr. P. refuses the petition then they will bring it in, but under great disadvantage, on account of the authority tacked to it.

Left my letters of introduction from Marshall, & cards, at the Earl of Chichester's, Stratton Street (he being at Stanmore 4 miles off, & not expected back for a week); and at General Dalrymple's at Boodle's St. James, he residing at Chelsea, where he has some office, but he comes to Boodle's every day, not getting out of his carriage.

At two went to the Catholic meeting at Lord Fingall's. All our past attending members were there with the addition of Lord Shrewsbury as Earl of Waterford and Wexford. Mr. Pitt had sent an answer to Lord Fingall's note, which he dated this day, presented his compts. to Lord Fingall, and that he will be glad to see him and the noblemen & gentn. who propose to accompany him, tomorrow at half past twelve o'clock.

Took the letter into consideration and agreed to meet tomorrow at eleven to consider further, & then to go to Mr. Pitt. Read John J. Dillon's letter[1] upon the construction given by the late Atty. and Solicitor General (Scott & Mitford) to the Test Laws agst. the Cathc. interest— proposing that we should insist upon Mr. P.'s having it revised and altered—Submitted his letter to the meeting as he desired—they thought it better to defer it for the present, lest it should seem as if we were soliciting a partial concession if we were to request such revision.

Repeated Mr. Addis's offer of services this day, & it was again approved of & accepted.

After much discussion, the following heads of discussion with Mr. Pitt for tomorrow were agreed upon –

First

– that the object of our mission should be fully stated to him

– to make a remark, by way of personal compliment, upon the causes which have induced the Caths. to apply first to him

– to state that the Caths. are very earnest & feel deeply interested in this petition—that they do not come forward to embarrass Ministers but from a deep sense of their situation & of the necessity of the measure.

– that it will not be dropped by them on any account—that they have conceived great hopes & expectations from his past conduct & declarations in their favour—and the sacrifices he has made for them.

Secondly

If he will not go the whole length of carrying the bill for us, to propose his introducing the petition & grounding upon it a Declaratory Vote of both Houses recognising the justice and policy of the measure—to press this

[1] Reproduced in *The Catholic Question*, p.92.

very strongly upon him as something of this kind or some such parliamentary pledge or sanction will be necessary to conciliate the Caths.—to hold out hopes to them etc.

Thirdly

If he will not do even this, then shew our great desire to conciliate Ministers, to give him the authority we have the power to give him, mentioning it then only for the first time, and to repeat that the Irish Caths. will not drop the matter—that they will persevere from session to session—and to explain to him, that they intend, by not pressing the immediate adoption of it at this moment, merely to give [time] for the removal of any objections which may now exist.

At the end, to say, that if he should wish to re-consider the subject, or to revolve in his mind what has passed, we will give him another interview.

At half past four returned home from Lord Fingall's, being set down by Lord Shrewsbury. Found the cards of D. B. Daly & Earl of Kenmare.

Went towards Thayer Street and, in my way, met Mr. Ryan & Mr. John Roche—The latter gave me leave to put his name to the petition—said that he approved all our proceedings—that he was rather surprised he had not been communicated with or had notice of the meetings—He said that no alteration of the banking laws in Ireland is intended for this session. He & his lady are for the present at Kirkman's Hotel, in Bruton Street.

Went to Mrs. Bostock's in Thayer Street & staid an hour.

At seven went to the Salopian C. house, Charing Cross, & dined.

At half p. eight—called at Lord Buckingham's and found that Captain Dardis's return to town is quite uncertain. Afterwards returned home.

Tuesday, 12 March 1805

Breakfasted at nine at St. James's C. house—& afterwards called upon Mr. Fox—left my card—he not being up. Returned home and waited till eleven for Mr. Addis.

At eleven called upon the Marquis of Sligo—saw him & his Lady—told him of the appointment being made with Mr. Pitt—He thinks & has reason for it he says, that he will not bring in our petition. Talked upon the state of Ireland, Farmers etc—he gave me a frank for my father.

At a quarter past eleven went to the Catholic meeting at Lord Fingall's, & found the other members already come. Discussed several points of our subject—what is to pass to day with Mr. Pitt is not to be kept secret We are not to touch upon the union etc.

Mr. Addis got from me my copy of the petition, with orders to make out 3 or 4 copies of it. Put some more names to the petition.

At a quarter past twelve the 8 deputies went to Mr. Pitt's in Downing Street. In Lord Shrewsbury's coach went his Lordship, Ld. Fingall, Ld. Kenmare & Mr. Ryan. In Lord Trimleston's coach went Ld. Southwell, Ld. Trimleston, Sir E. Bellew & myself. Lord Kenmare's coach went empty—The procession looked very handsome and well.

I carried the petition, Ld. Fingall saying I was best entitled to do so.

We were received at Mr. Pitt's in some state, and ushered thro' several servants, into a small ante room—where we waited not five minutes, before we were introduced to him.

He sat in a large handsome library room—of oblong form—with pillars etc—He bowed very civilly, whilst Ld. Fingall (after his own name had been announced) introduced each of the deputies to him by name. He wore dirty boots, and odd-fashioned lank leather breeches—but otherwise well dressed & cleanly, his hair powdered etc. He was very courteous & cordial in words and looks, but his carriage was stiff & strait, perhaps naturally so—His face cold & harsh, rather selfish and active, but acute & sensible.

We took our seats, after much reciprocal ceremony etc—Ld. Fingall next to him—Ld. Shrewsbury was next to Ld. F. (but got up and desired me to take his place as being best prepared on the subject, and he said so aloud, before Mr. Pitt). He afterwards moved lower down to put Mr. Ryan next to me. Next sate Lords Kenmare, Trimleston, Sir E. Bellew, Lord Southwell, and at the lower part of the table Lord Shrewsbury took a seat.

Mr. Pitt's manner is very direct & distinct. He speaks rather in a measured articulation, and looks about incessantly at each person, whether he or another is speaking—indeed his eyes (tho' bad & ill coloured) are very busy and speaking He seemed to look most at Ryan & myself.

The conference was opened by Lord Fingall, who stated generally the object of our mission from Ireland, premising to him in the first instance that the Caths. wished to put their case and merits under his protection, as considering him their best friend—that under his administration almost all the relaxing statutes in their favour have been passed—that they have every hope and expectation that he will bring their petition before the Parliament. He dwelt upon the effects likely to result from the measure to Ireld. & to the Empire at large and pressed Mr. P's taking their case under his protection.

Mr. Pitt said, he understood the petition went to seek a total abolition etc. Lord F. answered that it does—Mr. Pitt owned having recd. the copy of it thro' Sir Evan Nepean and then said in a very frank and cordial manner, that he could not but feel highly flattered by the compliment paid to him by so very respectable a body as the Caths. of Ireland; that it was certainly very pleasing to him to be so considered—that it was true he had stated his opinion to be, that it would be a very salutary measure to take place whenever the proper time should arrive—that he thinks so still—that he did not consider it at all a question of right or justice, & he observed that we had not so put it in our petition—but that he considered it always, & solely, in a view of its policy & expediency—that, as such, the time must make a great consideration, for it must very much enter into the expediency of proposing it—That there exist strong objections against it at this moment, which he hinted pretty plainly to prevail in a certain quarter. That those objections have not been removed—that, in these circumstances, he must regret that he is under the necessity of declining the honour intended by us for him—that he cannot introduce our petition under such unfavourable circumstances, and when he cannot propose any measure grounded upon it—That he wished much that the determination of the Caths. of Ireland had been otherwise at this moment, & that they would have seen the unfitness of the present time for discussion as he does—but, they having so determined, he cannot but acknowledge, that the subject has been from the beginning conducted & brought forward in a manner the most moderate peaceable & commendable & such as to have claimed his strong approbation—He paid strong compliments to the conduct of the Caths. in their past proceedings—but repeated, that he considered the present time as extremely unfit for bringing forward the measure, that it is not for the advantage of the Empire & that it is injurious to the chance of eventual success, as many members who might otherwise have voted for it, will now vote against it. He said that, therefore, under all the circumstances, he cannot agree with the Catholics as to the propriety of the present time etc.

Mr. Ryan spoke of the general sense of the Irish Caths. in its favour at this time—of our having done our duty & shaken off responsibility from ourselves—of Sir Rd. Musgrave's book[1] & his misrepresentation of our views—of the *Dublin Journal* paid by Government (of this Mr. Pitt appeared ignorant)—of the legal & constitutional feelings of the Catholics etc, etc.

Ld. Fingall said it would be a most happy & desirable measure in every point of view—but that no doubt Mr. P. himself must be well aware of all these advantages & not need our enlarging upon them.

Mr. Scully [spoke] upon his past conduct and declarations in our favour—our considering him as our patron—the military and financial great advantages of the measure—the critical & perilous situation of Ireland & of the Empire at this moment—explained further what Mr. Ryan meant about the enemy mistaking or misrepresenting our views and hopes.

Lds. Kenmare & Fingall and Mr. Ryan—that the subject will not be dropped or lost sight of by the Irish Catholics, that they will persevere from session to session.

Mr. Pitt said there is no reason to suppose that the now subsisting objections will cease by that time—or how long they may last (here he smiled)—

[1] *Memoirs of the different rebellions in Ireland*, 1801.

After this part had been sufficiently urged Lord Kenmare then put to him the carrying a declaratory vote upon the policy & expediency of the measure—& said that something of this kind is necessary to conciliate the Cathc. mind in Ireland, & to hold out some hope of success.

Mr. Pitt said he was sorry he could not introduce the petition under such circumstances & that he cannot now carry such a vote—that the whole strength of Governt. would not carry it—that he cannot entertain any measure which must lead to a discussion, when the adoption is impracticable.

Mr. Scully put to him the advantages of his granting at least a Declaratory Vote—that it has struck several Caths. as a measure which he is perfectly able to carry if he pleases altho, from the peculiar objections existing, the adoption of the measure "in toto" is unattainable at this moment—that the vote of Parliamt. cannot infringe certain scruples existing in a particular quarter—that it goes to facilitate a measure which he himself has at heart, paves the way for its easy success whenever those objections shall be removed—that it must therefore perfectly consist with & forward Mr. P.'s own policy materially—that, as to his objection, that it must of necessity be followed by the adoption, we conceive that by its very nature it rather waves the adoption for the present, and rests upon a mere declaration of principle, therefore signifying that the adoption must for the present be postponed—that, it is precisely in such cases, a Declaratory Vote is used—it tends to guide & prepare the public mind, and gives the greater wisdom & efficacy to the proceedings which may in a subsequent session be deemed fit to be proposed, by having prepared men for it, & inducing them to turn it in their thoughts—that the case of the abolition of the slave trade is quite in point—there the House, not being prepared to take final and effectual measures, went as far as they could, and they declared in favour of the principle of the abolition[1]—yet they do not appear to have felt themselves committed or pledged by that vote, for the measure itself has not yet been reduced to a law—That, if in that case they deemed it expedient to declare in favour of the principle merely to indulge their feeling of humanity and to hold out hope to West Indian slaves, how much more expedient & necessary [is it] in the present instance to avert danger from the Empire, to unite all classes of subjects, & hold out at least a hope of relief to so substantial a class of people as those petitioned for.

Mr. Ryan also pressed it upon him.

Sir E. Bellew strongly pressed his carrying the declaratory vote for us—as useful to his Majesty's service & to the peace & security of the Empire—he dwelt upon the recognition of this very declaratory principle by the Parlt. of Ireld. 26 years ago.[2]

[1] On 2 April 1792 the Commons voted by 230 to 85 "That the Slave Trade ought to be gradually abolished", Pitt contributing with an eloquent speech (*Parliamentary History* XXIX, 1158). It was not until 25 March 1807 that parliament made the trade illegal.

[2] See the 5th paragraph of the petition, Appendix D.

Mr. Ryan stated that the reason why we do not press the adoption of the measure at this moment, is in order to give time for the removal of the objections, supposed now to exist before the subsequent session.

Mr. Pitt insisted that this is also impracticable, any discussion would be injurious, unless followed by the adoption of the measure itself—that, circumstanced as he is, he cannot carry the measure for us—that it will be his duty therefore to decline undertaking it.

After this second point also had been sufficiently pressed Lord Kenmare opened the third point to him, and proposed that, if he would introduce the petition and lay it upon the table, we would authorize him to state to the House that we do not press the immediate adoption of the measure prayed for. Lord K. added, that this proceeded from the extreme unwillingness of the Caths. to leave him, & their great reluctance to separate their cause from him, whom they have looked to as its patron and great prop—that they were determined to cling to him and to his Majesty's Governt., as long as they possibly could—that so far was it from being their inclination to embarrass Ministers, that they have preferred even to embarrass their own cause, and to clog its progress, than to subject themselves even to the imputation.

Mr. Pitt, with much apparent regret, said that he felt himself equally precluded from undertaking the matter in the manner now proposed—that he considered any step, which should on his part excite a discussion, as inconsistent with his duty—that the objections against the measure being adopted were equally strong against his originating a discussion of it—he hinted very plainly and broadly what these objections were.

Ld. Fingall pressed this last point upon him with great good sense & spirit—said that the Caths. were desirous that the question should be introduced thro' him—that they were at all events bent upon obtaining the notice and regard of the House—that even the entertaining the measure at all, tho' it should be rejected, would be more grateful & satisfactory to them, than total neglect and disregard—that they wished to be made known to their fellow subjects on this side—he thought, the more they were known the better they would be liked—he showed Mr. Pitt our instructions, which Mr. P. said he had not seen or exactly known, except from hearsay. Mr. P. kept the copy Lord F. gave him.

Mr. Pitt said still, that he could not introduce our petition even under these circumstances.

N.B.

In the course of his conversation he owned having got the copy of the petition which we sent him thro' Sir E. Nepean—asked whether any alteration had been made, and, when we said that we had softened the passage about trials by jury in it, he said he recollected the passage.[1]

[1] It is not in the petition itself but in a note accompanying paragraph 11 of it.

Mr. Ryan pressed his bringing in the petition in some way or other. Mr. Scully pressed it also upon him—Mr. P. has said that he only refuses it, because any discussion of it would be injurious to the cause & to the public good—now a discussion is inevitable, for we are bound to bring in this petition at all events, and then a discussion must ensue. It would be a favourable discussion, if brought in by him—unfavourable, if otherwise—he can guide and regulate it—Whether therefore he does not see the advantages of bringing it in—besides, it will keep the Catholics in his hand, under his patronage, looking up to him, and not likely to take any step embarrassing to Government etc.

Mr. Pitt did not deny or apply himself to this, but repeated his determination, & said, he himself would be less embarrassed, if the discussion should arise upon another member's introducing the petitn., than upon his doing so—that he must oppose it.

Ld. Kenmare (this point being fully urged) put very strongly that, if he will not bring it in, another will—that we are bound to it.

Mr. Scully (seeing him immoveable now) suggested that perhaps what has passed might be turned in his mind—that some things may have fallen which may afford matter for his attention—that he would perhaps wish to leave the matter thus for the present and communicate his final decision in a couple of days hence—that were he now on the instant to decide against us upon the first hearing, it would have the ungracious appearance, which he would not wish, of being abruptly resolved against, even before he had seen the deputies or a single Cathc. gentleman—that we cannot reconcile it yet to ourselves to consider ourselves entirely without hope of his support.

Mr. Pitt said, he has not decided it in a moment—he has been informed of our proceedings—has seen our petition, revolved it well in his mind, and fully deliberated on the course he should pursue. Mr. Pitt continued, that if he presumed to offer us any advice, it would be to withdraw our petition and postpone the presenting of it for the present.

He found that we were not to be moved from our purpose, and then adverted to the authority, which we can give to any other member, who introduces it, to declare etc[1]—and this he treated as a discretionary power which we may use as we please. He said that a discussion upon that authority would be less embarrassing to him, than if coming from his having introduced the petition.

He gave us to understand that Ministers will declare etc, if we get any other member to introduce the petition, and showed evidently by his way of treating it, that he will take advantage of that authority, to check or drown any discussion. "If I brought it in", said he, "I might have stated, it is true, that you do not press the adoption etc., but still any other member may take it up & press it".

[1] See the last lines of the Instructions (p.60).

Lastly—he expressed in parting with us, some difficulty as to the character in which we appear to the House—said, he supposed the persons, submitting the petition, do not petition save for themselves—lest any thing informal might be objected to—he advised us to take care & avoid objections upon this ground—that the petition can only come on behalf of those whose names are subscribed etc—that Parliament may only recognise us so. But upon our explaining, that we meant no more, he seemed satisfied—& Sir E. Bellew & others told him that, if he had any doubt, whether the Caths. of Ireland joined in this petition, he had only to let the experiment be tried & then he would see it. He was assured by others of the deputies, that it was really & warmly the sense of the Caths. of Ireland, but that, to avoid agitation & bustle, it was thought best to have no very great number of signatures, but that these should be respectable names.

Some observations were made to him upon the hostile spirit of the law in Ireland, & that every thing that regarded the execution of the laws was highly partial & abused—& Mr. Scully said, it was notorious and the deputies present would aver, that the act of 1793 has remained a dead letter & never been acted upon. Ld. Fingall mentd. that at the most perhaps 3 or 4 situations have, since that time, been given to Catholics. Mr. Pitt listened to this with much attention, seemed unapprized of the fact, but said he would be happy, at all times, to receive any representation from us, as individuals, upon the state of the country etc, etc.

After a conference with him of about 50 minutes, having pushed the different points enjoined upon us to the utmost, and finding that no impression could be made upon him at present, we rose & withdrew, he accompanying us thro' his room to the hall, with great favour and civility, bowing and smiling all the way.

We returned to Lord Fingall's in the same order, & continued there a short time in conversation upon Mr. P.'s refusal & conduct.

Lord F. expressed himself to be much disappointed & even deceived—that Mr. P. had acted with some duplicity in encouraging us thus far to come forward—and said he was much astonished at, & could not account for, Mr. P.'s mentioning the receiving the copy of the petition thro' Sir Evan Nepean, thereby recognizing all that transaction.

Ld. Kenmare expressed some resentment at what had passed—& spoke with much spirit—said Mr. P. had used a trick at the end in asking about our authority. Sir E. Bellew did the same.

At half p. two I returned home.

At three Mr. Fox called—& staid more than an hour and a half—I told him all that had passed today—he spoke very liberally upon the subject, said he has always been a friend to the relief of the Caths., even in 1780—seemed to wish much to have the management of the cause in his hands—as he could do it most service—said, if objections to him particularly should exist in any Cathc. he would recommend Lord Henry Petty, as by far the ablest of the young men now in public life—that he is laborious, regular & studious, & would take every pains to become master of the subject—He would also recommend Mr. George Ponsonby—he has reason to think that Mr. Grattan may be in Parlt. in a fortnight, & expects to be authorised tomorrow to write to him, offering a seat[1]—He would advise also our offering the petition to Ld. Cornwallis as a compt. in consequence of his pledges in Ireland[2]—tho' he will very probably decline it. Lds. Fitzwilliam & Grenville would do for introducing it. He would recommend the two persons selected in each House to be an Englishman & an Irishman. It can be introduced now, & laid upon the table, & the member introducing it can give notice of a specific motion to be made, after the recess, when the Irish county members shall have returned from their assizes—He said that the Prince & all whom he can influence will most certainly support it—but the Prince has some prejudices against the Dissenters, which he must give up—for we, Irish Caths., cannot look for success, without also including the Engh. Catholics, and therefore seeking a repeal or some modification of the Test Laws—that this repeal will of course admit the Dissenters[3]—that we must make up our minds to this course, that he can speak for the great body of the Dissenters, that they are favourable to our cause. Whilst he was with me, Mr. John Roche came in, joined in the conversation, and assured Mr. Fox of the very general & earnest wish prevailing in Ireland upon this point—that he thought we must now look to our sincere & real friends in Parlt.—as Mr. Pitt has thought proper to reject us. Mr. Roche spoke with much spirit upon this subject, and at some length.

When they had gone, I sent off my letters to my father & Mrs. Scully.

N.B. Ld. Kenmare visited me today & left his card.

At six, Lord Fingall, Col. Plunket & Mr. Domc. O'Reilly called & took me to the Crown & Anchor, to dinner with the Cisalpine Club.[4]

We found them just seated at dinner. At the head sate a Mr. Langdale, at the foot Mr. Wm. Throgmorton. The others were Lord Shrewsbury, Sir John Throgmorton, Mr. Chas. Butler, Mr. Cruise, Mr. Langdale Senior, Revd. Mr. Bellasis, Revd. Mr. Collins, Mr. Cox the brewer, Mr. Heneage, Mr Walmsley, Mr. Prugean. The dinner & wine were very good, the company civil, and, tho' not very mirthful, yet cheerful & well regulated. They drank the health of Lord Fingall & myself, and success to

[1] Fox wrote on 13 March telling Grattan that he would be in parliament in ten or twelve days (Grattan, *Life and Times* V, p.254).

[2] Of 13 February 1801 (see Chronological Table, Appendix I). Fox must have been aware of Cornwallis' imminent departure for India and known that his recommended gesture was an empty one.

[3] The sacramental test, abolished for the Irish Dissenters in 1780, was still in force for the English Dissenters.

[4] Founded in 1792 to resist the encroachments of the Roman curia on the civil power the club had become by now merely a dining club for the nobility and gentry. Lord Fingall was an early member of it.

our mission, & afterwards Mr. Chas. Butler proposed me to be balloted for as a member.[1]

Mr. Langdale Snr.[2] sate next to me—said he is an old acquaintance of Mrs. Scully's—talked much upon general subjects—does not seem very sanguine in hopes of our success—says that the King is quite firm upon this point—that he is greatly addicted to venery of late—that he has at this moment two very fine women at Kew, and his groom's wife at Windsor, one of the handsomest women in England.

At ten we came away.

Wednesday, 13 March 1805

Mr. Addis called upon me & brought me a copy of the petition—took directions for more copies & staid some time copying the signatures already affixed.

Mr. R. Scully also called, and I returned him his 5 guinea note as a bad one & not exchangeable.

At ten breakfasted at the St. James C. house—and afterwards called upon Stevens the hatter, & received the difference of my £50 bill, allowing him £1. 0. 5 for my hat etc. Returned to my lodgings.

At eleven called upon Lord Sligo, & communicated to him Mr. P.'s answer & all proceedings. He hoped we would not press our petition—that this is a very bad time—that it will ruin the measure—that Pitt ought to have conceded the declaratory vote to us—that the King's two great foibles (this said confidentially) are this subject & venery—that strange things are said upon the latter point—he will procure for me a full account of what Mr. Pitt thinks of the matter and his impression of our conversation.

At twelve went to the Cathc. meeting.

Ld. Kenmare warm for going strait to the opposition—Lds. Shrewsbury & Trimlestown & Mr. Ryan of the same opinion—Ld. Fingall thought it would be contrary to our instructions, but was not well able to shew how far. He felt for the opinion it might excite against us in Ireld.—and thought we should be very responsible for such a conduct—that it was an extremely serious step to take—wished for delay, and to wait for Sir Thomas French, from whom a letter from Holyhead had been received.

Lds. Kenmare etc. opposed this—Mr. Ryan said he would take it upon himself to answer for Sir T. French's approving of whatever we should determine upon the subject—all thought that any more delay would be injurious & none so strenuous as Ld. Kenmare—Ld. Southwell said that matters having gone thus far, no other course now remained but to go to the opposition as the most eligible quarter.

[1] Scully was declared elected at the next meeting on 26 April.

[2] Perhaps the father of the other. The club's minute book shows Thomas Langdale at the top of the table.

Sir E. Bellew very strenuous for going to the opposition.

Ld. F. then gave up his opinion and the following resolutions were then drawn up & agreed to.

1

that the Cath. deputies, having now executed that part of their instructions which relates to their requesting Mr. Pitt to introduce the Cath. petitn. into Parlt.—and having yesterday been distinctly given by him to understand, in a long conversation, that he declines introducing it at present under any qualification or authority whatsoever, and that he will feel it his duty to oppose it and any measure founded upon it, they do now take into consideration what other members are the most eligible to apply to for the introduction of it into Parlt.

2

that it does not appear, upon every inquiry and information within their power, that there is at present any member, of sufficient weight and talents for the introduction of the petition who is perfectly neutral & unattached to any political party.

3

that it appears, therefore, upon a full consideration of their instructions & an investigation of all facts necessary for their direction, that it is their duty to apply to the most eligible members in point of talents, character & personal weight, for the introduction of the petition.

4

that, acting upon this opinion, they conceive, that the most expedient method of proceeding, now to be adopted, is that of a communication to Lord Grenville & Mr. Fox, requesting them to introduce the petition and support it in Parlt., & that Lds. Fingall & Kenmare be authorized to make that request, and to procure a meeting between them & the deputies.[1]

This decided & clear line of conduct being adopted, I was desired to see Mr. Fox & appoint with him an hour for tomorrow when he could meet Lds. F., K., & myself.

[1] See Appendix B for a fuller report of this meeting.

I accordingly went to Mr. Fox's at three—He was out walking with his lady, and I left a message for him

I met Mr. Grey at the door, went in with him, & told him what had passed & our present state. He approved much of what had been done.

When I returned, I found the Marquis of Sligo's visiting card.

Mr. Fox shortly afterwards called, accompanied by Mr. Ryan. We conversed for half an hour on the subject & he was much pleased. Whilst he was with me, Ld. Kenmare came in, to whom I introduced Mr. Fox. They appointed half p. twelve for the meeting tomorrow. Mr. Fox then went away and soon afterwards Lord Kenmare.

At four Sir J. Throgmorton called & was highly pleased at my informing him of what had been resolved this day by the deputies. We talked half an hour upon the subject—He thinks we shall have the public writers with us—that he has a clergyman, a Mr. Jos[ep]h Berington, residing at his country house, who can & will write if necessary, to answer any pamphlets that may appear—that Cobbett is not venal, but might like a little compliment etc, that he would strongly recommend my writing to Cobbett, or else explaining matters to him, so as to interest him in support of the Catholics—and conciliate the Grenvilles & all their party.

At six I went to Mr. Cobbett's 15 Duke Street—found him at home & had a long conversation with him—explained the present state of our proceedings for his guidance & information—he had heard from Wyndham what had passed yesterday—He professed the strongest opinion in favour of our body—that our measure is right—and that discussion will be excellent—He said the public mind is with us—& (as Fox before observed) that no opinion of any consequence is against us—When I said that he had written down Addington's administration, he said, Aye! & I will have Pitt down too and Lord Sidmouth[1] along with him, perhaps not immediately, but at any rate before a year—said much of his former misconceptions agst. Irishmen & Catholics—which he imbibed in America, seeing only United Irishmen there, whom he opposed & abhorred—that when he came over here, he was got into the hands of Mr. Reeves, Mr. Gifford[2] etc, with finer talents & manner, the prejudices & false views of Duigenan & Musgrave etc—that he had written therefore in London in a daily paper against emancipation etc—that he is preparing something for the public to explain & account for his change of opinion—he will put it in a letter or address to Mr. Wyndham or Ld. Grenville etc—he says that from his knowledge of the public mind he can assure us of the most favourable reception etc—that he will print for us etc—that he will have his work out in about 3 weeks[3]

[1] Addington, the late Prime Minister, had become Viscount Sidmouth on 12 January 1805 and joined Pitt's administration.

[2] John Gifford, of the *Anti-Jacobin Review*.

[3] On 25 May the *Dublin Journal* attacked Cobbett for abandoning his former principles and now supporting the petition, but no article of the kind here described has been found.

that he will prove to the Church that the Test Laws, in their present state, may safely be modified in our favour—and in this he hopes fully to succeed—he took down my address.

At half p. seven I left him, & got from Byfield of Charing Cross some newspapers upon our subject. Then went to dine at the Salopian C. h. Charing Cross.

During my dinner, there were in the opposite box, drinking tea etc, a Colonel Rochfort or Burchell[1] of the Artillery, Ld. Newark, another Lord, and a Mr. Erskine of the Public Offices—Lord Newark ridiculed the King's scruples about Caths—said he had consulted the Bishop of London, the Archbp. of Canterbury[2] & a Dr. Majendie who had set him against us—that then the K. (in order to have a lay opinion) consulted also Lord Clare, who desired 24 hours to consider it, & afterwards gave him for answer, that he could not grant it without breaking his coronation oath.

Colonel Rochford spoke of General Huddleston[3] of the Artillery as a most worthy goodhearted fellow, in which Erskine joined—but the Colonel added that his foible is about the Plantagenets, that he is of a Cathc. family, tho' himself a Protestant, that they are all agog about Plantagenets, that the Colonel is the subject of great mirth about it—and he has sometimes told them at Woolwich (as it were in confidence) that in fact he has a nearer relationship to the throne, by descent, than the reigning family—he has lately got a battalion, which all are highly pleased at—but all say, that he would, in fact, much sooner give up his battalion than a scrap of his pedigree.

N.B Cobbett said, that, from his own knowledge, it would be highly important at this moment to pledge our friends in Parlt; not but that Fox, Grenville, Wyndham etc are really & heartily with us, but there are several others, who now vote with them, that we may not be sure of upon future occasions.

N.B. Whilst I was waiting today for Lord Sligo, Lady Sligo spoke in a most agreeable & interesting style of maternal affection of her son, Lord Altamont—said he has the finest heart possible—the sweetest temper that can be—that he is idle, but it is his only fault, & in his rank is not of much consequence. She spoke of her sister, a Mrs. Curzon Baroness Howe near Ashby in Leicestershire, whom she is much attached to, and who lately lost her eldest son, 17 years old & of the highest promise—she shed tears in speaking of him.

At half p. 9 returned home—Mr. Fox sent me a note to know whether we expected to meet him alone, or whether he might have other respectable men present, as Mr. Windham or Mr. Grey, favourers of our cause. I answered, that it

[1] Major General George Rochfort was in the artillery. Burchell has not been identified.

[2] Respectively Beilby Porteus (1787-1808) and John Moore (1783-1805).

[3] William Orchard Huddleston, who had been appointed Colonel Commandant on March 2nd 1805

would be perfectly agreeable to me, & that I do not see, why it should not be equally so to every one of my colleagues.

Wrote to Dr. Milner, the Bishop, at Wolverhampton, in consequence of his letter to Edw. Hay, which E. Hay showed me this morning—I explained to him, that I have not come through Wolverhampton, as he supposed, & that the Irish clergy are content with our forbearance—that the newspaper accounts are incorrect—that I expected to have met him here—that I much respect & esteem him, & feel his mention of me to be very flattering—that I leave town the 25th or 26th.

Thursday, 14 March 1805

At half p. ten Mr. John Dillon called and talked upon the Cathc. subject—he will decline going the circuit for the sake of preparing something upon it for the press.

I recd. a note from Lord Sligo desiring to see me.

At eleven called upon Lord Sligo—he was, as usual, very kind & gracious—enquired about our determination of yesterday, which I told him in part. He disapproved & deprecated our going at all to the opposition—it will ruin our hopes—it will make Mr. Pitt our enemy—he is now our friend, speaks most highly of our civility & politeness to him. and thinks most favourably of "our behaviour—even Mr. Ryan (from whom he had been taught to expect differently) was very civil & well behaved"—that our conduct has much attached him to us—that we ought to keep Mr. Pitt our friend—that we should get some friend of Mr. P.'s to bring it on—that then he will not oppose us—that it may then lie upon the table, and no discussion ensue—but he will oppose us violently if an opposition member is chosen—Lord Sligo recommended our consulting Mr. P. whom he would recommend to bring it in—If nobody else appeared more proper, he would recommend his own brother, Mr. Dens. Browne—Mr. G. Rose would be a good person, for that would be the same as Mr. Pitt. Ld. Henry Petty is now an oppositionist, but he would be a more desirable man, than Ld. Grenville or Mr. Fox. Lord Sligo much recommended our seeking another interview & keeping Mr. Pitt our friend, as we now have him so—He has heard Mr. P.'s sentiments through a third person, upon whom he can depend—and he will enquire further, & see me again tomorrow—he offered to call upon me, but I waved this, on account of his ill health.

Lady Sligo talked much about English and Irish servants etc. She reprobated the harshness & arbitrary conduct of the Irish squire, pitied the defenceless situation of the lower classes, and seemed familiarly acquainted with the subject, having known Ireland for 17 years—She appears to be a very honest, sincere, unaffected and goodhearted woman, of a very reflecting and well cultivated mind, of a tall and good proportioned figure, with a sensible good physiognomy, and rather small features, except that her eyes are of a good size and quick—but her features are not marked.

At half p.12 Lds. Fingall & Kenmare called upon me and we went to Mr. Fox's, to whom I introduced them. Mr. Grey and Mr. Windham were also there.

Ld. Kenmare communicated our resolution, in which Ld. Fingall concurred—and Mr. Fox undertook very handsomely to introduce the petition—Some conversation ensued in which Mr. Grey & Mr. Windham expressed themselves in the most zealous & cordial terms, as to the principles, upon which they would act—that it should not be a mere party question—they said they would consider it with relation to Ireland, to the interests of the Caths. & to the main success of the measure—Mr. Grey particularly threw it out for our consideration what effect such a discussion would produce in Ireland—it was finally agreed to meet at Ld. Grenville's on Saturday.

Went out at one with Lords Fingal & Kenmare—called with Ld. F. upon Mr. Whyte Bury Street, found him at home with Col. Plunkett & Mr. Domk. O'Reilly—the latter going tonight to Ireland offered to take letters for me.

I went home & wrote letters to Marshall, to R. MacDonnell, & to Mrs. Scully, all enclosed under cover to her—which I finished by five—and gave to Mr. Whyte to deliver to Mr. O'Reilly this evening. Wrote also to Doctr. Milner at Wolverhampton explaining our present prospect & case.

At five Mr. Wm. B. Ponsonby called. We talked much upon our subject: the state of parties—the hope of support—he thinks we have done perfectly right—we are not however to rely upon the Irish members—there are about 80 of them, who constantly vote with the Minister—a few of them may now vote against him upon this question—but still he would rather bring it on <u>during</u> the Assizes, to have them out of the way.

He contradicted completely the story of his having told G. Bagot that this is an improper time, for he has always expressed to him & to every other person the contrary opinion—and he particularly urged to Bagot that we ought now to apply—he spoke altogether warmly & honourably.

At a quarter before six, I was called upon by Lds. Fingall & Southwell & Col. Plunkett, & went to dine in the City at Mr. MacDonnell's, Lime Street Square Nr. 6 There were also, there, Alderman Rowcroft, Mr. Barnewall, Mr. Buchall,[1] Don Juan Justamenti (admiral of the Spanish captured frigates & now on parole), Mr. Kernan of Doctors Commons, Joseph Shee, Thomas Strange, Gordon, Jas. Ryan, & a little Spanish captain—The dinner & wine were capital—and the evening pleasant, with good conversation.

Mr. MacDonnell & Aldn. Rowcroft appear to be very superior men—acute, penetrating, quick & good speakers.

Returned with the same persons that I went with, at half p.ten.

[1] Possibly a misrendering of Bushell, the name of M. I. MacDonnell's business partner.

Friday, 15 March 1805

At nine went to Mrs. Bostock's. Afterwards left my name at Mr. Cooke's, North Row, Lord & Col. Hutchinson's, Park Street, Mr. Grey's, Lord Moira's, Mr. Guthrie's at Hatchett's hotel.

About eleven, breakfasted at St. James's C. house & then called upon Col. McMahon at Charles Street & Carleton House, but he was out.

Went at one to the Cathc. deputation at Ld. Fingall's—He wrote, by desire, a note to Ld Grenville, desiring an interview for the deputies—and it was agreed to interpret our instructions (to him, Mr. Fox etc) as mandatory upon us to give them the authority but not as mandatory upon them to use it in the House.

At 3 called upon Lord Sligo's & left my card, & returned to Great Rider Street. Went to Lincoln's Inn & returned Mr. Cruise's visit, saw him & Mr. W. Throgmorton. He sends me the Parly. Debates of Ireland upon the Cath. subject, which I am to send to Mr. Fox—He is also to give me, next Monday morning, some old valuable papers that he has had from Counsr. Macnamara.

Returned Mr. Chas. Butler's visit in Great Ormond Street, & Mr. Edward Jerningham's in Lincoln's Inn, and left my cards.

Dined at Gray's Inn C. house in company with H. Huddleston, & wrote an article for the *Morning Post*, which I gave him. At seven went with him to the Rolls Court, & saw Sir Wm. Grant (the Master), Richards & Romilly, who seem to be very able men.

At nine returned home. & found a letter from Mr. Grattan, brought by Sir. T. French—Lord Sligo's card, and one of Lady Kenmare's Sunday rout cards.

Saturday, 16 March 1805

At eight Mr. Addis called upon the Cathc. business and staid some time.

At ten, Lord Shrewsbury called and sate for a while, & by his desire I called upon Mr. Fox to speak about the conference to be held today.

Found Mr. Fox at home—He thinks our instructions very embarrassing to our friends in Parlt.—and wishes to have power to introduce the petition not clogged by any qualifications, and to have it given to him as we offered it to Mr. Pitt—He has appointed today to meet us at Lord Grenville's, and he has so told Lord Grenville.

Returned home, and told this to Ld. Shrewsbury—and he and I went to Lord Fingall's at eleven—we found him at home—and told him as above. We found with him some of the other deputies—he had had Lord Grenville's answer, appointing this day at noon for receiving him and Lord Kenmare.

We agreed to meet all together at three again, to consider upon the result of the conference about to be held by him & Ld. Kenmare with Ld. Grenville, Mr. Fox etc.

I accompanied Lord Fingall to Ld. Kenmare's—at twelve—found him & Lady Kenmare at home—he introduced me to her—she repeated her invitation for tomorrow evening—Her beauty is much declined—She seems wan & wasted about the eyes, and worn in the face generally, but her figure is fine. Having parted with Lds. Fingall & Kenmare, I returned the visit of Mr. Henry Dillon at his house Nr. 3 York Street, York place, Baker Street, & left my card.

Bought a couple of fowls for Mrs. Bostock, called upon her, and staid half an hour.

Called, between one & two, upon Lord Hutchinson, found him at home, & conversed half an hour with him. He thinks we ought not to take any middle line, but to put our shoulders now to the support of our cause in Parliament. He disapproves of our having brought it forward, because there will be a very angry discussion, and a renewal of all the invective used in the Irish Parliament—but, having come forward, we ought now to go through with it warmly & actively. He thinks no promise or inducement was held out to the Caths. at the union—and says that, of his own knowledge, the contrary was the case—And he seemed sore at my thinking that there was, upon the whole, sufficient in the different points of the conduct of the executive in Ireland at that time, to be fairly considered as a holding out of strong hopes to the Caths. to induce them to support the union. He intends to take an active part in the debate—says that the King is personally much prepossessed agst. him, considering him a Jacobin etc, etc.

At a quarter past 2 called upon Lord Dorchester, found him at home & staid half an hour. He disapproves of our proceeding to petition, unless we have Govt. along with us; because he says it is too good & great a cause to be the engine of opposition—Whilst I was there the Earl of Jersey came in to pay a morning visit—& I was introduced to him by Lord Dorchester. The E. of Jersey took no part in the conversation about Irish or Cathc. affairs, and seems a frivolous, mincing little man, slim and dapper—in countenance & manner resembling Lord Hardwicke—Ld. Dorchester was glad when he got rid of him—& then enquired much what we meant to do, what the prince thinks etc, etc and desired to see me often.

I then returned home, and found an invitation from Sir John & Lady Throgmorton to dine with them on Thursday next the 21st inst.

N.B. Ld. Shrewsbury has engaged me to take a family dinner with him on Saturday the 24, & a state dinner with the other deputies, on Tuesday, the 26. Also, I gave Lds. Shrewsbury & Kenmare copies of the petition, as made out by Mr. Addis.

At three attended the Catholic meeting—All the deputies attended, including Sir Thos. French, who was also present this morning, having come to town last night.

We found that Lds. Fingall & Kenmare, having waited upon Lord Grenville at 12, as appointed, found him at home, with Mr. Fox & Mr. Grey—that these persons expressed great difficulties how to act upon our instructions, as they are worded—that they desire to know, first, the sentiments of the deputies upon them, and then, as Ld. Grenville said, they will consider how to shape their course.

We debated this subject until 5 o'clock—The opinions of the deputies were very discordant—and we adjourned to tomorrow at one—The appointment for the deputies meeting Lord Grenville, Mr. Fox etc stands for 12 on Monday next.

Returned home & found that Lord Sligo had called, and afterwards sent a pressing message, desiring to see me when I should return. I called immediately upon Lord Sligo, and conversed half an hour with him—He is exceedingly uneasy at our giving the business to the opposition—says that they only want it as a switch for Pitt—that they have not our real interests at heart—that Pitt will always be powerful—that our conference with him made a great impression in our favour—that Pitt has told a friend of his (Ld. S.'s) that he would be content the petition should be introduced in any way most pleasing to the deputation—that we ought to cultivate this good disposition—that we should send to know, whom he would wish to bring it in—he advised our applying to Huskisson, Nepean or some person, who sees Pitt often and knows his sentiments—and advised that, at least, I should do so, and consider of this until tomorrow.

N.B. Lord Hutchinson observed this morning that the High Church party in England, who are highly bigotted, only want a leader of popular talents—that Pitt would be that man, if irritated by us—& that our applying to the opposition would most certainly irritate him highly—that he does not see at all events that a discussion can benefit our cause).

Went to the Cambridge C. house in Newman Street, & drank tea there about eight. At nine, returned home, & found a note from Sir. E. Nepean, desiring to see me tomorrow.

Sunday, 17 March 1805

At nine Mr. Hay, & afterwards Mr. Addis, called upon me and staid some time.

At eleven called upon Col. McMahon, found him at home, and staid nearly an hour with him. He said that the Prince returned yesterday from Donington with Mr. Sheridan, but Lord Moira is not come. He says that the Prince is actually under a promise to his father not to vote for or support our question during his father's life—that he conceives himself to be bound by this promise—that he, the Prince, thought hitherto, that Mr. Pitt and we had an understanding together and that we had come forward with Mr. Pitt's concurrence—that the Prince therefore did not imagine hitherto that we had looked to him at all in our proceedings—that he had been totally in the dark as to the steps we were taking and our hopes of success—that the Prince would rather, had he been [asked] to advise us, that we had not come forward at this moment—that McMahon of Dublin has been very much behindhand in his communications to the Colonel of what I told him from time to time—that he never mentioned me as his authority or that what he said upon the subject was upon any certain authority, but he rather stated it as a general opinion or a prevailing hope etc[1]—& that therefore what he wrote was not of that certain and fixed credit—that now it would embarrass the Prince much to have it brought forward as a party question—that the Prince certainly has a very great attachment to Mr. Fox and ranks him highest for abilities etc—and that he would probably make him the prime minister if he could—but that he had a particular interest in the good and careful management of this question—knows that Mr. Fox introducing it would at this moment injure it much—that therefore he would not wish Mr. Fox to be appointed for that purpose, as it would only increase the King's great antipathy to it—that certainly any other member of the opposition, especially Wyndham & Lord Grenville. would be far preferable in the Prince's opinion—that the Prince has that fair, real feeling in its favour as to have been very highly gratified if Mr. Pitt had actually brought in the petition & acted upon it—but that upon the whole, there is nothing he would deprecate more than making it a party measure.

At twelve went to Lord Sligo's & found him at home. He was still warm against going to the opposition—wishes us to stay with the ministry & agreed to procure me an interview with Mr. Huskisson to see whether some amicable arrangement might not yet be made between Mr. Pitt & the deputies.

At one went to the Cathc. meeting, which lasted till three & longer—There was much discussion of our instructions, and it was carried by a majority (Lords Fingall, Southwell & myself being in the minority) that we might tomorrow, if required by Ld. Grenville, Mr. Fox etc, empower them to introduce the petition <u>in whatsoever manner they shall deem most eligible</u>.

At half past three, went to Mrs. Bostock's, & dined with her *tete a tete*—She agreed to come with Mrs. Scully & me next summer to Richmond, and stay 2 or 3 weeks with us in lodgings there.

At five, went in a post chaise to Sir E. Nepean's at Broom House near Parson's Green and sate with him there about 50 minutes & returned to Thayer Street at a quarter before eight—he was confined to his bedchamber by the gout in his foot—and the croup in his throat, being an inflammation of the windpipe, which had nearly suffocated him last week.

He had only wished to see me to know what had passed with Mr. Pitt, as he had not stirred out all this week past—Lord Melville had called upon him today—He, Sir Evan, is desirous that we should remain upon good terms with Government—and will consider, & let me know, whether any middle way of proceeding can be struck out—He thinks we ought to have another interview with Mr. Pitt—that Mr. P. had told him before our former interview, that he would willingly agree to Lord F. or me having been introduced to him—& Pitt had written

[1] It would seem as if Scully had attempted to enlist the support of the Prince of Wales by feeding William McMahon, his colleague at the Irish bar, with material similar to that of Robert Marshall's minute on p.24.

to Sir Evan to come to him on Tuesday last at half past eleven (just before our conference with him) but Sir E. was not able to stir out—he thinks that, if he had been well enough, he might have prevented any misunderstanding, and been of service to each side.

He has not resigned his Chief-Secretaryship of Ireland, nor is his successor appointed—but the person whom he believes to have been treated with for the situation,[1] is his very intimate friend, and a very liberal & virtuous man—He is also (Sir Evan is) a very intimate friend of Mr. Wilberforce.

At nine returned from Thayer Street to my lodgings, & found the cards of Lord Southwell, Sir E. Bellew, Mr. Henry Dillon, Mr. Wm. Throgmorton and General Dalrymple. Also letters from General Dalrymple and Lord Sligo—the former says that in consequence of Marshall's desire to have me introduced to Lord Egremont, he has written to his Lordship, who will soon be in town & he will then introduce me.

Lord Sligo writes, that he has appointed tomorrow morning at ten o'clock for my calling upon Mr. Huskisson, Mr. Pitt's Undersecretary to see whether Mr. P. may not be led to take up some favourable course for the Catholic cause.

At eleven went to Lady Kenmare's Sunday party. It was rather thin and heavy.—There were Lady Buckingham, Clifford, Gerald, Mrs. Keating, Lords Fingall, Sir Mr. Throgmorton, Sir E. Bellew, Mr. J. Dillon, 2 Keatings, Mrs, O'Brien, Abbé Griffin—I heard no other names—Returned at half past twelve.[2]

Monday, 18 March 1805

At ten went to Mr. Huskisson's St. James's place—found him at home & staid an hour and a half—he repeated Mr. P.'s sentiments, expressed his own & Mr. Pitt's wish to be in favour of the measure—said that he & Mr. P. both thought the petition to be of singular merit, moderate, firm and dignified—they did not know that I wrote it—he wished to have the business managed amicably—said that we misconceived Mr. Pitt in thinking, that he was disposed to oppose the petition at all events—that was confined only to the principle—but as to the mode of having it introduced, he would cooperate with us—he wished it should not be put into the hands of persons known to act in systematic opposition to ministry—for that would be to make it appear a hostile measure—that there were neutral and indifferent persons to be found—that upon this head he would be very happy to speak with us—that, if so brought on, Mr. P. would be very ready to get up in the House & state his perfect approbation of the very honourable & patriotic manner in which we

[1] No doubt Nicholas Vansittart, who was appointed on 23 March.

[2] This paragraph was perhaps hurriedly composed before Scully went to bed. Clifford was probably Lord Clifford. Mrs Keating[e] was Lady Kenmare's sister and Gerald must have been her brother, Gerald Aylmer. If not relatives the other two Keatings could be the printers, father and son. Another peer is seemingly omitted after Fingall. Mrs O'Brien would have been the wife of Sir Edward's brother (see the next page).

had managed the business throughout—he would state his opinion to be in favour of the principle and expediency of the measure itself, and that he confined his objections merely to the point of time—He said that, in such case, Mr. P. would further oppose any person who should propose any violent resolution against the Catholics, or any proceeding negativing the prayer of the petition. We considered much upon the means of bringing about another interview with Mr. Pitt, as I could not propose it to the deputies without some authority—and at length it was settled that he should write me a note today (if so authorized by Mr. Pitt) to the effect, that "understanding from Lord Sligo, who had had conversation with me, that we had conceived Mr. Pitt bound to oppose our petition, not only in its principle but in every other manner, he was willing to take an opportunity of correcting that misconception in another interview, whenever we please".

At half p. eleven called at Col. McMahon, but he was just gone out, having waited half an hour, and been sent for by the Prince—left word that I would call again tomorrow at eleven.

At a quarter before twelve reached Lord Kenmare's, where I met all the other deputies.

A little after 12, we went to Lord Grenville's in Oxford Road, in 3 carriages, Lds. Kenmare's, Shrewsbury's & Trimlestown's.

We found there Lds. Grenville & Spencer, Messrs. Fox, Grey & Windham. The conference lasted nearly two hours. They agreed to present our petition, notice to be given in Parlt. tomorrow evening & to be presented on Monday next.

At two came with Ld. Trimlestown to Mrs. Bostock's—next went to Coghlans Brown & Keating, Duke Street, to direct them about printing the petition—Returned home—and wrote to Mrs. Scully and to Wm. McMahon of Holles Street. J. J. Dillon called upon me—found Mr. R. Selby's card.

At half p. five went to dine at the Crown & Anchor with the St. Patrick's Society. The Knight of Kerry[1] presided—I met Mr D. Bowes Daly, who introduced me to Sir Edw. O'Brien and to Mr. H. A. Dillon—I sate at the Steward's table. There were Marquis of Headfort, Sir Sydney Smith, General Doyle, Sir Wm. Douglas, Mr. Sheridan, Col. McMahon, Sir E. O'Brien's brother,[2] Mr. Robt. Thorley, Mr. Barnewall, Mr. Goulding, Mr. Paget, Mr. Goulding [*sic*], Revd. Mr. Glasse, a Mr. Bacon of Cumberland who has a house near Finchley Common, 9 miles off. Bacon was very civil, took my address, and said he would call upon me. I returned at twelve.[3]

[1] Maurice Fitzgerald, in the absence of Lord Moira.

[2] There were several brothers, the eldest of whom was Lucius.

[3] On the previous day the feast of St. Patrick had been celebrated in a grander 'entertainment' offered by the Marquis of Sligo. It was attended by all the principal members of the government (apart from Pitt), the leaders of the opposition and many members of the English and Irish aristocracy. According to the guest list published by the *Morning Post* Lord Fingall, but no other member of the deputation, was present.

Tuesday, 19 March 1805

Mr. Addis, Mr. Keating the printer & Mr. R. Scully called.

At half p. nine breakfasted with Mr. Cruise of Lincoln's Inn.

At eleven called upon Colonel McMahon and staid an hour with him.

At half p.12 called upon Mr. D. B. Daly & Mr. Fox, who were out.

Went to Lord Sligo's and sate half an hour with him.

Went to Lord Fingall's and staid there upwards of half an hour.

Left my cards for Ld. Southwell Fladong's Hotel, Lord Kenmare, Sir. E. Bellew 44 Upper Seymour Street, & Mr. R. Selby, 1 Bryanston Street. At three took some soup at Blenheim C. house, Oxford Street.

At half past 3 called upon Mr. Fox, and staid half an hour with him.

Afterwards called upon Mr. Dens. Bowes Daly, who had just called upon me.

Staid at home this evening writing and reading.

Wednesday, 20 March 1805

At twelve went to the Catholic meeting at Lord Fingall's & staid until nearly three. Ld. Kenmare, Sir T. French & Mr. Ryan were absent. Talked on several points but came to no resolution.

Wm. Bellew has written letters to Ld. Fingall & to Sir E. Bellew, disapproving of our going to the opposition and calculated to inspire a despondency & division amongst us, but Lds. Shrewsbury & Trimleston & Sir E. Bellew himself, set their faces against such opinions.

Called afterwards upon Colonel Martin and got a frank from him for Geo Vesey for tomorrow.

Returned home and wrote minutes until eight o'clock.

Afterwards, went to the Salopian Coffee House, Charing Cross—took coffee there—met Colonel Martin & talked about the Cathc. subject, Bagwell's Freeholder's Bill[1] etc. Returned home after ten.

Thursday, 21 March 1805

Mr. Addis called early.

At eleven Mr. Heny. Augustus Dillon called and staid some time—He means to speak next Monday upon the introduction of the petition—and wishes me to give him heads or topics, & to breakfast [with] him next Sunday at eleven.

At 12 went to the Catholic meeting & talked over our past acts & present state, until past 3—but came to no resolution.

At half p. three called upon Mrs. Bostock & staid half an hour. Afterwards called upon Mr. Dens. B. Daly, but he was out.

[1] A bill to regulate electoral certificates (*Hansard* IV, 124)

At six went to dine with Sir Jn. Throgmorton's. There were besides him & his lady, Lords Shrewsbury, Fingall, Petre, Southwell, Sir E. Bellew, Mr. Wm. Throgmorton, Mr. Errington, Mr. Ryan.

Sir John is a very gentlemanly & becoming man—his lady (who was a Giffard) is a little vulgar, very plain, with an overstrained warmth and force of civility.

Lord Petre is a heavy, stupid, sottish looking man, about 44 years old—Mr. Errington a very conversible and well bred intelligent man.

The dinner & wine were of the very first kind—services of plate all through—burgundy & champagne of the first quality at dinner—& claret, madeira, port etc very excellent afterwards. The solid dishes at dinner were a small saddle of mutton roast, a turkey roast, chicken boiled, wild fowl etc. There were several dishes of French cookery "fricandeau" etc.

The dinner was rather light, but sufficient, in quantity, & had a very good effect.

About half past ten Sir John had coffee introduced, which stopped the wine drinking—It happened well & is a good habit.

Sir John invited me to his house in Berkshire, whenever I shall happen to be on the Irish road.

At eleven we broke up.

Friday, 22 March 1805

At half p.10 called upon Col. MacMahon, but he was out.

Afterwards called upon Mr. Frogatt, Nr. 26 Castle Street, Leicester Fields, who is attorney for Dr. Troy in his actions against the printer etc of the *Anti-Jacobin Magazine*, for defamation. Frogatt was out, but I saw his head clerk, & gave him Dr. Troy's instructions & papers, relative to his Exhortations.[1]

At a quarter p. 11 breakfasted at the Oxford C. House, Strand—and afterwards went into the City.

Left my card at MacDonnell's Nr. 6 Lime Str. Square.

Visited Mr. Spooner in George yard & found him very well—Mrs. Spooner was in the country—They have sold their house at Southgate & now have one at Hamerton, beyond Hackney, about 3½ miles off—he pressed me to dine with him in town or country, but I declined.

Afterwards bought for Mrs. John Lloyd the Violet Soap at 102 Bank buildings—and changed some notes in the Bank of England.

Left my card at Joseph Shee's 8 Copthall Court.

Called at the Chapter & Peele's C. house, and read the reviews & Irish papers.

At three left my card at Mr. Charles Addis's, 13 New Boswell Court, Lincoln's Inn—and afterwards at Mr. Cruise's, Lincoln's Inn.

[1] Read in Dublin churches on 10 October 1803. The magazine accused him of having had advance knowledge of the Emmet rising in 1803 but failing to warn the government. On 11 July he was awarded £50 damages (*State Trials*, XXIX, 503).

Afterwards called upon Mr. Chas. Butler, and staid a few minutes with him. He offered his services as agent to the Catholic body and says he is composing 3 essays for the *M. Chronicle* in our favour.

At half p. 3 called upon Mr. E. Jerningham, saw him & his friend Mr. Carey & also Mrs. C.—She enquired very kindly after Mrs. S. & said they were old & warm friends. They pressed me much to dine with them next Sunday—they go shortly afterwards to a house they have taken out of town.

Afterwards called upon John Josh. Dillon, who fatigued me with arguments & narratives which he had told me of a week ago.

At four called upon H. Huddleston in Gray's Inn—Dined with him at the Gray's Inn C. house & we spent the evening together pleasantly. He has a cold & a bad cough. His brother Edward is now getting a renewal of his Crown lease for about £700—It is for 99 years from several years back, at the present rent for 20 years, his former term, and at a good advanced rent for the residue—but on the whole he has been highly favoured in it—and some of the houses will rise greatly in a few years.

H. Huddleston said that his father's present rental (including his estate in Dorsetshire) is £1600 per annum—and he was told 2 days ago by Pemberton his agent that his debts now stand thus

to Holford	3000
to Eyston	500
to 2 persons at Walden	
and in Cambridgeshire	1500
to me[1]	1500
	6500

which makes £325 to be deducted yearly for interest, & leaves him £1200 a year over—but then he owes a great deal yet to Pemberton for the expense of inclosing etc, etc. That the bill of this is not yet made out—but it may come to £2000 more—That he has lately sold a field or two in Pamperford to raise money for the enclosure, & is now about to sell another.

At nine returned home—wrote to Sir E. Nepean to enquire the state of his health.

N.B.—in these last three days I found the visiting cards of Lords Sligo & Hutchinson. Mr. J. Shee, Mr. D. B. Daly, V. Maher at Hatchett's hotel, E. Smyth at Steven's hotel—& Lds. Kenmare & Fingall had called.

I had this evening a card of invitation to dine with Ld. & Lady Trimlestown on Thursday next, to which I wrote for answer, that I leave town on Wednesday.

N.B. I wrote yesterday to Mrs. Scully and to Marshall under cover to Geo. Vesey.

[1] The balance of his wife's dowry.

Saturday, 23 March 1805

At half p. 9 left my note for Sir Evan Nepean at the Admiralty.

Afterwards called upon Col. Macmahon but he was out. At past ten went to breakfast at Lord Fingall's pursuant to his note of yesterday—he & Col. Plunket were there.

He and Lord Kenmare were yesterday with Lord Grenville, who had desired from them a written statement of the penal laws now remain[in]g against us. Ld F. wishes me to draw it up which I agreed to do.

Col. Plunkett is treating with Government for raising a regiment of 950 men in Ireland—he is to be allowed £19 a man—He may not sell any commission, but he may name officers, who shall raise men for rank, they being allowed £16 for each man, & the residue to go to the colonel[1].

At half past eleven called upon Mrs. Bostock & staid half an hour—She wishes me & Mrs. Scully to come in June in the short vacation, and for me to go back until September, & this will suit her best—as she may be removing from her house in September.

At twelve called upon Mr. Couche Nr. 2 North Street, Fitzroy square—& staid half an hour with him.

Afterwards called upon Mr. John Roche 73 Charlotte Street Fitzroy square—found him at home with Mrs. R. and Miss Whyte. He is attending his appeal here—very civil & friendly in his professions towards me—promised to put whatever business he can in my way in Dublin. He told me that Mr. Fonblanque, the great Chancery counsel & M. P. has absconded suddenly, greatly in debt.[2]

Walked with Mr. Roche to Castle Street, Leicester fields—called upon Mr. Frogatt about Dr. Troy's law suit.—Frogatt not at home, but saw his clerk.

At two returned home, & found Mr. Bushell's card, Nr. 6 Lime Street square.

Sir Thos. French & Col. Martin called & staid half an hour. At 3 left my cards at Lord Sligo's, at Mr. V. Maher's, Hatchett's hotel Dover Street, & at Mr. Ed. Smyth's, Steven's hotel, Clifford Street.

Afterwards called upon Mr. Dens. Bowes Daly, & sate with him upwards of half an hour. He is warm & earnest in our cause, & gave me a list he has made out of members of the Irish part of Parlt.—favourable, or doubtful, & marked. He said that Mr. Bagwell has complained to him that, tho' he did formerly support the Catholics in Parlt., yet he has lost some good county interest by it, and has not found a single Catholic to espouse his interests, save my father.

At six went to dine at the Rainbow Coffee house, King Street, Covt. Garden.

Returned at eight, and staid at home writing etc.

[1] See p.22, n.2. On 28 March Lord Hardwicke submitted the Colonel's formal application through the Home Secretary, who replied on 16 April that the Duke of York had rejected it (Hardwicke Papers, Add.MSS. 35,710, ff. 60, 76).

[2] This rumour proved unfounded.

Sunday, 24 March 1805

At eleven breakfasted with Mr. H. A. Dillon, 3 York Street, Baker Street.

At one went to mass at South Street, & met there Lord Fingall, Mr. Errington, Cruise, J. J. Dillon etc.

Afterwards left my cards at Mr. Grey's, Sir John Throgmorton's & Hon. H. G. Bennett's Nr. 9 Queen Street, Mayfair.

Returned at two, & found the V. cards of Mr. Cruise & Mr. MacDonnell. Afterwards left my V. cards at Mr. Colclough's, 39 Great Pulteney Street, Mr. E. Hay's, Portland Hotel & Mr. Evans's 20 Vere Street, & called at Mrs. Bostock's & staid half an hour.

Went to visit Ld. Trimlestown, & found him walking with a Bishop of Odessa,[1] a Frenchman apparently—walked with him a quarter of an hour. Returned home.

At six went with Hen. Huddleston to dine at Lord Shrewsbury's—the dinner etc were good & pleasant. There were Ld. & Lady Newburgh, a Mr. Salvin, & a young Mr. Blount. Returned at half p.ten.

Monday, 25 March 1805

Breakfasted at St. Jas. Coffee house & afterwards called at Mr. Fox's, and left my card. Called at Lord Fingall's and saw Colonel Plunket—after having before eleven called upon Lord Sligo and sate more than half an hour with him.

Returned home & at one Colonel Martin called upon me, also Mr. C. Addis, & Mr. Keating the printer.[2] Sent letters to Mrs. Scully, to D. O'Connell, and to Jer[3] about Noel's estate.

At two left my V. cards for Col. Macmahon at his house, and at Carleton House.

Afterwards called upon Sir Thos. French at the Salopian C. house—went to the House of Commons to see the Cathc. petition presented. The House & gallery were very full—and a little after four it was presented by Mr. Fox, with a very few words of preface. The clerk took 16 minutes in reading it—there was no opposition to its lying on the table, and Mr. Fox gave notice that on the 9th May he would make a specific motion upon the subject. Mr. Pitt said nothing, but by his looks & nods evinced great pleasure at the distance of the day named.

Returned home at half p. five. and, in my way, met Mr. Borrowes[4] who talked of his treaty with my father, said they will deal for the small lot, altho' my father declines to bid for the entire estate.

Found a note from Sir Evan Nepean, asking me to dine tomorrow with him.

[1] No such diocese, titular or otherwise, is listed in Eubel's *Hierarchia.*

[2] He was anxious to get copies of the petition to the booksellers before other printers saw it: see *The Catholic Question,* p.99.

[3] Scully's youngest brother, Jeremiah.

[4] Perhaps the Irish barrister, Peter Burrowes.

Went to dine—sought after coaches for Shrewsbury, Chester etc in Holborn, Bull and Mouth Street etc—and afterwards went to the play in Covt. Garden.

Returned at half p. 11.

Tuesday, 26 March 1805

Called upon Col. McMahon, Ld. Hutchinson, Mr. Cooke, Mr. Fox & some others. Dined at Ld. Shrewsbury's, in company with Lords Fingall, Southwell, Newburgh, Sir E. Bellew, Mr. Mostyn Browne & his 2 daughters, Colonel Plunkett, Mr. Ryan.

Wednesday, 27 March

Attended a conference at Lord Fingall's—there were present Lords Southwell, Shrewsbury, Trimlestown, Sir E. Bellew & Mr. Ryan.

We agreed to leave the managing of the Catholic petition in the hands of Lords Shrewsbury, Kenmare & Trimlestown.

The minutes, which I had drawn up, of our conference with Mr. Pitt & subsequent proceedings, were agreed to by all, except Mr. Ryan, and were deposited with Lord Fingall.[1]

Returned home & found a pressing message from Lord Sligo desiring to see me. I went to him and he told me he had some conversation the day before with Lord Hawkesbury, in which the latter spoke handsomely of me, and said he much approved of our not having got many signatures or sent about the petition. Lord Sligo said he would mention me also to Huskisson & Vansittart.

At 3 I dined with Mrs. Bostock, & H. Huddleston. Returned at 5.

At a quarter past 7 left the Golden Cross in the Holyhead mall.

Arrived at Holyhead at half p. 6 on Friday evening—sailed at 9 in the *Union* Capt. Skinner, & landed at Dunleary at 12 on Saturday the 30 March, whence I came home in a jingle.[2]

Source: Scully Papers, NLI, MS 27,514 (ii and iii).

[1] Their fate is unknown: see Appendix A for Scully's copy.

[2] In the meantime the Committee in Dublin had met on 21 March and taken cognizance of Scully's letter of 14 March to Randal MacDonnell, as well as letters from James Ryan and Lord Kenmare, none of which appear to have survived. In the expectation of soon receiving further news it had determined to meet again on the 23rd, and subsequently at frequent intervals, to take such action as the situation required: in particular, to follow up a suggestion by Scully that Irish MPs should be approached (see *The Catholic Question* pp.96-7).

III

THE PETITION IN PARLIAMENT

Lord Hawkesbury to Lord Hardwicke

[Extract] 1 April 1805

[The Home Secretary tells the Lord Lieutenant that the King says he is not to leave Dublin to receive the Garter recently awarded him, and continues:]

The Catholic petition will probably be discussed about the middle of the month of May, there is no reason to suppose however that we shall have any difficulty in the business in this country. The more I see the more I am convinced that if there was not an obstacle in its nature insurmountable at the present time, the opinion of the publick in this country is so decidedly against the measure of granting the Prayer of the petition, that it would not be in the power of the Government (even if they had the disposition) to carry it. The Catholicks will gain nothing by the attempt, and a great number of persons will feel themselves under the necessity of declaring their hostility to the Catholicks, who would have been very satisfied to have remained silent on the subject, if it had not been forced into discussion.

Source: Hardwicke Papers, Add. MSS. 35,706, f.197.

Lord Hardwicke to Lord Redesdale

[Copy] Dublin Castle, 4 April 1805

My dear Lord,

....

I have not seen Sir Evan Nepean's narrative which the Speaker has communicated to you, but I can easily conceive its tendency. Mr. Scully, whom I have seen since his return, was desirous to assure me that he had never communicated anything to Sir Evan Nepean with a desire that it should be concealed from me, that on the contrary he concluded that whatever he did communicate to Sir Evan was known to me, and that in fact it was the same thing. He told me that Mr. Pitt had used the same words that had been used in Lord Hawkesbury's letter, of which I gave Lord Fingall an extract; which I was glad to hear as it authenticates the declaration which I was authorised to make. Scully said another thing which I can hardly believe, that the Roman Catholic question is very popular in England: but he seems to expect & even to wish that a prorogation might take place before the question could be discussed. I believe there is no reason to apprehend any discussion or violence at the Assizes and it is wished that none should take place. Marsden tells me that he has sent you the information he possesses of the state of the Roman Caholic Church in Ireland. I think it very likely that some of the English Bishops may wish to obtain such information as can be furnished, and certainly if the Roman Catholics could consent to put their Church upon the same footing it is in England,[1] it would be a great point gained. Lest you may not have it, I send you a copy of McKenna's unpublished pamphlet on the subject of the clergy[2]. . . .

Source: Hardwicke Papers, Add.MSS., 35,778, f.107.

Lord Hardwicke to Charles Yorke

Private & confidential — Dublin Castle, 6 May 1805

My dear Charles,

You will receive enclosed the paper to which I referred in a former letter. It is a confidential communication from Mr. Bellew, who was himself a member of the R.C. Committee, attended all the meetings, and whose father [sic], Sir Edward Bellew, and uncle Sir Thomas French were members of the deputation of five who carried over the petition to England. This paper, added to the other information I have received, leaves not the smallest doubt upon my mind, that the secret and unauthorised communications of Sir Evan Nepean with Mr. Scully, first through Mr. Marshall and afterwards personally, were the real, and operative cause of the petition being brought forward. The circumstance of him asking for a copy of it in order to show Mr. Pitt, which copy was sent to him in the middle of January, after he had left Ireland, induced a belief that Mr. Pitt wished to see it in order to modify it into a form which might render it acceptable; and Mr. Scully told me after his return from England that he never supposed, that any communication he could possibly make to Sir Evan Nepean would be unknown to me: on the contrary, he supposed it was the same thing. . . . If you recollect my correspondence with Lord Hawkesbury, detailing my conversation with Lord Fingall, it must be apparent that nothing was intended but fairly to report to him the importance of keeping the Catholic q[uestio]n back from discussion, of which he was as well convinced as possible; I ever used an argument which must be obvious to everyone, namely the

[1] With a reduced number of dioceses governed by Vicars Apostolic.

[2] See p.67 n.2.

actual dependence of the Pope on our inveterate enemy, and his forced journey to Paris. I trust therefore if any attempt is made to fix duplicity upon Mr. Pitt that no part of that charge . . . can attach here. I certainly abstained from communicating with any other person than Lord Fingall, both because as an old acquaintance I knew him to be a man of the best and most honourable intentions, and because he was of the highest rank among the Catholicks and placed in the chair at all their meetings.

[Enclosure]

I have no doubt of the gentleman* in question having throughout the discussions which took place among the Catholicks relative to proceeding or not with their question at present, having uniformly, at least from the month of November, taken a very leading part in favor of proceeding immediately; and I am equally certain of his having repeatedly said, that in his opinion Mr. Pitt would support the measure, and having successfully denied that Lord Hawkesbury's letter to Lord Hardwicke was any authority to the contrary; and I have a full recollection, that on Friday the 15th of Feby., the day before the general meeting, when in the Committee of 31, a gentleman† in arguing against proceeding at the present moment, assumed as a fact from which he meant to reason, that the minister would at present oppose the question, the gentleman in question interrupted him by crying no no, and asserting the minister would not oppose, or words to that effect; and it is notorious that the doubt thus created in the minds of some of the Catholicks, as to what Mr. Pitt's sentiments really were, was one of the chief means by which a great part of the meeting were led to wish that some proceeding should be taken, and that the business should not be totally abandoned, when it was considered uncertain, whether if proceeded on, it would not ultimately meet with the support of the minister. It being argued by the gentleman in question and those with whom he acted, that though Mr..Pitt would not appear to promote the discussion, yet that he would not be sorry to have it pressed on him apparently without his interference, and that in such case he would at least probably give it his support.

[In Lord Hardwicke's hand]

* Mr. Scully, whose communication with Sir Evan Nepean commenced after the second meeting of the Roman Catholicks at Mr. Ryan's.

† Lord Fingall always assumed it as a fact.

Source: Hardwicke Papers, Add. MSS. 35,706, f.222.

Nicholas Vansittart to Lord Hardwicke

Secret & Confidential. Irish Office [London], 9 May 1805

My dear Lord.

[After some paragraphs about the threat to Ireland connected with the movements of the French Toulon fleet Vansittart continues]

The Catholic petition comes on tomorrow in the House of Lords & on Monday in the Commons. There is every reason to believe that the majority against it will be very large and the opposition are so well convinced of its unpopularity that they begin heartily to repent of having brought it forward & have debated about letting it drop.[1] Their friends are much divided about it. The Prince of Wales discountenances it privately. The Duke of Northumberland has declared himself openly & strongly. Upon the whole I have great hopes that it will be decided so as to set the question at rest for many years.

Source: Hardwicke Papers, Add.MSS. 35,716, f.63.

Dr John Milner to Archbishop J. T. Troy

10 Queen's Street, Bloomsbury, 8 May 1805

My Lord,

I have not been idle during the fortnight I have spent in this metropolis, yet I wish I cd. prove that I have done any essential good. My Pamphlet[2] has been distributed to members of both Houses & I have conferred with all those to whom I cd. procure access. Still it seems a settled point that we shall not be able to command more than one third in either house. In this state of affairs I have endeavoured to rouse the

[1] See the *Dropmore Papers* Vol.VII, p.268 for a report by Thomas Grenville on a meeting at Fox's house at which he himself, Grey, Windham, [Robert, Lord] Fitzgerald and Lord Temple had canvassed the possibility of deferring the petition without fixing a precise period or until next session, if the Catholics then required it. "What I hear of the indisposition of our whole party to it, as well as its general unpopularity, incline me to this; but this is much encreased by the eagerness and irritation of the Prince, who called in Windham and myself in Pall Mall after the meeting, and shewed me in his conversation the extreme to which he pushes the matter. . . . My conviction is that in persisting you will make the future possessor of the Crown as adverse to it as the present".

[2] *A short view of the chief arguments against the Catholic petition.*

attention of the legislature to the greatest of our practical grievances, the state of about 200,000 poor Catholic soldiers & seamen. All whom I have conversed with, to a man, admit the impolicy as well as the injustice of the religious persecution they suffer, & I have no doubt that the same might be removed, if in the impossibility of carrying everything, the deputies of the Irish Caths. wd. unite their efforts to obtain this & certain other specific benefits. I have not omitted the opportunity of stating one of our cheif English grievances, namely the state of the marriage act in our regard, & Bishop Horseley has kindly undertaken to negotiate that business, as far as it is practicable with the judges & Protestant Bishops. Lord Buckingham, of course, is disposed to lend his aid.

Mr. Grattan is deeply immersed in the study of the Councils of Lateran & Constance & other matters of the same nature, as our adversaries dwell so much upon them. I have begged him not to spend his vast talents on questions of this nature, but he says he must be armed at all points. Indeed I expect he will not have recourse to these weapons except in case of necessity & that he will make one of the most brilliant speeches ever heard in our or any other senate, in which amongst other things he will turn the charge of perfidy on the Legislature itself, or at least Mr. Pitt and his friends.

The policy of deferring the motion in the House of Commons until Monday [13 May] is to enable Lord Grenville to substantiate this charge in the upper House on Friday [10 May].[1] I hope to attend both discussions. Mr. Fox will confine himself to the grand question of national policy as I gathered from what he said to me.—The Methodistical party appears to be hostile to us, accordingly I have met with much coolness among their leaders. The worst business, however, is that we are not united & energetical ourselves. The return of the deputies to Ireland, & the little figure they made in London is generally blamed. Add to this that there is great jealousy at least amongst the English Catholics, viz. on one side amongst the old Commitee people,[2] & the Episcopate or orthodox party, & on the other amongst the lawyers, all of whom wish to stand foremost when any great business is to be transacted.

Of course Yr. Grace will see Mr. Plowden's pamphlet[3] with the Frontispiece, containing amongst other things a severe satyr on Mr. Ch. Butlers pamphlet, known by the name of <u>The Great Now</u>. Mr. McKenna is on the point of publishing a short

[1] Having resigned with Pitt on the Catholic question Grenville was in a stronger position than Fox to make such a charge, although he does not seem to have done so.

[2] Charles Butler, Sir John Throckmorton and others of the pre-1791 Committee.

[3] *A Letter to Sir Richard Musgrave Bart.*, published by Vincent Dowling. The frontispiece shows Cerberus with three mouths representing the *Anti-Jacobin, British Critic* and *Irish Rebellion* outpourings of Musgrave. On page 63 Plowden claims that Lord Sidmouth had engaged Butler to write his 1803 pamphlet, *A Letter to a Roman Catholic Gentleman of Ireland*, which urged that with the enemy at the gate the GREAT NOW should take precedence over all other considerations.

pamphlet,[1] so also is Dr. Coombs.[2] By this time Yr. Grace will have recd. under Sir John [Hippisley]'s franko a copy of my pamphlet. Dr. Hamil will send you other copies as opportunity serves.

Mr. McKenna has twice done me the honor of calling here, but both times I was from home. Tomorrow I will endeavour to see him at his own house. Being much pressed for time, of which my writing is a proof, I beg leave to subscribe myself, with desiring my compts. to Mr. D'Arcy & begging a share in yr. pious thoughts.
PS. Our four V[icars] A[postolic] are all now in London. I wish their meeting may be of [paper torn] to the common cause.

Source: DDA, Troy Papers, 29/9 f.58.

Lord Fingall to Lord Grenville

Thayer Street, 10 May 1805

My dear Lord,

Not having had the honour of seeing your Lordship when I had the honour of calling yesterday on your Lordship, I take the liberty of enclosing a copy of the resolutions entered into at the last meeting of the Catholics in Dublin. It is merely in case anything should be urged against the measure being brought forward at this moment.

[Enclosure]

Dublin, 20 April 1805

At a general meeting of Roman Catholics

> Resolved That the thanks of the meeting be and are hereby given to our delegates the Earl of Fingall, Lord Visct. Southwell,[3] Sir Edw. Bellew, Sir Thos. French, Denys Scully & James Ryan Esqs. for the zeal and ability with which they executed the important trust reposed on them, to have the petitions of the Roman Catholics of Ireland presented to both Houses of the Impl. Parliament.

[1] *An abstract of the arguments on the Catholic question.*
[2] Dr Coombes contributed to Cobbett's *Political Register* under the pseudonym of British Observer, but owing to lack of space the article did not appear until 26 October.
[3] Only this resolution classes him as one of the appointed deputies.

Resolved That the thanks of the meeting be and are hereby also given to the Earls of Shrewsbury & Kenmare & Lord Visct. Trimlestown for their zealous cooperation with our other Delegates in having the said petitions presented.

Resd. That understanding there is no likelihood of Mr. Pitt's objection as to time being removed in the next session of Parliamt, we fully approve of the decision taken by our said Delegates in authorising Lord Grenville & Mr. Fox to take an early opporty of having our said petitions taken into consideration.

Resd. That the said Delegates & the Earls of Shrewsbury & Kenmare, Lord Trimlestown & R. MacDonnell Esq.[1] be requested and are hereby authorised & empowered, during the present session of Parliamt. to direct & assist in the management & conduct of our said petitions in both Houses of Parliament in such measures as may appear to them or the majority of them to be necessary & useful for obtaining the full & complete repeal of all the penal statutes which affect the Catholics of Ireland agreeably to the Prayer of the said petitions.

Signed by Thomas Fitzgerald

Chairman[2]

Source: Dropmore Papers, Add. MSS. 59,255, ff.210,216.

[1] It is not known which of the other elected delegates, apart from MacDonnell and Lord Fingall, went to London, but Scully did not. They were still there on 23 May when the *Morning Chronicle* reported their imminent departure

[2] This is the last record of the Committee that has been found. Plowden writes in his *History* (II, p.296): "After the return of the delegation some select partial assemblies were holden at Mr. Ryan's to receive the report of the delegation; but most of the very persons, who had usually attended those meetings, became so dissatisfied, that they refused to attend to vote thanks to the delegates for their upright and honourable conduct in the fulfilment of their important mission. Soon after which, they called a final meeting and dissolved their committee". Plowden fails to make it clear whether he is referring to the mission of the first or the second deputation.

Randal MacDonnell to Lord Grenville

Bloomsbury Square, 13 May 1805

My Lord,

I hope the paper herewith[1] will sufficiently convey to your Lordship the information desired on the points of which it treats. I regret it is so long but there was not time to compress it.

Source: Dropmore Papers, Add.MSS. 59,255, f.181.

Alexander Marsden to John King

[Extract] Dublin Castle, 15 May 1805

....

We have got the first part of the debates in the House of Lords on the Catholic petition, & are anxious to have the sequel—We give equal praise to the ability of Lord Grenville's & Lord Hawkesbury's speeches—The subject you may suppose excites an interest here, but as yet no agitation.[2]

Source: HO 100/128, f.165.

[1] Not found. Grenville was about to reply to the debate in the House of Lords that evening. See also p.121 n.1.

[2] Marsden was no doubt thinking only of Catholic agitation, for at the Dublin Quarter Sessions John Giffard had made a violent speech on 26 April against the petition and on 3 May Lord Hardwicke had dismissed him from his post at the Customs. The present letter is the last dealing with the Catholic subject in the Home Office file, which ends in October. In correspondence on other matters there are several references to the peaceful state of the country.

Dr John Milner to Archbishop Troy

[London] 17 May 1805

My Lord,

The newspapers will have informed you of the fate of the petition & of the nature of the debate that occurred upon it. On our side was all the sp[l]endor of high birth, extensive possessions, brilliant talents & public virtue. On the part of our adversaries were natural imbecility for the most part & sordid interest. I wish I cd. give yr. Grace an idea of the sublimity of Fox, the finished oratory of Grattan & dignified energy & generosity of Lord Grenville. If I had no other reason to thank yr. Grace for the honorable commission you imposed upon me, it wd. be that you have afforded me the opportunity of becoming acquainted in the last mentioned personage, with one of the most illustrious statesmen, most humane of men & warmest of friends to Catholics amongst our legislators. I must not omit to mention, as an additional satisfaction, that I had the honor of being abused by Dr. Duigenan & that in company with yr. Grace.[1] You did not stand in need of an advocate: yr. known character was a sheild to you, but as I wanted an advocate, so I found an able one in Dr Laurence.[2] I hope you will have a tolerable account of the whole debates in a work which I am told is shortly to be published. Although defeated in our object, all the Caths who heard the discussions, as I did in both houses, have departed from it with the highest satisfaction. Our loyalty, fidelity & conscientiousness have been loudly proclaimed by our very enemies: indeed it was upon that very ground Ld. Sidmouth & the Attorney General opposed us in each of the houses.[3]

But to proceed to some thing practicable. As I was assiduous in my visits to all the leading men of each chamber, so I was more frequent in my attendance on our best friend Lord Grenville. I found him after the first debate cheifly taken up preparing an answer to Lord Redesdale[4] & I furnished him with such documents as I cd. procure for this purpose from yr. venerable Vicar Genl Dr. Hamil, or as occurred to myself. In consequence of such instruction his Lordship denied in his

[1] *Hansard* IV, 873.

[2] Ibid 982. Dr French Laurence, MP for Peterborough and Professor of civil law at Oxford, upheld certain qualifications made by Dr Milner regarding the validity of oaths.

[3] Lord Sidmouth said he gave the petitioners full credit for loyalty but questioned what their sentiments might be under different conditions. Spencer Perceval argued that even their conscientious regard for oaths suggested that in an orderly way they would omit no opportunity to advance their religion (Ibid. IV, 695, 941)

[4] Ibid. 1061. Lord Redesdale claimed that the Irish hierarchy, in contrast with the Vicars Apostolic of England, flouted the constitution by their very existence, and that they aimed to substitute themselves for the protestant establishment.

reply of Monday night that the Cathc. prelates aimed at the revenues or temporal distinctions of the Protestant Bishops, which subject as stated by Ld. Redesdale had greatly excited the jealousy of the Bench of Bishops & induced even our friend Dr Horseley to change his resolution of voting for us.[1] At present Ld. Grenville is in the country, but his brother the Marquis of Buckingham tells me in his name that it is requisite yr. Ldps the Catholic Bishops of Ireland, shd "redeem Lord Grenville's pledge"[2] by testifying in that distinct letter of thanks which I have assured his Lordship he might expect from your Rt. Revd. corpses [*sic*] for his generous exertions in our behalf, a disavowal of all such claims, pretensions or expectations of the revenues privileges rank distinctions &c by law annexed to sees of Dublin, Armagh, Cork &c.—2dy whereas much has been alledged against us from the supposed decrees of the Councils of Lateran & Constance, from the Decretals & from Belarmine & other schoolmen by Dr. Duigenan & a shoal of pamphleteers, [t]he wish is that in the sd. letter you wd. not only disclaim these perfidious & immoral tenets as they are in themselves, but also as they are supposed to grow out of the said Councils, Decretals &c. Lastly the Marquis is extremely anxious that in the said letter, yr. Grace & yr. colleagues the Archbishops & Bishops wd. assume such styles & titles as might mark yr. spiritual authority without clashing with the civil distinctions of the establishment (Yr. Grace will perceive that I am here merely stating the opinions of others, not my own). Having consulted Dr. Hamil he proposed four different schemes for this purpose: viz (1) J. T. Troy DD., Dublin; (2) J. T. T., R. Cath. A. B. of Dublin; (3) J. T. Troy DD., R. Cath. A. B. in the Ch. of Dublin (as in yr. *Vindication*);[3] (4) J. T. T., A. B. of the R. Cath. Church of Dublin. Amongst these the Marquis prefers the last, only substituting in for of before Dublin.

I must add that it is conceived it wd. be well taken & have good effect if in such a letter you were to express yr. sense of the liberality & kindness for Catholics expressed by the House of Peers in general & particularly His Grace the A.B. of Cantry. & the Bench of Bps. in common. Lord Somerford[4] may not be possessed of this spirit, but as I was informed, means were found to gag him.

[1] Ibid. 794. Dr Horsley, alluding to the difficulties raised by Lord Redesdale, argued that compliance with the petition would be the worst thing for the Catholics themselves in view of the rancour that it would revive.

[2] In his closing speech Lord Grenville replied to two allegations against the Bishops: that they had not signed the petition because they were not willing to subscribe to the sentiments of loyalty expressed in it; and that they regarded the clergy of the reformed religion as usurpers. Probably on the strength of assurances from Dr Milner and MacDonnell (see p.116) he told the House that he had the means of proving the contrary (Ibid. 837). See p. 124 for the letter signed by all the Irish Bishops, addressed to Lord Grenville in response to Dr Milner's request.

[3] The title of an anonymous pamphlet of 1804 defending Dr Troy against an attack on his Exhortation (see p.101 n.1).

[4] *Recte* [Viscount] Somerton, Archbishop of Dublin, from 1806 1st Earl of Normanton.

have no doubt but that you will fulfill my pledge, in writing to Ld Grenville in quality of Cathc Prelates & heads of the Cathc. Church, & I dare say you will think it just to thank also Mr. Fox, if not Mr. Grattan. But how far you will think it expedient to fulfill his Lordship's pledge you in your wisdom will determine. It seems to be the wish of the Marquis that you wd. transmit a draft of yr. letter to Lord Grenville previously to signature. But perhaps that might lead to unpleasant discussions. At any rate you will be pleased to address yrselves immediately to that nobleman, as I expect to leave London in the course of a week.[1]

I have paid particular attentions in the course of my visits amongst our great men to the persecution under which our soldiers & sailors labour, & there is but one opinion of the justice & policy of redressing that grievance. Indeed it has been often mentioned in the late debates, & I believe the government has already sent orders to the head officers &c of a different tenor to those which I believe they previously sent. I am led to believe that when the Mutiny bill next comes round proper clauses will be added to enable these poor men to practice their religion. Our friends however do not wish us to introduce any new bill at the present moment, whatever prospect we might have of carrying it. This advice refers as well to the desired modification of the marriage act, as to the relief of the soldiers. I am told however that the Hon. Augustus Dillon is bent on bringing in a bill immediately for the latter object, without consulting either friends or enemies. This is unwise & may have bad consequences.[2]

I have too good reason to fear that whenever the moment of Emancipation comes we shall have fresh difficulties to encounter from the policy of statesmen & the jealousy of the establishment. In short, I expect they shall be for abridging the Pope's power as well with respect to the nomination of our prelates, as to the sending of any rescripts whatever, in a manner that we shall not be able to agree to.

My pamphlet is nearly sold off & I believe some of the 300 copies yr. Grace &c undertook to answer for have also been sold, as the whole number of 300 was not distributed gratis. Of course there will not be so many to pay for. I cd. have no objection whatever to the republication of my pamphlet in Ireland except what arose from my wish of correcting its errors. The most material of these consists in my twice calling the Antinomians—Anomeans.

I have had some conversation with Ld. Fingall concerning yr. Grace's cause which is to come on next Thursday [23 May] & in consequence of what fell from

[1] There are two drafts in Dr Troy's hand (DDA 29/9, f.49) and Dr Troy refers to one by Scully (*The Catholic Question, p.118*). For the final version see p.124. By 'immediately' Milner means 'direct'.

[2] Among the Troy Papers (29/9, f.48) there is a protest from the four Archbishops to Lord Hardwicke regarding the soldiers, minuted as not presented 'for prudential reasons'.

his Lordship I have requested Mr. MacKenna to wait upon him.[1] I have several times seen Mr. MacDonell, but have never yet had the pleasure of seeing Mr. Troy, though he has been here once or twice to pay me a visit. All our Cath Bishops are here in London, God grant we may meet for his glory.

I must not forget to say that I hope yr. Grace or some other person will inquire into the truth of those extraordinary stories told by Ld. Redesdale in Pt, which I presume you have remarked in the newspapers.[2] I must by this time have wearied yr. Grace with my wretched scrawl, I therefore hasten to subscribe myself . . . .
P.S. Sir John [Hippisley] begs his kind compts.

Source: DDA, Troy Papers, 29/9 f.59.

Nicholas Vansittart to Lord Hardwicke

Private. Irish Office, 18 May 1805

My dear Lord

The great question of the Catholic claims is settled (at least for the present) by the decision of both Houses. Your Excellency is already apprized of the debates and division in the House of Lords. In the Commons we divided at four this morning 336-124 a number which, considering how much the house must have been exhausted by a debate during the greatest part of the night, shews the strong interest taken in the subject. The general majority was quite as large as could be expected, but the number of Irish members who supported the petition appeared to me larger than I hoped it would have been. . . . I am persuaded that several gentlemen, for the sake of gaining a little popularity, voted for the petition against their own judgement under the conviction that they should be extracted by the English members. This disingenuous conduct has several bad effects: it creates prejudices against the Union & against English connection in general—it furnishes a ground for popular complaint & clamor—it will ultimately lead to the success of the Catholic claims themselves (contrary to the wishes of those gentlemen, who will find it impossible to retract when they become sensible of the danger) as there can be no doubt a great part of the English members would withdraw their opposition if they conceived them to be popular in Ireland.

[1] See p.101. The case was not heard until 11 July. Lord Fingall gave evidence as the principal witness (*State Trials*, XXIX, col.515).

[2] He cited several cases of Irish Catholic bigotry (*Hansard* IV, 1067,1072,1081).

The public feeling here was extensively and decidedly against the application though not very strongly expressed: which is principally to be attributed to the influence of government being employed to discountenance any discussion of the question, & to the general conviction that the sense of Parliament exactly agreed with the prevailing sentiment.

Source: Hardwicke Papers, Add.MSS. 35,716, f.67.

Dr John Milner to Archbishop J. T. Troy

[Wolverhampton] 13 June 1805

My Lord

It has been very contrary to my wishes to have remained so long a time without writing to your Grace. The fact is, that during the whole of my continuing in London after I had last the honour of writing to you I was taken up with some business or other consequent to the grand business in which you did me the honour to employ me. As soon as I could by any means get away from that metropolis I hastened down to my dear friends & parishioners & by [*sic*] beloved abode at Winchester, where I enjoyed every comfort in this life calculated to refresh me after my preceding fatigue, except the prospect of being allowed to remain there. In one word, I had at Winchester all I cd. wish for in this life; here I have most things that I dislike.

I must begin my narrative by informing yr. Grace that in my last interview with Mr. McDonnel I perceived symptoms of that disposition in him which Mr. Clinch had previously told me existed in him & some of his colleagues. I believe he thought I acted too independent & conspicuous a part in my negociations with the members of both Houses. What he said to me was, that the matter had not been properly arranged by yr. Grace for the purpose of forming a joint cooperation. I might have answered that yr. Grace & the Prelates of Ireland had been neglected by the lay gentlemen as persons of no interest or weight in the business going forward, till our common enemies were on the point of availing themselves of the neglect, when you generously stepped forward & covered them with the sheild of yr. authority from the disgrace they might otherwise have suffered.[1] This, however, I did not say, nor I hope anything else to give displeasure to that gentleman or any other deputy; I barely state the circumstances under which I had transacted one

[1] Dr Milner had evidently been authorised to assure Lord Grenville that the Bishops, as they later confirmed in writing, endorsed the petition of the laity.

particular affair with Lord Grenville, which I believe that gentleman thought wd. have been more properly done by himself. The truth is I was sent for by his Lordship & expressly commissioned to act as I did.[1]

Now that I am upon the subject of Mr. McDonnel I must mention that Dr. Hamil had said something to him on the subject of my expenses. What I said was that I previously refused, as I still do, to receive one farthing myself on that or any other score; but that having given up the copyright of my pamphlet to Keating (with stipulation, however, in favor of what has been done in Ireland) I hoped that some means wd. be devised for defraying the expenses of the 900 copies distributed amongst members of Pt. I must add that yr. Grace's last letter reached me just as I was setting out from London, so that I had no opportunity of communicating to any of yr. friends the melancholy news it contained & that I never had the opportunity of paying my compts. to your nephew, though we mutually took measures for that purpose.

I now proceed to more important business—Though I used my best endeavours for the common concern, yet as I intimated to yr. Grace before I set off to London, I tremble at the prospect of its succeeding, for fear of the evils that might follow such an event. I have already mentioned to yr. Grace some of the schemes which our friends have already devised, in the event of future success, for regulating yr. Hierarchy & our common discipline. God forbid that you shd. give up any point that ought really to be maintained out of compliment to those friends or for any other consideration whatsoever. In my last conversation with the Marquis of Buckingham, Lord Grenville being then in the country, I found he was willing (& I understood that he spoke the sentiments of the A. B. of Canterby)[2] to admit <u>of</u> for <u>in</u> with respect to yr. titles. According to this plan your Grace might subscribe yrself Archbishop of the R. Cathc. church of Dublin. His Lordship added that your titles being once settled, he wd. have you adopt them on every public occasion whether in addressing yr. flocks or his Majesty's Ministers. I was at particular pains to discover what plans were in contemplation, with respect to the filling up of vacant sees. One is that of his Majesty being allowed a negative, the other that of his being at liberty to choose, but being confined to the corps of Grand Vicars, it being supposed there shall be two in each Bishopric. I represented that neither these nor any other changes cd. take place but by a concordatum with the H. See. A still more alarming proposition is, that all our communications, of whatever nature, shd. be revised by the Ministry, in order to see whether they contain any thing hostile to the nation, & the example of France before the Revolution and the authority of the Statute of

[1] See Randal MacDonnell's letter of 13 May (p.116). Grenville replied to the debate in the House of Lords on the evening of that day and evidently sought the assistance of Dr Milner as well as of MacDonnell.

[2] Charles Manners-Sutton, Archbishop since 2 February 1805.

Praemunire[1] were adduced to show that this may be done. It is proper to mention these matters to yr. Grace, & I make no doubt that you will communicate them to yr. M. Rev. & Rt. Rev. Brethren at yr. approaching meeting in order to be prepared yrselves & in order to instruct yr. agents & friends shd. such proposals be made, at a future time in a more public manner. For my part, I tremble for the consequences of them, knowing that there is a party amongst ourselves, I mean us English Catholics at least, who are ready to go all lengths, for temporal purposes, perhaps even to humble & restrain us clergy. I find that directions have been given in some parts to allow the poor soldiers to practice the Cathc. religion, but by a strange inconsistency they are required also to practice the Protestant. I indend [*sic*] making some representations on that subject shortly. I have not leisure or patience to discuss the business of marriage. I have reason, however, to think that it is very possible for us to be relieved without yr. being aggrieved. If not I wish to forego the advantage.

I have been requested to mention a Mr. Sheridan to yr. Grace & Mr. D'Arcy, who was formerly on the stage, afterwards in the Friars Habit at Douay, & who is now a candidate for a situation at Maynooth. What I can say with truth of him is, that in the first mentioned station, he conducted himself with a decency, honesty & respect for religion very unusual in persons of that profession.

When you meet yr. venerable confreres I beg to be most respectfully named to them, as likewise to Mr. D'Arcy.

P.S.

Sir Jn. continues to write to me, as I understand he also does to yr. Grace & our good friend Bp. Moylan, on the subject of his intended publication.[2] His kindness & service to me when in London are beyond description. I am surprised that Cuthell & Martin's acct. of the debates do not appear & that I hear nothing of yr. Grace's action against the *Antijacobin.*[3] My three brethren met me in London; but Dr. D.[4] continued firm in his resolution of not corresponding with me, though he owns I never wrote to him but in terms of the utmost respect. Hence yr. Grace will perceive that there can be no cordial cooperation in our little body. The only remedy seems to be for me to resign. I sincerely wish to do it.

Source: DDA, Troy Papers, 29/9 f.61.

[1] Of 1353 and later, against encroachments of the Holy See.

[2] Sir John Hippisley had caused to be printed for private circulation *The substance of additional observations* which he had been unable to deliver in the debate on the petition. In response to demand, this was published in 1806.

[3] See p.120,n.2.

[4] John Douglass, Vicar Apostolic of the London district. Because of "the violence, bullying and insults" he had seen in Dr Milner's letters he had thought it best for both of them that no further letters should pass between them (B.Ward, *The Eve of Catholic Emancipation*, I, p.27, citing a contemporary letter in the Clifton archives).

The Roman Catholic Archbishops and Bishops of Ireland to Lord Grenville

Dublin, 5 July 1805

We the undersigned Archbishops and Bishops of the Roman Catholic Church of Ireland, beg leave to convey to your lordship our testimony of sincere and respectful gratitude. . . . The principles contained in the Catholic petition we avow as our principles, agreeably to those reiterated and solemn oaths whereby we have bound ourselves to our sovereign and our country. But if, notwithstanding such pledges, we still be charged with tenets immoral or anti-social in consequence of canons and decretals misunderstood, or of divines and schoolmen delivering their own particular opinions, our answer is, that we have long since abjured all such tenets, maxims and sentiments.

However we may wish for the speedy accomplishment of the measure petitioned for, yet we never did, nor do intend to disturb the security of the established Church. We ambition not its preeminence, nor repine at our own situation, neither do we seek to exalt our Church by means of wealth or power. The tithes, precedence, and privileges of the established clergy, conferred by the laws of the land, we freely acknowledge in our intercourse with them, nor have we ever refused to them their rights and distinctions. The jurisdiction we exercise over our respective congregations is purely spiritual, and this, in its extent and nature, we conceive to be in perfect analogy with that necessarily exercised in every other religious society, when any member is segregated for his disorderly life or obstinate criminality, but we do not assume or pretend to enforce such sentence of removal otherwise than by spiritual coercion.

The principles of our holy religion as taught and practised by us are not only compatible with the most faithful allegiance to our most gracious sovereign, but are also amongst the most powerful incentives to the conscientious discharge of that sacred duty. It will, morever, be found that the best instructed Catholics are the most loyal of subjects, and the most virtuous of the community. These, our principles and practices, have long been submitted to the severest scrutiny.

We earnestly solicit a full enquiry into our past conduct, in order to an exculpation from the charges which are said to have been lately preferred against us; charges heretofore unheard of in Ireland, and of which we are confident our country will acquit us, for we know them to be groundless.

And surely we may presume to express our confident hope, founded upon the known wisdom of the legislature, that no imputations contrary to these our solemn disavowals, will be admitted against the Roman Catholic hierarchy in Ireland, the spiritual teachers and comforters of such a large proportion of his Majesty's European subjects,[1] without full investigation and substantial proofs.

We may doubtless be permitted to hope that such imputations so unsupported, so contrary to fact, will not be allowed to prejudice us, or the laity of our communion; or to postpone the long-wished-for enjoyment of the entire benefit of the British laws and constitution.[2]

Richard O'Reilly
J. T. Troy
Thomas Bray
Edward Dillon

Pat.Jos. Plunkett
D. Delany
F. Moylan
Domk. Bellew
John Cruise
Jas. Caulfield
M. P McMahon
Edmund French
Pat. McMullen

James Lanigan
Jas. Dillon
John Young
C. O'Donnell
Thos. Costello
James Murphy
J. Power
N. J. Archdeacon
Charles Lynah
Edm. Derry
C. Sughrue
P. McLaughlin
W. Coppinger.

Source: Dropmore Papers, Add.MSS. 59,256, f.5.

[1] A reminder that George III also had Hanoverian Catholic subjects.

[2] This letter, accompanied by another saying that thanks had also been sent to Fox, is printed in the published selection of the *Dropmore Papers* (VII, p.290),but without the signatures.

APPENDICES

APPENDIX A

MINUTES OF THE MEETINGS OF THE DEPUTATION

Tuesday, 5 March

A conference took place between the delegates already arrived, viz. Lds. Fingall & Southwell, Mr. Scully & Mr. Ryan.

Wednesday, 6 March

At one o'clock, a conference was held, the same deputies attending, & also Sir E. Bellew.

Friday, 8 March

At two o'clock a conference was held—present Lords Fingall, Kenmare, Southwell & Trimlestown, Sir E. Bellew, Mr. Scully, Mr. Ryan.

It was agreed that Lord Fingall should write a note to Mr. Pitt to request an interview with him on behalf of the noblemen & gentlemen who compose the Cathc. deputation from Ireland.

Saturday, 9 March

At two a conference was held—Present the same deputies as yesterday.

Discussed the outline, or heads of the conversation proposed to be had with Mr. Pitt, pursuant to the instructions.

Sunday, 10 March

At two a conference was held—The same deputies attended save Mr. Ryan.

A letter from Mr. Chars. Addis was read, offering his services in a confidential situation—It was agreed to accept his offer, and to employ him, as occasions should require.

Monday, 11 March

At ten a conference was held—Present: the Earl of Shrewsbury (Waterford and Wexford in Ireland), E of Fingall, [E of] Kenmare, Visct. Southwell, Lord Trimlestown, Sir E. Bellew, Mr. Scully, Mr. Ryan.

A note from Mr. Pitt to Lord Fingall, in answer to that of Friday last, was read.

It was dated this day, & purported, that Mr. P. will be glad to see Lord Fingall, and the noblemen & gentlemen who propose to accompany him, tomorrow at half past twelve o'clock.

This note was taken into consideration. The heads, or topics, to be urged to Mr. Pitt, were further discussed & prepared.

Tuesday, 12 March

At eleven a conference was held—The same deputies attended.

The heads, or topics, to be urged to Mr. Pitt, were finally agreed upon and methodized.

At a quarter past twelve the eight deputies attending went to Mr. Pitt in Downing Street, and had an interview with him, which lasted about 50 minutes.

He declined, first, to introduce the petition in the ordinary way.

Secondly to introduce it and procure a Parliamentary sanction, or declaration in favour of the principle or policy of the measure prayer [*sic*] for.

Thirdly, to introduce it, even under the authority expressed in our instructions or in any other manner whatsoever.

Wednesday, 13 March

At twelve a conference was held, which lasted three hours.

The same delegates attended—and they came to the following resolutions unanimously, vizt.

1

that the Cath. deputies, having now executed that part of their instructions which relates to their requesting Mr. Pitt to introduce the Cath. petitn. into Parlt.—and having yesterday been distinctly given by him to understand, in a long conversation, that he declines introducing it at present under any qualification or authority whatsoever, and that he will feel it his duty to oppose it and any measure founded upon it, they do now take into consideration what other members are the most eligible to apply to for the introduction of it into Parlt.;

2

that it does not appear, upon every inquiry and information within their power, that there is at present any member, of sufficient weight and talents for the introduction of the petition who is perfectly neutral & unattached to any political party;

3

that it appears, therefore, upon a full consideration of their instructions & an investigation of all facts necessary for their direction, that it is their duty to apply to the most eligible members in point of talents, character & personal weight, for the introduction of the petition;

4

that, acting upon this opinion, they conceive, that the most expedient method of proceeding, now to be adopted, is that of a communication to Lord Grenville & Mr. Fox, requesting them to introduce the petition and support it in Parlt., & that Lds. Fingall & Kenmare be authorized to make that request, and to procure a meeting between them & the deputies.

[Inserted note][1]

Present at the Conference of 12 March, 1805 with Mr. Pitt:
Earl of Shrewsbury,
Earl of Fingall,
Viscount Gormanstown,[2]
Viscount Southwell,
Lord Trimlestown,
Sir Edward Bellew,
Counsellor Denys Scully,
Mr. Ryan.

N.B. Lord French came too late to London to be of any service and was not present at the meeting with Mr. Pitt, nor then arrived.

Thursday, 14 March

At half past twelve, Lords Fingall & Kenmare (and Mr. Scully) waited upon Mr. Fox by appointment, & found him in company with Mr. Grey and Mr. Windham.

Lord Kenmare communicated to them the resolution of the deputies pursuant to the proceedings of Wednesday last, and requested Mr. Fox to bring the petition into Parlt.—in which request Lord Fingall concurred.

Mr. Fox undertook to do so in the handsomest manner.

Mr. Grey and Mr. Windham also expressed themselves in very cordial terms upon the subject and professed that they would espouse the cause, upon principles of a genuine interest, not by any means as a party question that they would hold the attainment of the measure wholly in view, having for their object the interests of the Catholic body, and of Ireland at large.

Mr. Grey particularly threw out, for the consideration of the deputies, what effect the discussion of the measure, at this time, would produce in Ireland.

It was finally agreed to meet at Ld. Grenville's on Saturday next.

[1] The list and the note, occupying an empty page, were inserted after Sir Thomas, on the death of his mother, became a baron on 8 December 1805.
[2] A slip of the pen: the third ranking deputy was Lord Kenmare (see p.81).

N.B
Mr. Grey & Mr. Windham were present at the meeting in consequence of Mr. Fox's letter to Mr. Scully, intimating a wish for permission to request their attendance upon this occasion.

Friday, 15 March

At one, the deputies met at Lord Fingall's.

It was agreed that Ld. Fingall should write a note to Lord Grenville desiring an interview between him and the deputies, which his Lordship did accordingly.

It was further agreed, preparatory to our interview with Lord Grenville, Mr. Fox etc, that, in such interview, we should treat our instructions as mandatory upon us to give them the authority to declare etc, but not mandatory upon them to use that authority.

Saturday, 16 March

At three, the deputies met, including Sir Thomas French, who came last night to town.

It appears, from the report of Lds. Fingall & Kenmare, that they had this day waited (by appointment) upon Ld. Grenville, & found him in company with Mr. Fox & Mr. Grey

that these persons expressed great embarrassment how to act upon our Instructions, and found great difficulty in the wording of them;

that they desire to know, in the first instance, the sentiments of the deputies upon the Instructions, and how far they will accompany the request to introduce the petition, with the restriction or qualification contained in those Instructions, or not;

that they will then, as Ld. Grenville said, consider how to shape their course.

The deputies discussed this subject two hours, but came to no determination.

Sunday, 17 March

The deputies met at one—and sate 2 hours and a half.

It was finally resolved (but not unanimously) that, in the conference which is to take place tomorrow between the deputies & Lord Grenville, Mr. Fox etc, the deputies may authorize them (if required by them) to introduce the petition in whatever manner they shall deem most eligible.

Monday, 18 March

At a quarter before 12 the deputies met at Lord Kenmare's, and shortly afterwards proceeded together to Lord Grenville's.

Lord Grenville was in company with Ld. Spencer, Messrs. Fox, Grey & Windham.

They and the 9 deputies[1] conferred together nearly two hours. They undertook, explicitly, to present and support the petitions in Parliament—Monday next the 25th, was appointed for presenting the petitions, and notices to that effect are to be given tomorrow evening in both Houses by Lord Grenville & Mr. Fox.

Mr. Fox took down the following minute, by consent of the deputies, as the authority under which he & his friends are understood to act –

> The noblemen and gentlemen here present on the part of the Irish Catholics, understanding that there is no likelihood of Mr. Pitt's objections to time being removed in the next session, declare that it is their wish and, as they believe, that of the Catholic body in Ireland that, after presenting their petitions, Lord Grenville & Mr. Fox should take an early opportunity of moving to take the said petitions into consideration.

Here ended the functions of the deputies.

The petition was presented accordingly in both Houses on Monday the 25th March.

The debates, in every body's hands, took place in May following.[2]

Source: Scully Papers MS. 27,514 (i).

[1] The eight previously mentioned plus Sir Thomas French.

[2] These last four lines, plainly inserted at a later date, are entered on a new page.

APPENDIX B

THE DEPUTIES' MEETING OF 13 MARCH 1805

The deputies held a conference together which lasted 3 hours.

They considered that they had now fully executed that part of their instructions which related to their requesting Mr. Pitt to introduce the petition—and that there remained no hope whatsoever of their prevailing upon him so to do under any qualification or authority that they could give him

That it next became their duty to consider how to execute the second part of their Instructions, which enjoined their procuring the introduction of the petition thro' such other Member as shall seem most eligible.

They reflected upon Mr. Pitt's positive declarations of the preceding day, that he would oppose the petition in the House.

That he gave no intimation or prospect whatever, as to the time when he shall be able to support it, nor any hint as to any particular quarter, thro' which it could be introduced without meeting his decided opposition, and they felt that in those circumstances, they could not apply to any Ministerial Member to introduce it with any prospect of advantage, credit or dignity to the Catholic cause.

That, if introduced through such a channel, it would probably receive contemptuous treatment, as Mr. Pitt would oppose it, and no powerful body of Members would, in that case, be inclined to support or even to countenance it.

That it appeared, from the general sense of the public in England, that the cause of the Catholics would lose ground very considerably, if they applied to any other ministerial Member to introduce the petition with a certainty of Mr. Pitt's opposing it—for they would ridicule and reprobate such a step as weak, servile and irresolute.

That, at that critical time and posture of public affairs, it behoves them not to take any step, which would risk the credit and consequence of the cause in the public estimation, or endanger or impair the attachment and zeal for their interests well ascertained to pervade a very powerful description of members not in the habit of supporting the Ministers.

They therefore resolved, that it did not appear to them, that they could, with any prospect of advantage to the Catholic cause, procure the introduction of the petition thro' any Ministerial Member of Parliament—and that such a Member, far from being the most eligible, which they were bound by their Instructions to seek, would on the contrary be very ineligible.

They next considered, whether there was to be found in Parliament any Member of neutral character and unattached to any political party, who possesses consequence, personal weight, and talents adequate to the patronage of so great a cause, and whether such a Member would be most eligible.

It did not appear, upon every inquiry and information they had, hitherto, had, that there was any such Member.

Persons of weight or talents have committed themselves with one or other of the political parties, which now divide the Parliament.

There might, perhaps, be a few Members, who voted sometimes with Ministry, & sometimes against them, but those men had no place in the public estimation, they were not men of talents or of considerable weight or in the habits of Parliamentary attendance.

Besides, it was perceived, that a Member of this description having once obtained the patronage of so powerful a cause, without having in any wise earned it, might underrate its importance and discredit it considerably.

That he might very easily and probably be induced to sacrifice the cause to personal views and considerations; that he would bestow no importance upon the cause, whereas the cause would raise him to great importance—that thus he alone might be the gainer by such an arrangement; for it might render him a very different person from what he was before—that tho' it should find him apparently neutral and unattached to party, it would put him in a situation to dispose of his neutrality, to great personal advantage, and to attach himself to a party, who would reward his services at the expense of the Catholic cause.

That this arrangement would cast a temptation in his way, too dangerous for any political character to encounter—that it would probably end in his exchanging his independent character for a dependent one.

That thus the whole character of the present measure and perhaps of the Catholic body (upon which the public attention is now fixed) would be degraded and cast into contempt and derision.

That, in fine, such a measure, without ingratiating the Catholic cause with the Ministerial side, would for ever alienate from the Catholics the esteem and affection of those great and powerful characters in both Houses, who differed from Ministers.

That it would be felt by them as a stigma and unmerited proscription.

That it must wound them deeply, and they might resent it accordingly, at a day, possibly not distant, when their hostility (altho' at all times to be avoided) would be a fatal and insurmountable obstacle to relief.

That it can be no object to the Catholic body to affront, proscribe, and stigmatize any description of Members.

That it might perhaps gratify the party feeling of those, who were determined to oppose the Catholics themselves, but that this would be extremely unwise & ridiculous in the Catholics to do.

That, as they had not chosen to court opposition by slighting the Ministers, there was no better reason, why they should court the Ministers (now irrevocably adverse) by offending the opposition, who were still their warm and unaltered friends.

That, on the whole, it did not appear in all the circumstances to be for the advantage to the Catholic cause to procure the introduction thro' any Ministerial member (even if Mr. Pitt had countenanced such a proceeding).

That it was still less for the advantage of the cause to procure its introduction thro' any Member reputed to be neutral and unattached to party, supposing such a member could be found.

That in both those cases the discussion (which it was the sense of the Catholic meeting in Dublin should take place) would materially suffer, inasmuch as the opposition, irreparably lost to the Catholics, would probably stand aloof; Mr. Pitt would oppose, other Members connected with Government could indulge in the most violent and inflamed hostility against the Catholics, without restraint nor resistance, and the Member introducing it, would probably be either unable or unwilling to do justice to the merits of the petitioners, or possibly might even impair the credit of the Catholic cause and stamp disgrace and injury upon it by some timid sentiment or unlucky admission into which his dismay or negligence might betray him.

The Deputies, after full and mature consideration, satisfied their minds, that in truth there now exist in Parliament only two descriptions of political members, the Ministerialists and the Anti Ministerialists, or united opposition party.

That no option or alternative was then left to them seeing that they had positively been rejected by the Ministerialists.

They saw, that the opposition party, as now constituted, is of vast and increasing power and influence in the country—that it comprizes an assemblage of the first men in points of talents, rank, honour, personal weight, wealth and experience,

That it is nearly connected with an Illustrious Personage, who is the sincere well wisher and patron of the Catholic cause.

That, as it is at present constituted, it is admitted, even by its political opponents, to concentrate a great proportion of the respectability of the country.

That three members of this party, namely Lords Spencer, Grenville & Mr. Windham, have actually been, until within a short time, members of the same cabinet with Mr. Pitt, had resigned office together with him, and upon one common principle, the Catholic question—that therefore they were peculiarly eligible to be applied to next after Mr. Pitt.

That Mr. Fox was known to stand the highest in the confidence and regards of the Prince of Wales; that his merit has been admitted, even by Mr. Pitt, within this last year, inasmuch as he proposed Mr. Fox to his Sovereign as a fit and eligible person to sit in the cabinet—that therefore he cannot but be a fit and eligible person, in the eyes of the Ministerialists (setting aside his talents and rank) to communicate with, upon the subject of the introduction of the petition.

That, upon the whole, the Deputies conceive it to be most clearly expedient and for the advantage and future prospects of the Catholic cause, to deposit the petition at this juncture in the hands of this assembled and united body of opposition members of both Houses, and to commit it to their protection and support.

That they also conceive it will tend to the better and more effectual exhibiting of the Catholic cause to the public, to leave it to those members to choose and settle among themselves, which of them shall introduce the petitions in both Houses or propose any measures thereon.

That it will render those Members the more able and inclined to perform their respective parts, according as they shall have cast their parts among themselves—That it is, besides, more grateful to their feelings & complimentary to their judgements—That it is not for the Deputies, who are unskilled in Parliamentary tactics, to select or proscribe any particular member of this body—and that their interference in this respect would probably injure and impede the cause, which it is their duty to promote.

That therefore, leaving it to the members of this powerful body to act in this respect as they shall see best for the general good, they conceive that the most eligible members for the introduction of the petition will be such members as shall have been chosen and agreed upon by their Parliamentary supporters in the above mentioned manner.

That they conceive themselves to be bound by their Instructions to take this course of proceeding, and no other.

That they should have deviated from their Instructions very widely, were they to procure the introduction of the petition thro' any other than the most eligible Members.

And that they are well persuaded, that not only the Members to be chosen in the above mentioned manner, will be found the most eligible Members for the introduction of the petitions and for supporting them throughout a full and able discussion in Parliament, but that the course now adopted, is the only one now remaining that can secure the eventual and ultimate attainment of Catholic relief and establish a solid foundation for future discussion and support.

That, acting upon these opinions, they conceived that the most expedient method of proceeding, then to be adopted, was that of a communication with Lord Grenville & Mr. Fox, as the heads of the respective great partiescomprizing the coalesced talents, rank and weight of all those great characters.

That they should be requested to cause the petitions to be introduced and supported in Parliament in the most advantageous manner—and that Lords Fingall and Kenmare be authorized to make that request and to procure a meeting between them and their friends on the one part, and the deputies on the other part.

It was further agreed that Mr. Scully, who enjoyed the private acquaintance of Mr. Fox, should introduce Lords Fingall and Kenmare to him, and arrange with Mr. Fox the time and place of the meeting.

Source: Scully Papers, NLI, MS. 27,514 (i).

APPENDIX C

PARAGRAPHS IN THE *MORNING POST*

4 March 1805

We understand that the Catholic petition will be very favourably received in Parliament. A **great personage**, who was supposed to have entertained difficulties upon the subject, has been heard to say, within the last few days, that he highly approves of the language of the petition, (as it has been represented to him) which the Catholic committee has prepared, and the quiet and unaffected moderation of their proceedings has prepossessed his mind with an advantageous opinion of their intentions and principles. It must be a happy omen to the commencement of the measure, that the deputies appointed to manage the petition, are personally agreeable to the heads of the different political parties, and equally respected by the Ministry and the opposition.

The Earl of Fingall, Sir Edward Bellew, Counsellor Scully, and Mr. Ryan arrived in town on Saturday. The fifth deputy, Sir Hon. Thomas French, being detained by indisposition, was not expected to leave Dublin till Friday last. He will probably reach London on Wednesday, and the whole will then obtain their first audience of Mr. Pitt. The measures to be grounded upon the petition will come at this season with a peculiarly good grace. The union of the parties in supporting and promoting these measures, must afford a substantial pledge to the people of Ireland of the happy temper of Parliament towards the feelings and interests of four millions of H. M.s subjects, who have by the late union between Great Britain and Ireland, committed the superintendence of their concerns to the liberal and protecting care of the Imperial parliament.

We hope that every Member, of either House, will feel it his duty to attend to this Petition, and to urge such measures as may appear best calculated to promote the honour, safety and happiness of the Empire. The facts contained in it are, we understand, exceedingly important and interesting, and they are authenticated by the signatures of men of eminence, wealth, landed and commercial, of the highest honour and probity, and of known and experienced attachment to the constitution. We could name very many among them who have exposed their lives to imminent peril in the support of his Majesty's Government; and all are willing to repeat the hazard, if any occasion should afford an opportunity of evincing their attachment to their Sovereign.

5 March 1805

It is not true, as stated in some of the papers of yesterday, that the Catholic Deputation, in the event of Mr. Pitt's declining to present their Petition to Parliament, mean to apply to Mr. Fox for that purpose. We are well assured that the gentlemen who compose the Deputation, true to the trust imposed on them, are determined that no feature of faction, or party, shall extend to any part of their proceedings. If Mr. Pitt should decline, the Petition will be presented by an independent country gentleman.

7 March 1805

The Hon. Sir T. French is not yet arrived in town but is expected Friday next.

The Marquis Cornwallis yesterday waited on the Earl of Fingall and had a long conference with his Lordship on the subject of the Catholic petition. In the course of the day several of our Nobility and Gentry left their cards at Lord Fingall's house, in George Street, Hanover Square, and also at Mr. Scully's, Great Ryder-Street, and Mr. Ryan's, Clarges-Street.

Viscount Southwell, a nobleman assisting the Catholic deputation, is arrived at Fladong's Hotel, Oxford street.

The Earl of Kenmare and Lord Trimlestown are also preparing to attend at the meetings of the deputation.

14 March 1805

Mr. Pitt, it is said, has expressed himself in such terms to the noblemen and gentlemen who compose the Catholic deputation as to leave no doubt of the success of their application at a proper period; in consequence of which their Petition is expected to be presented by some independent gentleman, unconnected with either party, and laid upon the Table of the House, but the subject will not be agitated with the consent of the petitioners.

The four Deputies who waited upon the Minister (Sir T. French not yet being arrived) were attended by Lords Shrewsbury, Kenmare, Southwell and Trimleston. Lord Fingall opened the business to Mr. Pitt, who, in giving his reason for the postponement of the application, declared, that he still adhered to the sentiments he has always expressed on the subject. The difficulty to be now surmounted is that [*sic*] the opinion of certain Members of Parliament, who have declared their resolution to oppose the measure, if brought forward at present. We shall in our next offer a few observations upon this subject.

15 March 1805

The reception of the Catholic Deputation by the Prime Minister, on Tuesday last, we learn, was of the most courteous and cordial nature, and marked by every form of respect, as well as by every expression of personal kindness. He did not immediately undertake to introduce or support their Petition to Parliament, but will probably deliberate upon the answer to be given. Perhaps he may have deemed it most respectful to the individuals with whom he conferred, as well as most suitable to the dignity of his high office, to avoid coming to any abrupt or precipitate decision upon the application of that great body of subjects. He paid many and high compliments to the temperance, coolness and deliberate circumspection which have marked their first proceedings. These, he said, had claimed his fullest approbation; and further observed, that such a personal compliment to himself as the present application from so respectable a body, who had manifested such meritorious intentions towards their country in the preparatory steps, must be considered, as he felt it to be, highly gratifying to his mind. What his ultimate or fixed decision will be, we cannot take upon us to pronounce. All that is known at present is, that he has had a copy of the Petition some weeks in his possession, (having sent for it to Dublin while the Catholic gentlemen were deliberating upon the mode of presenting it) and has expressed his perfect approbation of its form and language. The Catholic Noblemen and Gentlemen must, therefore, in coming to London, have entertained sanguine hopes of finding in him a patron of this great measure, and which there is every likelihood of his ultimately proving himself to be. We understand that so very reluctant are they to withdraw their case from Ministry, or to embarrass the Government in any respect, that they have offered, if Mr. Pitt will present their petition, to waive the adoption of the measure for the present, leaving it to Parliament to sanction the principle of it by any declaration that may be judged proper for that purpose.

16 March 1805

Mr. Pitt has spoken in the handsomest terms of the courteous and becoming deportment of the Deputies; and in a manner highly creditable to his feelings and liberality of sentiment, has declined, for the present, presenting their petition to Parliament. It is remarkable, that this has been the only conference with Catholics, officially granted and held by the Prime Minister for two centuries past.

The Catholics, in their present application, were encouraged by certain very striking circumstances which have occurred within the last two months, and which we are not yet at full liberty to disclose. The tenor of their petition had found favour in the eyes of a Great Personage, in whose mind conscientious objections to the measure, objections deservedly to be held sacred, are supposed still to exist in a certain degree. We re-assert this fact upon no light authority; but though pre-possessions may have been created in favour of their conduct, and approbation of their petition may have been drawn forth, it does not follow, nor did we ever assert, that the prayer of the petition has yet been deemed reconcileable to certain solemn engagements which the Catholics themselves most highly respect.

For the paragraphs of 4,7 and 16 March see respectively pages 66, 72 and 94.

APPENDIX D

TEXT OF THE PETITION TO THE HOUSE OF LORDS[1]

To the Right Honorable the Lords Spiritual and Temporal of the United Kingdom of Great Britain and Ireland, in parliament assembled

The Humble Petition of the Roman Catholics of Ireland whose names are hereunto subscribed, on behalf of themselves and of others his Majesty's subjects, professing the Roman Catholic Religion

<u>Sheweth</u>

[1]

That your petitioners are steadfastly attached to the person, family and government of their most gracious Sovereign, that they are impressed with sentiments of affectionate gratitude for the benignant laws which have been enacted for meliorating their condition during his paternal reign, and that they contemplate with rational and decided predilection the admirable principles of the British Constitution

[2]

Your petitioners most humbly state that they have solemnly and publickly taken the oaths, prescribed by law to his Majesty's Roman Catholic subjects as tests of political and moral principles; and they confidently appeal to the sufferings which they have long endured, and the sacrifices which they still make, rather than violate their Consciences (by taking oaths of a religious or spiritual import contrary to their belief) as decisive proofs of their profound and scrupulous reverence for the sacred obligations of an oath

[1] Paragraph numbers have been inserted. The footnotes are based on those of Keating's edition of the petition to the House of Commons.

[3]

Your petitioners beg leave to represent that by these awful tests, they bind themselves in the presence of the all-seeing Deity whom all classes of Christians adore,

> "to be faithful and bear true allegiance to their most gracious Sovereign Lord, King George the third, and him to defend to the utmost of their power against all conspiracies and attempts whatsoever, that shall be made against his person, Crown or dignity; to do their utmost endeavours to disclose and make known to his Majesty and his heirs all treasons and traiterous conspiracies, which may be formed against him or them, and faithfully to maintain support and defend to the utmost of their power the succession to the Crown in his Majesty's family against any person or persons whatsoever: that by those oaths they renounce and abjure obedience and allegiance unto any other person claiming or pretending a right to the Crown of this Realm; that they reject and detest as unchristian and impious to believe, that it is lawful in any ways to injure any person or persons whatsoever under pretence of their being hereticks and also that unchristian and impious principle that no faith is to be kept with hereticks; that it is no article of their faith and that they renounce reject and abjure the opinion, that princes excommunicated by the Pope of Rome or any other foreign prince, prelate, State or potentate hath, or ought to have, any Temporal or Civil Jurisdiction power superiority or preeminence within this realm,[1] that they firmly believe that no act, in itself unjust immoral or wicked can ever be justified or excused, by or under pretence or colour, that it was done for the good of the church or in obedience to any ecclesiastical power whatsoever, and that it is not an article of the Catholic faith, neither are they thereby required to believe or profess, that the Pope is infallible, or that they are bound to obey any order in its own nature immoral, though the Pope, or any ecclesiastical power, should issue or direct any such order, but on the contrary they hold, that it would be sinful to pay any respect or obedience thereto, that they do not believe that any sin committed by them can be forgiven at the mere will of any Pope or any priest or of any person or persons whatsoever, but that any person who receives absolution for the same, without sincere sorrow for such sin and a firm and sincere resolution to avoid future guilt and to atone to God, so far from obtaining thereby any remission of his sin, incurs the additional guilt of violating a sacrament;

[1] The citation up to this point follows the oath framed by the Irish Parliament in 1773, the remainder what was added in 1793.

and by the same solemn obligation they are bound and firmly pledged to defend to the utmost of their power the establishment and arrangement of property in their country as established by the laws now in being;[1] that they have disclaimed, disowned and solemnly abjured any intention to subvert the present Church-establishment for the purpose of substituting a Catholic establishment in its stead; and that they have also solemnly sworn, that they will not exercise any privilege, to which they are or may become entitled, to disturb or weaken the Protestant religion or Protestant government in Ireland"[2]

[4]

Your petitioners most humbly beg leave to shew, that, however painful to their feelings it is, that it should still be thought necessary to exact such tests from them, and from them alone of all his Majesty's subjects, they can with perfect truth affirm, that the political and moral principles, which are thereby asserted, are not only conformable to their opinions and habits, but are expressly inculcated by the religion which they profess; **And** your petitioners most humbly trust, that the religious doctrines, which permit such tests to be taken, will be pronounced by Your Lordships to be entitled to a Toleration, not merely partial but complete, under the happy constitution and government of this realm, and that his Majesty's Roman Catholic subjects holding those principles will be considered as subjects, upon whose fidelity the State may repose the firmest reliance

[5]

Your Petitioners further most humbly shew, that twenty-six years have now elapsed, since their most gracious Sovereign and the Honorable Houses of Parliament in Ireland, by their public and deliberate act, declared,[3] "that from the uniform peaceable behaviour of the Roman Catholics of Ireland for a long series of years it appeared reasonable and expedient to relax the disabilities and incapacitates under which they laboured, and that it must lead not only to the cultivation and improvement of this Kingdom, but to the prosperity and strength of all his Majesty's dominions, that his Majesty's subjects, of all denominations, should enjoy the blessings of a free constitution, and should be bound to each other by mutual interest and mutual affection", remains to be carried into effect (altho' your

[1] This clause was introduced purposely "to consign to eternal repose" apprehensions circulated in 1793 regarding Catholic claims to the confiscated estates.

[2] A footnote adds that by this clause the Catholics were "sworn to a maintenance of the Protestant religion and Government in Ireland."

[3] The citation follows the preamble of the Irish Act of 1778.

petitioners are impressed with a belief, that the apprehensions which retarded its beneficial operation previous to the Union, cannot exist in the parliament of the United Kingdom).

[6]

For your petitioners most humbly shew that, by virtue of divers statutes[1] now in force, his Majesty's Roman Catholic subjects, who form so great a proportion of the population of Ireland and contribute so largely to the resources of the State, do yet labour under many of the incapacities restraints and privations, which affect them with peculiar severity in almost every station of life; that, more especially, they are denied the capacity of sitting or voting in either of the Honorable Houses of parliament, the manifold evils consequent upon which incapacity they trust it is unnecessary to unfold or enumerate to your Lordships.[2]

[7]

They are disabled from holding or exercising (unless by a special dispensation) any corporate office whatsoever in the cities and towns in which they reside; they are incapacitated and disqualified from holding the office of Sheriffs and Sub-Sheriffs and various offices of trust, honour, and emolument, in the State, in his Majesty's military and naval Services, and in the administration of the laws, in this their native Land.

[8]

Your petitioners, declining to enter into the principal detail of the many incapacities and inconveniences, avowedly inflicted by those Statutes upon his Majesty's Roman Catholic Subjects, beg leave however most earnestly to solicit the attention of your Lordships to the humiliating and ignominious system of exclusion reproach and suspicion, which those Statutes generate and keep alive

[9]

For your petitioners most humbly shew, that, in consequence of the hostile spirit thereby sanctioned, their hopes of enjoying even the privileges, which, thro' the

[1] The principal disabilities inflicted by these were collected together and re-enacted in 1793 by the Irish Statute Geo.3, 21 Sect.9 et seq.

[2] A footnote adds that exclusion from Parliament confirmed exclusion in practice from offices and employments for which Catholics were capacitated by the statute of 1793.

benignity of their most Gracious Sovereign, they have been capacitated to enjoy, are nearly altogether frustrated, inasmuch that they are in effect shut out from almost all the honours, dignities and offices of trust and emolument in the State, from rank and distinction in his Majesty's army and navy, and even from the lowest situations and franchises in the several cities and corporate towns throughout his Majesty's dominions

[10]

And your petitioners severely feel, that this unqualified interdiction of those of their communion from all municipal stations, from the franchises of all the guilds and corporations, and from the patronage and benefits annexed to those situations, is not an evil terminating in itself; for they beg leave to state that by giving an advantage over those of their communion to others, by whom such situations are exclusively possessed, it establishes a species of qualified monopoly, universally operating in their disfavor, contrary to the spirit, and highly detrimental to the freedom, of trade

[11]

Your petitioners likewise severely feel, that his Majesty's Roman Catholic subjects, in consequence of this exclusion from the offices of Sheriffs and Sub-Sheriffs and of the hostile spirit of those statutes, do not fully enjoy certain other privileges of the British constitution, which the law has most jealously maintained and secured to their fellow subjects[1]

[12]

Your petitioners most humbly beg leave to solicit the attention of your Lordships to the distinction, which has conceded the elective, and denies the representative franchise to one and the same class of his Majesty's subjects; which detaches from property its proportion of political power, under a constitution, whose vital principle is the union of the one with the other; which closes every avenue of legalized ambition against those who must be presumed to have great credit and influence amongst the mass of the population of the country; which refuses to peers of the realm all share in the legislative representation, either actual or virtual, and renders the liberal profession of the law a mere object of pecuniary traffic, despoiled of its hopes and of its honors

[1] A footnote adds that no right was so dear as that of trial by jury, by a jury "composed of fair, impartial men, indifferently chosen."

[13]

Your petitioners further most humbly shew, that the exclusion of so numerous and efficient a fraction of his Majesty's subjects as the Roman Catholics of this realm from civil honors and offices, and from advancement in his Majesty's army and navy, actually impairs, in a very material degree, the most valuable resources of the British Empire, by impeding his Majesty's general service, stifling the most honorable and powerful incentive to military and civil merit, and unnecessarily restricting that bright prerogative of the Crown, which encourages good subjects to promote the public welfare, and excites them to meritorious actions by a well-regulated distribution of public honors and rewards

[14]

Your petitioners beg leave most humbly to submit, that those manifold incapacities restraints and privations are absolutely repugnant to the liberal and comprehensive principle recognized by their Most Gracious Sovereign and the parliament of Ireland,[1] that they are impolitic restraints upon his Majesty's royal prerogative; that they are hurtful and vexatious to the feelings of a loyal and generous people; that the total abolition of them will be found not only compatible with, but highly conducive to, the present security of every establishment, religious or political, now existing in this realm.

[15]

For your petitioners most explicitly declare, that they do not seek or wish, in the remotest degree, to injure or encroach upon "the rights, privileges, possessions, or revenues, appertaining to the bishops and clergy of the protestant religion, as by law established, or to the churches committed to their charge or to any of them,"[2] the sole object of your petitioners being an equal participation, upon equal terms with their fellow subjects, of the full benefits of the British laws and constitution.

[16]

Your petitioners beg leave most humbly to observe, that, altho' they might well and justly insist upon the firm and unabated loyalty of his Majesty's Roman Catholic subjects to their most gracious Sovereign, their most profound respect to the legislature, and their dutiful submission to the laws, yet they most respectfully

[1] In the preamble of the Irish Statute of 1778.

[2] This passage is taken from the King's coronation oath.

rest their humble claims and expectations of relief upon the clear and manifest conduciveness of the measure which they solicit, to the general and permanent tranquillity, strength and happiness of the British Empire; and your petitioners, entertaining no doubt of its final accomplishment from its evident justice and utility, do most solemnly assure your Lordships, that their most earnest solicitude for it, at this particular crisis, arises principally from their anxious desire to extinguish all motives of disunion and all means of exciting discontent

[17]

For your petitioners most humbly state it as their decided opinion, that the enemies of the British Empire, who meditate the subjugation of Ireland, have no hope of success save in the disunion of its inhabitants, and therefore it is, that your petitioners are deeply anxious, at this moment, that a measure should be accomplished, which will conciliate the principle of religious animosity, and animate all descriptions of his Majesty's subjects in an enthusiastic defence of the best constitution, that has ever yet been established.

Your petitioners therefore most humbly presume to express their earnest, but respectful, hope that your Lordships will in your wisdom and liberality deem the several statutes now in force against them no longer necessary to be retained, and that his Majesty's loyal and dutiful subjects professing the Roman Catholic religion, may be effectually relieved from the operation of those statutes, and that so they may be restored to the full enjoyment of the benefits of the British constitution, and to every inducement of attachment to that constitution, equally and in common with their fellow subjects throughout the British Empire.

And your petitioners will ever pray

[signed] Shrewsbury, Waterford and Wexford; Fingall; Kenmare; Gormanston; Southwell; Trimlestown; Thomas Barnewall; Edwd. Bellew[1]

Source: House of Lords Record Office, Main Papers, 25 March 1805

[1] The names and addresses of seventy-five signatories follow on separate sheets. See Appendix E where they are rearranged in alphabetical order along with additional names from the petition to the House of Commons.

APPENDIX E

SIGNATORIES TO THE TWO PETITIONS

(rearranged in alphabetical order)

Aylmer, Gerald	Derry, Co. Tipperary
Bagot, Gerard Wm.	Castle Bagot, Co. Dublin
Barnewall, Thomas	
Barron, James	Georgestown Co.Waterford
Barron, Pierce	Faghagh, Co. Waterford
Barron, William	Carrick Barron, Co. Waterford
Bellew, Christopher D.	Mount Bellew, Co.Galway
Bellew, Edward, Bart.	
Bellew, William, barrister	Gardiner's Street, Dublin
Bolger, Richard	Balliane, Co. Wexford
Brennan, John	Kilkenny
Burke, Edwd.	City Waterford
Burke, John	City Waterford
Butler, Pierce O'Brien	Bansagh, Co. Tipperary
Byrne, Charles	Ballyspellan, Co. Kerry
Byrne, James	of the City of Kilkenny
Byrne, John	Merrion Square, Dublin
Caddell, Rob.	Harbourstown, Co. Meath
Coleman, Fran.	Dame Street
Corbally, Elias	Cookstown, Co. Meath
Cronin, Daniel	Park, Co. Kerry
Cruise, Francis	Belgarth, Co. Dublin
Dillon, Thomas	Dublin
Donelan, Anth[ony]	Ballyartagh, Co. Galway
Donelan, Malachy	Ballydonelan, Co. Galway
Dowdall, Walter	Carn Isle, Co. Meath
Duffy, Jno.	North Frederick Street, Dublin
Egan, Thomas M.D.	Sackville Street, Dublin

Fingall, [Earl of]	
Fitzgerald, Thos.	Snowhaven, Kilkenny
Fitzgerald, Thos.	Geraldine, Co. Kildare
Fleming, Nicholas	Mountjoy Square, Dublin
French, Thomas, Bart.	
French, Robert	Rahasane, Co. Galway
Galway, Thomas	Killarney, Co. Kerry
Gannon, Nicholas	Ballyboy, Co. Meath
Goold, Francis Bart	
Goold, George	Old Court, Co. Cork
Gormanstown. [Viscount]	
Grainger, J.M.	Cawestown, Co. Meath
Hartney, John	Somerville, Co. Limerick
Hinchy, David	Rockvale, Co. Dublin
Keating, R.S.	Ballyneety Castle, Co. Limerick
Keatinge, R.S.	County of Tipperary[1]
Kenmare, [Earl of]	
Lalor, John	Cranagh, Co. Tipperary
Lynch, M.F., barrister	Mountjoy Square, Dublin
MacDonnell, Eneas	Westport, Co. Mayo
MacDonnell, R[andal]	Allens Court, Dublin
MacDonnell, Randle P.	Westport, Co. Mayo
Moore, Ambrose	York Str. Dublin
Moore, Edward	Temple Street, Dublin
Nangle, James	Kildalky, Co. Meath
Nowlan J[unio]r, James	Dublin
O'Brien, D. Thomas	Rutland Square, Dublin
O'Connell, Daniel barrister	Dublin
O'Connell, Maurice	Derrynane, Co. Kerry
O'Connor, Hugh	Dominick St.,Dublin
O'Connor, Thomas	Dublin
O'Connor, Val	Dominick Street
O'Connor, Valentine Junior	Rutland Square, Dublin
O'Donel, Antony M.D.	Sackville Street
O'Donoghue of the Glins	Kerry
O'Brien, D. Thomas	Rutland Square, Dublin
O'Ferrall, Ambrose	Ballyna, Co. Kildare

[1] This is the entry in the House of Lords MS, the preceding one being from the petition to the Commons.

O'Mahony, Daniel	Dunloe, Co. Kerry
O'Reilly, Dom. Wm.	Kildangan Castle, Kildare
O'Reilly, John	Lower Mount St., Dublin
Plunkett, Robert	
Purcell, John M.D.	Sackville St. Dublin
Redington, Thomas	Kilcornan, Co. Galway
Rice, Domk. barrister	Dawson Street
Roche, Charles	Limerick
Roche, John	William Street, Dublin
Ryan, Jeremiah	City Waterford
Rorke, Jno.	Ushers Quay, Dublin
Ryan, Chas.	Church Street, Dublin
Ryan, Edw	Corkerenstown, Co. Kildare
Ryan, James	Marlborough Street, Dublin
Ryan, James	Newtown, Co. Kildare
Ryan, Thomas	Ballinakill, Co. Kildare
Sause, Richard	Annsborough, Co. Kilkenny
Scully. Denys, barrister	Dublin
Scully, James,	Kilfeacle, Co. Tipperary
Shrewsbury, Waterford and Wexford, [Earl of]	
Southwell, [Viscount],	
Strange, Richard	Eccles Street, Dublin
Taaffe, John	Smarmor Castle, [Co.Louth]
Taylor, Bartholomew	Castlepollard, Westmeath
Taylor, Chris.	Swords, Co. Dublin
Taylor, Jos.	Nonsuch, Westmeath
Trant, H.	Co. Dublin
Trimlestown, [Baron]	
Ward, James P.	Stafford Street, Dublin
Ward, Lewis	Ballinderry, Co. Galway
Warren, Thomas	Cottage, Co. Kildare
Whyte, John	Loughbrickland, Co. Down

Sources: House of Lords Record Office, Main Papers; *The humble petition of the Roman Catholics of Ireland*, Keating, 1805.

APPENDIX F

VOTING OF THE IRISH MEMBERS ON FOX'S MOTION
at 4.30 a.m. 15 May 1805

46 Against the motion

Acheson, Hon. A., Armagh Co.
Archdall, M., Fermanagh Co.
Archdall, Richard, Dundalk
Boyle, Viscount, Cork Co.
Burroughs, Sir. W., Enniskillen
Bagwell, J., Tipperary Co.
Bernard, Thomas, King's Co.
Chinnery, Sir B., Bandon
Castlereagh, Visct., Down Co.
Canning, Rt. Hon. G., Tralee
Clements [H.J.], Leitrim Co.
Duigenan, P., Armagh City
Falkiner, John F., Dublin Co.
Foster, Rt.Hon. J., Louth Co.
Fortescue, W.C., Louth Co.
Fetherstone, Sir T., Longford County
Hardman, Edw., Drogheda
Hill, Sir G., Londonderry City
Hamilton, Sir C., Dungannon
Hamilton, Hans, Dublin Co
Jones, T. Tyrwhitt, Athlone
Jones, Walter, Coleraine.
Jephson, Denham, Mallow
Keane, Sir John, Youghal.
Knox, Hon. G., Trinity College, Dublin
King, Hon. Edward, Roscommon County
Longfield, M., Cork City
Leslie, C.P., Monaghan Co.
May, Edward, Belfast
Macnaghten, E.A., Antrim
Neville, R., Wexford town
Ormsby, Charles, Carlow tn
Pole, Hon. W. Wellesley, Queen's County
Ram, Abel, Wexford Co.
Rochfort, G., Westmeath
Sneyd, Nath. Cavan County
Savage, Francis, Down Co.
Sudley, Visc., Donegal Co
Shaw, R., Dublin City
Stewart, Hon. C.W., Londonderry County
Stewart, Rt Hon. Sir John, Tyrone County
Stewart, James, Tyrone Co
Tottenham, C., New Ross
Vereker, C., Limerick City

and probably

Beresford, Lord George, Londonderry County
Beresford, Rt. Hon John, Waterford County

29 For the motion

Bagnell, W., Carlow County
Burton, Hon. F., Clare Co.
Butler, Hon. J., Kilkenny Co.
Butler, Hon, C., Kilkenny City
Bligh, T., Meath County
Caulfield, Hon. H., Armagh Co.
Crosbie, J., Kerry County
Corry, Right Hon. I., Newry
Dillon, Hon. [H] A., Mayo Co.
Fitzgerald, Rt.Hon. J., Ennis
Fitzgerald, Right Hon. M., Kerry County
French, A., Roscommon Co.
Greene, Wm., Dungarvan.
Hume, W.H., Wicklow County
Hutchinson, Hon. C. H., Cork City
Hawthorne, C.S., Downpatrick
Latouche, D., Carlow County
Latouche, R. Kildare Co.
Latouche, P., Leitrim Co.
Latouche, J., Dublin City
Lee, E., Waterford Co.
Matthew, Rt. Hon Viscount, Tipperary County
Martin, R., Galway County
Newport, Sir J., Waterford City
Odell, W., Limerick County
O'Brien, Sir E., Clare Co.
Ponsonby, Right Hon. W.B., Kilkenny County.
Ponsonby, G., Wicklow Co.
Somerville, Sir M., Meath Co

25 Not recorded as voting

Bagwell, W., Clonmel
Beresford, J.C., Dublin City
Browne, Hon. D., Mayo Co.
Chichester, Lord S.S., Carrickfergus
Cole, Col. Hon G.L., Fermanagh County
Cooper, J.E., Sligo County
Coote, Sir E., Queen's Co.
Daly, D. B., Galway City
Dawson, R., Monaghan Co.
Dunlo, Visct, Galway Co.
Fitzgerald, Lord R.S., Kildare County
Fitzgerald, R.U., Cork Co.
Handcock, W., Athlone
Loftus, Viscount, Wexford County
O'Hara, C., Sligo County
Oliver, C.S., Limerick Co.
O'Neill, Capt. J.B.R., Antrim County
Parsons, Sir L., King's Co.
Rowley, S.C., Kinsale
Saunderson, F., Cavan Co.
Smyth, W., Westmeath County
Tyrwhitt, Thomas Portarlington
Wickham, W., Cashel
Wynne, Owen, Sligo City
Yarmouth, Earl of, Lisburn

Source: Freeman's Journal 25 May 1805.

APPENDIX G

ROBERT MARSHALL'S NOTES ON THE IRISH CATHOLICS (COMPOSED IN 1806 AND UPDATED IN 1807)

Private and confidential.

The nobility, country gentlemen, barristers, merchants, traders and respectable farmers influence the clergy, and the clergy the lower classes of the people.

The influence of the nobility is much less than that of the country gentlemen, and the influence of the country gentlemen much less than that of the merchants & traders etc.

The barristers in general are of consequence at public meetings.

The individuals of the body of most importance are as follows:

Nobility

* The property of each individual is here inserted merely to show the quantum of influence which he derives from it, and may not in some instances be very accurate.

Earl of Fingall

Has a large property much encumbered & can scarcely spend 4 or £5000 per annum.

A zealous & faithful subject of the Crown and very liberal as to religious opinions—amicable in private life—has lost much of his influence in consequence of his having employed it in providing for his relations and friends, and little importance should be attached to it—insignificant at public meetings—at those of last year a general disposition to show him disrespect—ambitious of being employed by Government in the channel of communication with the Catholic body—may be so employed with less jealousy on the part of others, on account of his being first in rank—apt to be much irritated when communications are made by Government to other Catholics. Great caution therefore necessary.

18 April 1807 Lord F. was at the head of the Catholic deputation who communicated with Mr. Pitt. His Lordship's influence has been greatly increased of late in consequence of his having supported the petition, though in reality he could not help it & it was against his inclination.

Viscount Gormanstown about £7000 p.a. Premier Viscount—attainted in 1697, attainder reversed 1800.

Viscount Netterville, Viscount Southwell 2 or 3000 p.a.

Viscount [*sic*] Kenmare, great property

Baron Trimleston

Taafe

French, one of the 5 deputys.

all good subjects & ready to cooperate with Govt. in deferring the petition[1] provided they would not stand alone in so doing.

With regard to Lord French in particular, he is rich, unsteady, not much respected. Catholics have little confidence in the integrity of his public character—owes his consequence to the mere violence of his opposition to Lord Fingall—has some following & should be particularly attended to.

Country Gentlemen

Sir Edward Bellew Bt. about 2000 p.a.

Inclined rather to the popular party—strong Catholic feelings & impatient for Emancipation—of a good private character, and considered as a very respectable country gentleman. Shd. be much noticed. One of the 5 deputys.

Sir Thomas Burke, Bart, about £7000 p.a.

Mr. Power of Waterford, about 15,000 p.a.

Mr. John Burke (son of the late Edwd. Burke) from 12 to 15,000 p.a.

Mr. Corbally at 12,000 p.a.

	£
Col. O'Brien Co. Kilkenny	10,000
Mr. O'Shea	7000
Mr. Nich. Maher	6000
Mr. Donellan Co. Galway	4000
Mr. Cruise of Belgarth nr Dublin	4000
Mr. Taylor of Swords	4000
Mr. Wyse of Waterford	4000
Mr. Mansfield of Naas	4000
Mr. Cadell near Drogheda	4000

[1] On 18 February 1806 Fox had advised the Irish Catholics to defer their petition and a meeting of 4 March 1806 resolved to drop it (Plowden, *History*. II, p.305).

Mr. Strange—father in law of Sir E. Bellew, rich, very respectable—should be noticed particularly when opportunity offers.

Nangle 2000

Bagot, of Castle Bagot near Lucan, a young man obliged to leave the country having lost much by gaming. 2000

18 April 1807 he is returned to Ireland.

<u>Barristers</u>

Mr. McKenna
Mr. Wm. Bellew
Mr. Martin Lynch

Pensioned, all their influence therefore gone—scarcely allowed to speak at public meetings—ought not to be seen much at the Castle—Little reliance upon their representation of Catholic feelings, but Mr. McKenna should not be entirely neglected as he writes very well and may do much mischief by anonymous publications—may go to Mr. Marsden as usual, but as little as possible to the Secretary and Lord Lieutenant.

Mr. Scully

Eldest son of an eminent grazier in Tipperary who has very much influence in all the southern counties—strongly Catholic feelings, anxious for Emancipation—attentive to his religious duties and therefore much respected by Bishops and clergy—of great weight at public meetings, where he has generally carried all his points—by far more intelligent than any other Catholic upon the Penal Laws & their consequences—has been very kind in sending me a detailed account of everything that has passed at the meetings; & tho' I have often received accounts from other quarters I have always had reason to rely upon Mr. Scully's as the most correct—wants neither honors nor emoluments—ambitious of being communicated with by Government—a valuable man & should be much cultivated, but with great caution as to Lord Fingall and the leading Catholics.

D. Rice

A warm and zealous Catholic—might be led by management.

O'Connell

An intimate of the Currans, talents, property, impatient for Emancipation—ambitions very warm—uncle rich—probably a J[acobi]n—fled about time of the rebellion.

Farrell

also very impatient—young—studious—diligent—promising son of a respectable Dublin farmer.

George Moore

of the Cty of Mayo has written well, supported the Union, attached to His Royal Highness the Prince of Wales.

Laffan

McKenna's brother in law, without much ability or much talent.

Keogh [Michael,

A Catholic merely in name, good property—no influence or exertion.

Fitzsimmons [?Fitzsimon] ditto ditto ditto.

O'Gorman

probably a J[acobi]n

<u>Physicians</u>

The physicians were mostly J[acobi]ns till cured by the late events in France. If any opportunity should occur some personal attention might be bestowed on Dr. Purcell who for many months has had the first practice in Dublin; and upon Dr. Dromgoole who sometimes attends public meetings. *18 April 1807* Dr. Purcell is since dead.

<u>Merchants</u>

This class very impatient for Emancipation—increasing daily in influence & number. possess much influence on the clergy to whom they are very hospitable.

Mr. McDonnell

worth above £100,000. Very respectable, attends all meetings & has great weight—shd be much attended to.

James Ryan

Served his time to McDonnell. Son of a Roman Catholic gentleman in Kildare—very impatient—of unsound political principles—till lately thriving in trade—a very embarrassed speaker—Talents not much above mediocrity—owes the little importance he possesses to his connexion with McDonnell & to his having been the first to call a meeting to petition—one of the 5 deputys.

Mr James Scully,

An eminent grazier in Tipperary—very loyal—of an excellent private character—old and feeble—shd be treated with great respect if an opportunity should offer, as he can influence most of the southern counties.

Mr. [John] Keogh merchant

abt. 2000 p.a.

Is much listened to at public meetings—feeble and unable to attend them much—impatient—was formerly a J[acobi]n—should be much noticed—lives near Dublin—ambitious of being the head of the popular party

Mr Roche

ditto worth about 100,000, very respectable

Mr. James Connolly do. do.do.

his son	abt 20,000
D.T. O'Beirne [? O'Brien]	abt 50,000
Richd. Mahon	abt 30,000
John McLoughlin	abt 30,000
Thos. Dillon	abt 20,000

Bishops & clergy

The Catholic Primate Dr. O'Reilly resides at Drogheda. He is a man of mean birth & of less consideration. Dr. Troy, the Catholic Archbishop of Dublin, has great influence over the Bishops & clergy of Ireland & therefore well deserves much attention; but he is not much respected by the country gentlemen and the merchants, who know that the providing handsomely for his nephew is a very great object with him at the Castle.

Dr. Moylan, the Catholic Archbishop of Cork, is a highly respectable character. Such of the Bishops as are trustees of the Catholic College, at Maynooth, come up to town every year in the month of [blank] If some notice were to be taken of them on these occasions it would have a good effect.

R. M.

Source: Richmond Papers, NLI, MS 60 f.264

APPENDIX H

IRISH PRELATES' RESOLUTIONS OF 1799

At a meeting of the Roman Catholic Prelates held at Dublin on the 17th, 18th and 19th of January, 1799, to deliberate on a proposal from Government of an independent provision for the Roman Catholic clergy, under certain regulations not incompatible with their doctrines, discipline, or just influence, it was admitted:—

That a provision through Government for the Roman Catholic clergy of this kingdom, competent and secured, ought to be thankfully accepted.

That in the appointment of Prelates of the Roman Catholic religion to vacant sees within this kingdom, such interference of Government as may enable it to be satisfied of the loyalty of the person appointed is just, and ought to be agreed to.

That to give this principle its full operation without infringing the discipline of the Roman Catholic Church, or diminishing the religious influence which prelates of that Church ought justly to possess over their respective flocks, the following regulations seem necessary:—

1st. In the vacancy of a see, the clergy of the Diocese to recommend, as usual, a candidate to the prelates of the ecclesiastical province who elect him, or any other they may think more worthy, by a majority of suffrages: in the case of equality of suffrages, the presiding Metropolitan or senior Prelate to have a casting vote.

2nd. In the election of a Metropolitan, if the provincial prelates do not agree, within two months after the vacancy, the senior prelate shall forthwith invite the surviving metropolitans to the election, in which each will then have a vote: in the equality of suffrages the presiding Metropolitan to have a casting vote.

3rd. In these elections the majority of suffrages must be *ultra-mediatatem*, as the canons require, or consist of more than half the electors.

4th. The candidates so selected to be presented by the President of the election to Government; which within one month after such presentation will transmit the name of the said candidate, if no objection is made against him, for appointment to the Holy See, or return the said name to the President of the election for such transmission as may be agreed upon.

5th. If Government have any proper objection against such candidates, the President of the election will be informed thereof within one month after the presentation, who in that case will convene the electors to the election of another candidate.

Agreeably to the discipline of the Roman Catholic Church these regulations can have no effect without the sanction of the Holy See; which sanction the Roman Catholic prelates of this kingdom shall, as soon as may be, use their endeavour to procure.

The prelates are satisfied that the nomination of the parish priests, with a certificate of their having taken the Oath of Allegiance, be certified to Government.

[signed] Richard O'Reilly, J. T. Troy, Edward Dillon, Thomas Bray, P. J. Plunkett, F. Moylan, Daniel Delaney, Edmund French, James Caulfield, John Cruise

Source: Hansard XXX, 487.

APPENDIX I

CHRONOLOGICAL TABLE

1559

The Act of Supremacy declares Queen Elizabeth to be the only supreme governor of the realm in spiritual and ecclesiastical as well as temporal matters and prescribes an oath to be sworn by anyone taking office.

1661

13 Ch.II St.2, Ch.1 (the Corporation Act) requires members of municipal administrations to take an oath abjuring rebellion and affirming receipt of the sacrament according to the rites of the established church.

1667

17 & 18 Ch.II Ch.2, 82, an Irish act confirming the Corporation Act, excludes Catholics from municipal offices by requiring them to take the Oath of Supremacy.

1672

25 Ch.II Ch.2 (the Test Act) requires all holders of office under the crown to receive the eucharist according to the usage of the Church of England, to take the oaths of Supremacy and of Allegiance, and to make a declaration against Transubstantiation.

1692

3 Will. and Mary Ch.2, an English act for abrogating the Oath of Supremacy in Ireland and appointing other oaths, excludes Irish peers and commoners from parliament unless they take the oaths prescribed by the Test Act, and declare against invocation of the virgin and saints etc.

1697

9 Will. III Ch 1, an Irish act, banishes the Catholic clergy.

1703

2 Anne Ch.6, an Irish Act to prevent the further growth of Popery. Sons turned Protestant are given rights over their father's property; tenure is restricted to leases of 31 years; holders of any office, civil or military, must make the oath and declaration prescribed by *3 William & Mary*; oaths of allegiance and abjuration are to be taken by voters at elections.

1707

6 Anne Ch.6, an Irish act to strengthen *10 Will.III* against papists practising as solicitors.

1709

8 Anne Ch.3, an Irish act, amending the 1703 act, prescribes that when a child of Catholic parents conforms to the established church the Court of Chancery may oblige the father to declare his income and make an order for the child's support; a papist teaching school is to be prosecuted as a convict; rewards are offered for 'discovering' clergy and teachers; and papists who refuse to reveal where masses are celebrated and the names of those present may be sent to gaol for up to a year.

1715

Jacobite rising in Scotland. Ireland quiet

1719

6 Geo.I Ch.9, an Irish act, discharging holders of office from the penalties incurred if they have failed to qualify under *2 Anne Ch.6*, relieves Dissenters (but not in practice Catholics, no Catholics being in such employment).

1727

1 Geo.II Ch.9, Sect.7, an Irish act which completes the disenfranchisement of the Catholics by laying down that no papist shall vote at elections without taking the Oath of Supremacy.
1 Geo.II Ch.20, an Irish act, prescribes that barristers are to take the Oath of Supremacy.

1745

Jacobite rebellion in Scotland. Ireland again quiet.

1756

March Formation of a Catholic Association by Charles O'Conor, Thomas Wyse and John Curry.

1757

A 'Declaration of Catholic Principles' drawn up by leading Irish Catholics as a reply to 'the misrepresentations and calumnies which they labour under'.

1774

June 1 Entry into force of *13 & 14 Geo.II Ch.35*, an Irish act enabling H.M. subjects of whatever persuasion to testify their allegiance by taking a prescribed oath and signing a declaration in which among other things they abjure allegiance to the Stuarts.[1]

22 The Quebec Act gives Canadian Catholics religious and civil rights.

1775

April 19 First battle in the American war.

[1] In his *Statement of the Penal Laws* Scully dates this statute 1773.

1777

October — Irish Catholic peers and more than three hundred of the gentry address the King complaining of their inability to purchase land or improve their farms, and of the informers who drag them into court.

1778

February 2 — Alliance between American colonists and France.

May 2 — Loyal address of English Catholic peers and commoners to the King followed by the formation of a committee which holds discussions with the ministry and presses for concessions in regard to property rights. These are granted in *18 Geo.III Ch.46*, an act for "allowing further time for inrollment of deeds and wills made by papists and for the relief of Protestant purchasers."
Representing the Scottish Catholics, Sir John Dalrymple and Lord Linton fail to get Scotland included but Sir Henry Dundas, the Lord Advocate for Scotland, undertakes to introduce a bill for the Scottish Catholics in the next session of parliament.

August 14 — *17 & 18 Geo.3 Ch.49*, an Irish act, referring in its preamble to the 'uniform peaceable behaviour' of the Catholics over a long period of years, enables them to take leases of up to 999 years and inherit in the same way as Protestants; and revokes the special privileges accorded to conforming children.
The Volunteer movement spreads from Scotland to Ireland.

1779

Owing to opposition from numerous Presbyterian synods the bill proposed for the Scottish Catholics is dropped.

July — Arms issued to the Volunteers in Ireland.

1780

March — *19 & 20 Geo.III Ch.6* relieves Irish Dissenters from the sacramental test.

June 2 — Gordon Riots in protest against the extension of the 1778 act to Scotland.

1782

		Establishment of an English Catholic Committee for a term of five years.
February	15	Convention of the Volunteers at Dungannon.
May	4	*21 & 22 Geo III Ch.24* (Gardiner's Irish act) allows Catholics to acquire land except in parliamentary boroughs and abolishes a number of obsolete laws, but reaffirms provisions against proselytism, the assumption of ecclesiastical titles, wearing vestments outside chapels etc.
		21 & 22 Geo.III Ch.48, Sect.3 enacts that all clauses in English statutes relating to oaths and declarations shall continue in force according to their existing tenor.
		21 & 22 Geo.III Ch.62 (Gardiner's second act) allows Catholics to keep school upon taking the Oath of Allegiance and obtaining a licence from an ordinary of the established church.
July	27	An amendment of Poyning's Law of 1494 concedes legislative independence to the Irish parliament.

1783

February	15	End of the American war.

1787

May	3	New English Catholic Committee with Charles Butler as Secretary.

1788

May	9	The English Catholic Committee is received by Pitt, who says that the government will not object to their claims being brought before parliament in the next session and advises them to obtain in the meantime the opinion of foreign universities on the Pope's dispensing powers.
December	7	The declaration of Catholic principles called the Protestation is approved by the English Catholic Committee and sent out for signature.

1789

July	14	Outbreak of the French Revolution.

1790

January	19	Irish Catholic Committee draws up a programme.
March	2	Fox's motion for repeal of the Test and Corporation acts defeated.
August	22	Tone's *An Argument on behalf of the Catholics of Ireland.*
November	9	First meeting of the Dublin Society of United Irishmen.

1791

February	11	The General Committee of the Irish Catholics prepare a petition to be restored "at least to some of the rights and privileges . . . granted to others who dissent from the established church". This is turned down by the Chief Secretary, Lord Hobart, and no Irish MP can be found to present it.
June	10	*31 Geo.III Ch.32* allows the English Catholics to practise their religion openly, frees them from the fear of informers and admits them to the bar.
November		John Keogh in London November-December engages Richard Burke, son of Edmund Burke, as Secretary to the Committee.
December	27	Lord Kenmare and over forty of the principal gentry of the Catholic body secede from the Catholic Committee.

1792

January	23	The Committee's petition, drafted by Richard Burke, is presented to the Irish parliament by Charles O'Hara, but is withdrawn on being found informal and giving offence.
February	4	The General Committee resolves to confine the application for relief to four objects: (1) admission to the profession and practice of the law; (2) the capacity to serve as county magistrates; (3) the right to serve on petty juries; (4) the right to vote for Protestant county members of parliament. There is also an Address to the Protestants, accompanied by the answers of the foreign universities asked for by Pitt in 1788.
	20	Presented by John Egan, an alternative petition, signed by fifty respectable Dublin merchants, asks only for the removal of some of the grievances, but is rejected by a huge majority.
March	17	Republication of the 1757 Declaration of Catholic Principles, which is adopted by the General Committee of the Irish Catholics. Article VIII of it renounces all claims of the Catholics to their ancestors' forfeited estates.

		This is followed by a circular announcing reunion with the seceders and calling upon all local Catholic committees to elect delegates to a convention to meet towards the end of the year.
April	2	Declaratory vote by the English House of Commons for the gradual abolition of the slave trade.
	12	Foundation of Cisalpine Club in London.
	18	*32 Geo.III Ch.21* (Langrishe's Irish Act) admits Catholics to the Irish bar subject to their taking the 1774 oath; permits mixed marriages; and allows Catholics to teach school without obtaining a licence from an ordinary of the established church.
July		Wolfe Tone is appointed agent of the Catholic Committee.
December		Catholic Convention sends five delegates with a petition to the King. Signatories include Dr Troy and Dr Moylan.

1793

January	2	The Catholic delegates (Edward Byrne, John Keogh, James Edward Devereux, Christopher Bellew and Sir Thomas French) present the petition to the King.
February	1	France declares war on England and Holland.
April	9	*33 Geo.III Ch.21* (Hobart's Irish Act) extends the parliamentary franchise to Catholics on the same terms as for Protestants; enables them to hold civil and military offices not specifically excepted; makes them eligible for the magistracy, jury service and membership of bodies corporate; and opens the University to them—all subject to their subscribing both to the Oath of Allegiance of 1774 and to a new oath and declaration, based on the 1792 Declaration of Catholic Principles. They continue to be excluded from all the high offices of state, judgeships, the positions of King's Counsel, Sheriff and General on the Staff, and the right to sit in parliament. (Irish Catholics in the army and navy, moreover, could not exercise their new rights outside Ireland as an act of George I still excluded Catholics from any military situation elsewhere).
		In the course of the debate on the bill C. K. Bushe argues that any full participation in power by the Catholics must be accompanied by an ecclesiastical establishment paid for by the Treasury.
June	3	Catholic relief act for Scotland confers peaceful possession and free distribution of property.
August	16	*33 Geo.III Ch.29* (the Convention Act) prohibits any assemblies of delegates purporting to represent the people under the pretence of preparing or presenting petitions.

1794

December	23	Dublin Catholics, followed by Catholics throughout Ireland, decide to petition for repeal of all the penal laws.

1795

January	4	Arrival of Lord Fitzwilliam as new Lord Lieutenant with instructions to favour the Catholics.
February	2	Grattan moves for leave to bring in a relief bill.
	6	Memorandum by the King declaring his opposition to the government's proposed Irish measures. John Fitzgibbon, the Irish Chancellor, draws his attention to his Coronation Oath.
	19	The Cabinet in London decides on Lord Fitzwilliam's recall.
March	25	Fitzwilliam leaves Ireland and is replaced by Lord Camden.
April		On hearing that the government intends to postpone a relief bill until a legislative union is accomplished, a meeting of Irish Catholics resolves that they would rather forgo their own emancipation than acquiesce in a surrender of the liberties of their country.
May	20	Wolfe Tone leaves for America.
	24	Grattan's relief bill is defeated on its second reading.
October		Opening of the Royal College of St Patrick at Maynooth

1796

February	1	Wolfe Tone lands in France.
March	24	An Insurrection Act is passed.
September	21	Foundation of the Orange Order.
October	26	Habeas Corpus is suspended.
December	25	On the appearance of a French fleet in Bantry Bay Francis Moylan, the Catholic Bishop of Cork, urges his flock to resist the invaders. The fleet is driven off by contrary winds.

1797

March	13	Disarming of Ulster begins.
October	11	Dutch fleet that was to invade Ireland is destroyed at Camperdown.

1798

March	12	Fifteen leading United Irishmen are arrested, including T. A. Emmet and Dr W. J. McNevin.
	30	Proclamation of martial law.
May	6	Lords Fingall, Gormanston, Southwell and Kenmare, Sir E. Bellew, and others publish a declaration protesting against any imputation of the Catholic body's abetting rebellion.
	19	Arrest of Lord Edward Fitzgerald.
	24	Outbreak of the rebellion. Notices in the press that an address to the Lord Lieutenant will lie open for signature at Fitzpatrick's and the houses of Lords Fingall and Kenmare, Malachy Donelan and William Bellew.
	27	Dr Troy orders an address to be read from all altars on Sundays exhorting rebels to give up their arms.
June	20	Arrival of Lord Cornwallis as Lord Lieutenant and Commander in Chief.
August	23	French expedition under Humbert lands in Killala Bay, Co. Mayo.
September	8	The French invaders surrender at the battle of Ballinamuck.
October	8	The Irish Chancellor, Lord Clare, sails for England to persuade Pitt of the advantages of a legislative Union, in which however Catholic emancipation is to have no part.
	12	Wolfe Tone is captured on board a ship of a French fleet in Lough Swilly.
November		A draft Treaty of Union is sent from London to Dublin Castle. Publication anonymously of Edward Cooke's pamphlet *Arguments for and against an Union.*
December	22	Catholic meeting held at Lord Fingall's adjourns *sine die* after judging it inexpedient at the moment to publish any resolution on what line the Catholics as a body should take on the Union.

1799

January	17	The four Catholic Archbishops and six senior Bishops accept Lord Castlereagh's proposal for giving the government a role in nominations to vacant sees and paying stipends to the clergy.
	23	The proposal for a Union is defeated by two votes in the Irish parliament.
	31	Pitt's speech in the House of Commons moving resolutions for a Union. In the present state of things, he says, full concessions cannot be made to the Catholics without endangering the state: how soon such concessions might be properly discussed depends

on the conduct of the Catholics and the temper of the times, but it is obvious that a question which might shake the government of Ireland in its separate state might be less dangerous in a united parliament.

April 15 A motion to provide a permanent endowment for the Maynooth seminary is defeated in the Irish House of Lords after a speech by Lord Clare.

17 Lord Hardwicke forbids membership of societies and lodges to his regiment stationed in Dublin.

August 3 At a meeting called by the Sheriff of Co. Tipperary James Scully signs a declaration supporting the Union.

1800

January 13 At the Corn Exchange in Dublin a Catholic meeting with Ambrose Moore in the chair, James Ryan as Secretary and Daniel O'Connell as the main speaker, resolves that "having hereto determined not to come forward in the distinct character of Catholics" they now think it right to make it clear that Catholics "cannot give any concurrence whatsoever to so foul and fatal a project" as the Union.

February 26 The Union carried by 158 to 115 in the Irish House of Commons.

March 7 Lord Fingall asks the Lord Lieutenant that the Catholic peers of Ireland shall be allowed to vote for representative peers: otherwise they will be deprived of a right which every freeholder enjoys.

April 17 James Scully of Kilfeacle one of the signatories to an address urging the sheriff of Co. Tipperary to refuse to convene an anti-Union meeting requested by Lord Lismore and others.

August 1 The Act of Union (*40 Geo.III Ch.38*) receives royal assent. Under Article V there is to be one protestant episcopal church called The United Church of Great Britain and Ireland; and "the continuance and preservation of the said united church, as the established church of England and Ireland, shall be deemed and taken to be an essential and fundamental part of the union."

1801

January 1 The Act of Union enters into force.

22 Opening of the first Union parliament. In the House of Commons the sixty-four county members and the two each for Dublin and Cork retain the seats they held in the Irish parliament, the borough members being chosen by lot. In the House of Lords there are

		twenty-eight Lords Temporal elected by their (non-Catholic) peers; and four Lords Spiritual (one of the four Archbishops and three of the twenty-eight Bishops, sitting in rotation for each session). Peers not elected as representative peers are eligible to sit in the House of Commons.
		Lord Fingall is urged by the Lord Lieutenant to dissuade Catholics from petitioning.
January	31	Pitt offers his resignation on the refusal of the King to countenance his cabinet's proposed Catholic measures (repeal of the test acts, admission to parliament etc, replacement of the old oaths by a new one which includes a renunciation of Jacobin principles, payment of the clergy and a right for the King to fill vacant sees by choosing one of three names submitted to him).
		Lord Grenville, Sir Henry Dundas, Lord Spencer, William Windham and Lord Castlereagh also resign.
February	13	Lord Cornwallis gives Lord Fingall and Dr Troy two papers for circulation among the principal Catholics: (1) a summary of Pitt's sentiments; and (2) "the sentiments of a sincere friend to the Catholic cause", namely himself. In this he urges the Catholics to be "sensible of the benefit they possess by having so many characters of eminence pledged not to embark in the service of government, except on the terms of the Catholic privileges being obtained . . . "
		The King's illness: Pitt promises not to agitate the Catholic question again.
March	17	Addington's administration takes office.
May	25	Lord Hardwicke sworn in as Lord Lieutenant. Charles Abbot Chief Secretary.

1802

February	13	Lord Redesdale Chancellor for Ireland; William Wickham Chief Secretary.
March	25	Peace of Amiens
July	13-26	General Election.
November	16	The new parliament meets.

1803

March	7	*43 Geo.III Ch.30* enables Roman Catholics subscribing to the Declaration and Oath of the English Relief Act of 1791 to take the benefits of the 1778 act *18 Geo.III Ch.46.*

March	15	The Irish militia is called out.
May	18	England declares war on France.
July		Meeting of English and Irish Catholics at Lord Kenmare's house in London endorses a petition to the King drafted by Francis Plowden, asking for equal religious rights in the armed forces. After being submitted to the Home Secretary, Lord Pelham, it is dropped when he returns it with alterations.
	23	Robert Emmet's rising in Dublin.
	26	Denys Scully transmits to the Lord Lieutenant his father's offer to raise a regiment of up to 500 men.
	28	Suspension of Habeas Corpus in Ireland.
August		Denys Scully publishes his pamphlet *An Irish Catholic's advice to his brethren,* urging the latter not to side with the French in the event of an invasion.
	15	Lord Redesdale's first letter to Lord Fingall, on appointing him a magistrate.
	18	Charles Yorke, Lord Hardwicke's half-brother, is appointed Home Secretary.
	24	A loyal address to the Lord Lieutenant is presented by Lord Fingall, Dr Troy and other prominent Catholics. Theobald McKenna and Denys Scully criticise it for appearing to forgo emancipation.
October	10	Dr Troy's Exhortation on the duty of patriotism, to be read at Mass on the two following Sundays.
November	23	Reopening of parliament. The motion on the address is moved in the House of Lords by the Marquis of Sligo.

1804

February	1	Sir Evan Nepean arrives in Dublin.
May	2	Pitt writes to the King confirming his promises of 1801 regarding emancipation.
	14	Pitt's new government is announced. The appointment of John Foster to the Irish Exchequer is seen by some as a sign of his determination to lay emphasis on the Protestant ascendancy.
July	31	Parliament prorogued.
September	30	The King informs George Rose of Pitt's having recently told him that he might be perfectly at ease on the subject of Catholic emancipation.
October	10	The leading Roman Catholics of Kilkenny express to Grattan their grateful recollection of his past services in the cause of their common country.

October 24 Preliminary Catholic meeting at James Ryan's house.
27 First general meeting at Ryan's house.
November 2 James Ryan and Randal MacDonnell call on Marsden.
3 Second general meeting at Ryan's house.
4 Nepean sends minutes of 1st General Meeting to the Home Office for transmission to Pitt.
13 Two private meetings are held in Lord Fingall's house this week to prepare resolutions to submit to the meeting of the 17th.
15 The Home Secretary authorises Lord Hardwicke to tell the Catholics that Pitt will resist the petition to the utmost of his power.
17 The Home Secretary's letter is received but Lord Fingall cannot be informed as he is ill.
Third general meeting at James Ryan's house. A Sub-committee of twenty-five is to prepare a petition and report on 14 December.
18 Nepean transmits minutes of this meeting to Pitt
20 The Lord Lieutenant sees Lord Fingall and communicates to him the contents of the Home Secretary's letter.
25 First meeting of Select Committee (with others) at Lord Fingall's house. Lord Fingall tells it of Pitt's sentiments as communicated in the Home Secretary's letter of 15 November.
December 2 The Second meeting of the Select Committee at Lord Fingall's debates the merits of a petition as opposed to a statement of facts and appoints a sub-committee of five to draw up in the form of a petition a statement of the still existing penal laws. A report of the meeting, signed by Marshall, is in the Home Office file 100/99.
3 MacDonnell, Lynch and Fingall inform Marsden that the general disposition of the meeting was against a petition.
8 Nepean tells King at the Home Office that he has sent direct to Pitt the report of the Sub-Committee which will be read to a meeting next day.
9 The report of the Sub-Committee of Five is read at a meeting in Lord Fingall's house.
15 A General meeting at Lord Fingall's approves the draft petition, appoints a superintending committee of thirty-one and adjourns to 2 February.

1805

January 14 Nepean, in London, is sent a copy of the petition.
15 Reopening of parliament.
17 Randal MacDonnell suggests to Marsden that the Catholics might,

instead of petitioning, transmit a statement of their case through the Lord Lieutenant. On 20 January the latter asks the Home Secretary for instructions.

January 26 The Home Secretary agrees to a transmission of representations.

27 MacDonnell's proposal is put before a meeting. While it receives less support than expected there is much difference of opinion and the meeting adjourns to the 30th.

30 No decision is reached. Another meeting is to be held on 1 February preparatory to the General Meeting.

February 2 The General Meeting adopts the petition and adjourns for a fortnight, when the time of presenting it will be decided.

3 Lord Hardwicke breaks off relations with Sir Evan Nepean.

16 The General Meeting nominates deputies to present the petition to parliament and lays down their terms of reference.

March 5 First meeting of the deputies in London.

12 The deputies are received by Pitt, who refuses to present the petition and says he will oppose it if presented by any other member.

13 The deputies decide to entrust the petition to the the opposition.

17 By a majority vote the deputies agree to authorise the opposition to introduce the petition in whatever manner they deem most eligible.

18 At 10 a.m. Scully sees Huskisson to discuss the possibility of a compromise with Pitt. At noon the opposition leaders formally undertake to present and support the petition in parliament.

19 Lord Grenville and Fox give notice in their respective Houses.

21 In Dublin the Committee considers reports from James Ryan, Lord Kenmare and Scully, and will meet again at frequent intervals.

25 The petition is presented in both Houses

27 Last meeting of the deputies. Scully leaves for Ireland.

April 1 Lord Grenville names 10 May for his motion on the petition.

8 The Assizes in Ireland. Scully sets off on the Leinster circuit.

20 A General Meeting in Dublin endorses the action of the deputies and authorises them, with the addition of Randal MacDonnell, to assist in the management of the petition in both Houses.

May 10 Debate on the petition in the House of Lords begins.

13 Resumed debate in the Lords continues until 6 next morning. Lord Grenville's motion is defeated by 178 to 49 votes.

The debate on Fox's motion opens in the House of Commons

14 The resumed debate in the Commons ends at 5 the next morning. Fox's motion is defeated by 336 to 124 votes.

APPENDIX J

BIOGRAPHICAL NOTES

In the following notes careers are summarised only up to the change of government in 1806. In contrast with the Index, peers are entered under their titles and wives under their married names. Names appearing in the Dictionary of National Biography *are marked with an asterisk.*

ADDINGTON,* Henry (1757-1844) While Speaker of the House of Commons he was one of those who in January 1801 influenced the King's mind against Pitt's Catholic policy, but he favoured payment of salaries to the Catholic clergy as 'a measure of influence rather than indulgence.' Prime Minister from 14 March 1801 to 10 May 1804. Created Viscount Sidmouth in January 1805, when he joined Pitt's second ministry and supported it with some forty followers until he resigned in July.

ADDIS, Charles A Catholic attorney of Gray's Inn who had done some work for Lords Kenmare and Trimleston and was later employed by Scully.

ARUNDEL, Lord Henry Arundell (1740-1808), 8th Baron, of Wardour.

AYLMER, Gerald Son and heir of Michael Aylmer of Lyons, Co. Kildare, by his 3rd wife; brother of Lady Kenmare and Mrs Keatinge.

BAGOT, Gerard William Son of John Bagot of Castle Bagot, Lucan, who was one of the seceders of 1791-2.

BAGWELL, Mr/Lt-Colonel John (1752-1816) MP for Tipperary County 1792-1806 and Colonel of the Tipperary militia 1793-1805. After changing sides twice he had supported the Union.

BAILLIE,* Dr Matthew (1761-1823) A well known pathologist, Physician Extraordinary to the King.

BARNEWALL, Thomas (1773-1839) Son of the 14th Baron Trimleston, whom he succeeded in 1813.

BELLASYSE, Revd Dr Charles DD (*d.* 1815) A London priest, son of a merchant of Leghorn. A founder member of the Cisalpine Club. Succeeded his brother in 1810 as 6th Viscount Fauconberg.

BELLEW, Sir Edward (1760?-1827) 6th Baronet, of Barmeath Castle Co. Louth. His wife was daughter and heiress of Richard Strange. He had three uncles in the Austrian service and an aunt married to Malachy Donelan, Lord Fingall's brother-in-law.

BELLEW, Robert Probably the son of Patrick Bellew, Ballindinas, Co. Cork who was admitted to the Middle Temple in 1787 and called to the Irish bar in 1791.

BELLEW, William (*d.* 1835) A younger brother of Sir Edward. Admitted to Lincoln's Inn 1782 and called to the Irish bar after the relief act of 1792. For dissuading the Catholics from declaring against the Union he was promised a county court judgeship in Co. Louth, but the local gentry prevented the appointment and he was awarded a pension in lieu. In the pension list published in June 1801 this stood at £300.

BENNETT, Henry Grey (1777-1836) Second son of the Earl of Tankerville.

BERESFORD,* John (1738-1805) The 'King of Ireland', dismissed from office by Lord Fitzwilliam in 1795 but reinstated after the latter's recall; retired in 1802.

BERINGTON,* Joseph (1746-1827) A priest at this time stationed at Buckland, Sir John Throckmorton's seat in Berkshire. He had played a prominent part in the religious controversies of the previous century and was twice suspended, but he made a full retractation in 1801.

BOSTOCK, Mrs Mary Huddleston (*c.* 1738-1817), widow of Henry Bostock (*d.* 1803) and aunt of Denys Scully's wife. Thayer Street, where she lived, lay just north of the junction between New Bond Street and Oxford Street.

BROWNE, Denis (1763-1828) A younger brother of the Marquis of Sligo; MP for Mayo. He failed to vote on the petition, a footnote to the list published in the press explaining that he had been obliged by indisposition to leave the House of Commons before the division.

BROWNE, Mostyn Second son of Sir Edward Mostyn. He assumed the name of Browne under the terms of the will of Sir Charles Browne.

BROWNE, Wogan (*d.* 1812) His Christian name was Thomas but he was generally known as Wogan Browne. His seat was Castle Browne, Naas, renamed in 1814 Clongowes Wood. He had been under suspicion during the 1798 rebellion and was dismissed from the magistrature. His wife was a rich Protestant. Although he abandoned his Catholic faith he continued actively to support emancipation.

BUCKINGHAM, Lady Mary Elizabeth (*d* 1812), daughter of Robert Earl Nugent and wife of the Marquis of Buckingham. In 1800 she was created Baroness Nugent in the Irish peerage.

BUCKINGHAM, Lord George Nugent-Temple-Grenville* (1753-1813), the 1st Marquis. Lord Lieutenant of Ireland 1782-3 (as Lord Temple) and again in 1787-9. His seat was at Stowe, Buckinghamshire, where Revd Charles O'Conor DD, nominally the chaplain of his Catholic wife, was working on the Irish manuscripts in his library.

BURKE, Sir Thomas Of Marble Hill, Loughrea, Co. Galway. Created a baronet in 1797.

BUTLER,* Charles (1750-1832) Of Lincoln's Inn. A nephew of Alban Butler and son of a French mother. His wife was Mary Eyston, by whom he had two daughters as yet unmarried. A conveyancer who after the Relief Act of 1791 became the first English Catholic to be called to the bar. Secretary of the Catholic Committee dissolved in 1791 and moving spirit in the Cisalpine Club.

BYRNE, John Son and heir of the rich Dublin merchant Edward Byrne, who died in December 1804.

CARLISLE, Lord Frederick Howard* (1748-1825), 5th Earl. Lord Lieutenant of Ireland 1780-2 and Lord Privy Seal in 1783, but out of office since then. An author and patron of the fine arts. He spoke against the Union in 1800 and in favour of the 1805 petition.

CARY, John (1770-1820) A Catholic of the Tor Abbey family, married since 1799 to Sophia Sulyard of Haughley Park, Suffolk.

CASTLEREAGH, Lord Robert Stewart* (1769-1822), styled Viscount Castlereagh as son of the 1st Marquis of Londonderry. MP for Co. Down. After carrying the Union when he was Chief Secretary in Ireland he had resigned with Pitt on the King's refusing to countenance further Catholic relief, but he joined Addington's ministry as President of the Board of Control in July 1802. On 13 May 1813 he told the Commons that he had then accepted office on the understanding that his intended payments to Catholic and Dissenting clergy would be introduced, adding that the Irish Bishops declined to accept the offer while the claims of the laity remained unsatisfied. Pitt retained him in the same office and made him concurrently Secretary for War in July 1805.

CHICHESTER, Lord Thomas Pelham* (1756-1826), styled Viscount Pelham from 1801 until he succeeded his father as 2nd Earl on 8 January 1805. Chief Secretary in Ireland 1795-8 and Home Secretary under Addington from 30 November 1801 to 7 August 1803.

CLARE, Lord John Fitzgibbon* (1749-1802), 1st Earl. Lord Chancellor of Ireland before the Union.

CLIFFORD, Charles (1759-1831), 6th Baron, of Chudleigh

CLINCH, James Bernard (1770-1836) Educated in Rome and a professor at Maynooth 1795-1802. Having taken up law he was about to enter the Middle Temple.

COBBETT,* William (1762-1835) The celebrated journalist and political radical.

COLCLOUGH, Mr John Colclough (1767-1807), rather than his brother Caesar, who was not yet back from imprisonment in France. He stood for Wexford in 1807 but was killed in a duel with another candidate.

COLLINS, Revd Mr John Collins, entered in the minute book of the Cisalpine Club immediately after Charles Belasyse, also a priest.

COOKE,* Mr Edward Cooke (1755-1820), Secretary of the Military and then of the Civil Department at Dublin Castle, from which he resigned in 1801. Lord Cornwallis complained of his narrow minded jealousy and his unwillingness to delegate responsibility, and Lord Hardwicke, who suspected him of misapplying secret service money, wrote in June 1804 that Cooke's return to the Castle would be the signal for his marching out of it. He was however a favourite of Castlereagh, who in July 1805 gave him an appointment in the War Office. His correspondence with Castlereagh shows him as a strong advocate of Catholic relief.

COOMBES,* Dr William Henry Coombes DD (1767-1850), of Meadgate, near Bath; author of devotional tracts and a contributor to Cobbett's *Political Register* under the pseudonym of British Observer.

CORNWALLIS,* Lord Charles Cornwallis (1738-1805), created Marquis in 1792. Second in command in the American war and Commander-in-Chief in India. As Lord Lieutenant and Commander-in-Chief in Ireland he dealt with the aftermath of the 1798 rebellion and the French landing in Killala Bay. Having pushed through the Union he resigned with Pitt when this was not followed by a settlement of the Catholic question. Since then he had negotiated the Peace of Amiens. By February 1805 it was already settled that he should return to India and he sailed in the *Medusa* on 14 April.

CORRY,* Isaac (1755-1813) Chief speaker for the government in carrying the Union. through the Irish parliament. MP for Newry. Chancellor of the Irish Exchequer 1802-4.

COUCHE, Mr Probably Thomas Couche who had corresponded with the Huddlestons on testamentary matters, some of them perhaps affecting the interests of Scully's wife. A Mr Couche, 'a most cheerful companion', was staying with the Huddlestons at Sawston Hall in August 1805.

CRUISE,* William (*d.* 1824) Second son of Patrick Cruise of Rahue, Westmeath. Admitted to Lincoln's Inn 1773 and practised as a conveyancer; called to the English bar 1791. He published in 1804 a Digest of the property laws of England which passed through three editions in his lifetime. An original member of the Cisalpine Club.

CURRAN,* Mr John Philpot Curran (1750-1817), the Irish barrister, best remembered as the defender of the leading United Irishmen. Appointed Master of the Rolls by the Grenville government in 1806. Richard Curran was his son.

DALRYMPLE, General William Dalrymple (1736-1807), a brother of the Earl of Stair. As Colonel of the 47th Foot, he had been in command at Belfast in 1795 and Cork in 1796 when the French fleet appeared in Bantry Bay. Now retired as Lieutenant-Governor of Chelsea Hospital.

DALY, Denis Bowes (*c.* 1745-1821) Of Dalystown, Loughrea, Co. Galway. Since 1802 MP for Galway city but being about to contest a vacancy for Galway county (for which he was elected on 8 June) he was probably not in parliament for the debate on the petition. A founder member of the Irish Whig Club and a friend of the Prince of Wales, whom he had approached in November 1804 on behalf of Catholic relief. Joint Mustermaster General of the Forces in Ireland when the Whigs came into power in 1806. His wife was a sister of George Ponsonby.

D'ARCY, Mr The Revd Morgan D'Arcy, missioner at Wolverhampton at the time of Dr Milner's appointment there but recalled by the Irish Bishops to become president of the lay college of Maynooth.

DARDIS, Captain Employed at Stowe as a writer or secretary and used sometimes.as a confidential agent. Lord Buckingham, as also Charles Butler, called him plain Mr Dardis.

DIGNUM,* Charles (1765?-1827) A celebrated tenor, associated with Drury Lane Theatre. He had wanted to become a priest but his father, a master tailor, was too poor to pay for his training.

DILLON, Mr Hon. Henry Augustus Dillon-Lee* (1777-1832), son of 12th Viscount Dillon, whom he succeeded in 1813. MP for Mayo. A supporter of Catholic claims, he had already in 1801 published a pamphlet on the Catholic question and according to Francis Plowden was on the point of introducing a bill for the repeal of penal laws affecting Catholics in the armed forces when the return of Pitt to power induced him to abandon it.

DILLON, John Joseph (*d.* 1837) A younger son of William Mervyn Dillon of Proudstown, Co. Meath. From Lincoln's Inn he was called to the English bar in 1801, in which year he published two pamphlets on the admission of Catholics to parliament. Later a strong vetoist writing under the name of Hibern Anglus.

DONELAN, Malachy Of Ballidonelan, Ballinasloe, Co. Galway. A brother-in-law of Lord Fingall, who obtained for him a post in the Customs worth £300 a year. He had also a house in Mountjoy Square, Dublin, where along with the residences of Lord Fingall and William Bellew, the loyal Catholic address of 24 May 1798 was laid open for signature.

DORCHESTER, Lord George Damer (1746-1808), son of the builder of Milton Abbas in Dorset, whom he succeeded as 2nd Earl in 1798. He was educated at Trinity College Cambridge and as Baron Milton of Shronehill he accompanied Lord Fitzwilliam to Ireland in 1795. In the rebellion of 1798 the Dorset militia served under his command. Shronehill was an estate in County Tipperary near Denys Scully's home at Kilfeacle and Scully's father, who entertained the Earl to dinner in January 1799, found him 'good humoured and pleasant'.

DROMGOOLE,* Dr Thomas (*c.* 1750-*c.* 1826) A doctor trained at Edinburgh. A Dublin Catholic of extreme religious views, prominent later in the Catholic movement.

DUIGENAN,* Dr Patrick (1735-1816) MP for Armagh City. Grand Secretary of the Orange Order. Judge of the Prerogative Court in Dublin, which as well as ecclesiastical matters also dealt with marriage and testamentary cases affected by the penal laws. He led the opposition to Fox's motion on the petition and attacked Scully by name.

EGREMONT, Lord Sir George O'Brien Wyndham* (1751-1837), 3rd Earl. A patron of the fine arts and a successful stockbreeder at Petworth.

ERSKINE, Mr, of the Public Offices Possibly David Montagu Erskine* (1776-1855), later 2nd Baron Erskine, a Commissioner of Bankruptcy 1805-6. The term Public Offices, mainly applied to petty sessions courts, was also used for Bankruptcy offices.

EVANS, George (*d.* 1842) Eldest son of Captain Hampden Evans and nephew of Eyre Evans of Portrane House, Co. Dublin. On 21 August 1805 he married William Parnell's sister, Sophia.

EYSTON, Basil (1748-1817) Of East Hendred. A brother-in-law of Charles Butler and related to the Huddlestons through his wife, a niece of Ferdinand Huddleston.

FINGALL, Lord Arthur James Plunkett (1759-1836), 8th Earl and senior Irish Catholic peer, of Killeen Castle, Co. Meath, married to Frances Donelan. His father, whom he succeeded in 1793, had been one of the seceders in 1791-2. His yeomanry helped defeat the rebels at Tara Hill in 1798 and he supported the Union. Procured a post worth £300 a year for his wife's brother, Malachy Donelan. He had been much in the news during 1804 following the leaking to the press of an exchange of correspondence with Lord Redesdale, regarding the latter's contention that Catholics could not make good subjects of a Protestant king.

FITZGERALD,* Maurice (1774-1849) 18th Knight of Kerry and MP for that county. A friend of Lord Castlereagh, he had supported the Union and in 1801 was made a Lord of the Treasury in Ireland, an office which he retained when Pitt returned to power. In February 1804 he made an offer to raise a corps but it was not taken up. A supporter of emancipation, he was now disillusioned by the outcome of the Union.

FITZGERALD, Thomas Probably either Major Thomas Fitzgerald (1735-1812) of Snowhaven, Co. Kilkenny, who had had a distinguished career with the East India Company; or his son (*d.* before 1839) who was taking an active part in the Waterford committee in 1806.

FITZWILLIAM, Lord William Wentworth Fitzwilliam* (1748-1833), 2nd Earl Fitzwilliam, whose short-lived viceroyalty caused the crisis of 1795 in Ireland.

FLETCHER, William (1750-1823) A follower of Grattan who had been made a KC by Lord Fitzwilliam in 1795 and became Justice of the Common Pleas when the opposition came into power in 1806.

FONBLANQUE,* John de Grenier (1759-1837) An equity lawyer who was MP for Camelford 1802-6.

FOSTER,* John (1740-1828) The last Speaker of the Irish House of Commons, where he had opposed emancipation, now Chancellor of the Irish Exchequer.

FOX,* Charles James (1749-1806) Leader of the 'Foxite' as opposed to the Whig element of the opposition and a long standing friend of the Prince of Wales. Although he might have joined Pitt's second administration if the King had allowed it, he came out of retirement in June 1804 to speak against Pitt's Additional Forces bill and remained to oppose his other measures. A supporter of Catholic relief and opponent of the Union, he was already in December 1803 hoping to bring Grattan into parliament to give a lead on the Irish question.

FRENCH, Arthur (1764-1820) Of Frenchpark, Co. Roscommon and MP for the county since 1783.

FRENCH/FFRENCH, Sir Thomas/Lord (*c.* 1765-1814) Of Castle French, Co. Galway. Prominent in the Catholic Convention of 1792 and a member of the deputation sent to petition the King. For his later moderating influence on the Catholic Committee his Protestant mother was awarded a barony in 1798, the King refusing to raise a Catholic directly to the peerage: when she died on 8 December 1805 he succeeded to the title. After the Union he opened a private bank in Tuam, Co. Galway and in 1804 a branch at 23 Lower Dominick Street, Dublin. His wife was Margaret Redington, daughter of Thomas Redington of Kilcornan.

GEORGE III* George William Frederick (1738-1820), King since 1760. He had a first attack of mental illness in 1765 and a second in 1788. In 1795, when confronted with Lord Fitzwilliam's proposed concessions to the Catholics, he first fell back on his coronation oath to protect the established church. In 1798 his opposition to the direct creation of a new Catholic peer had to be met by bestowing a peerage on Sir Thomas French's Protestant mother instead of on him. In January 1801 his coronation oath scruples were revived when he saw the cabinet's proposals for Catholic relief and despite Pitt's resignation he suffered his third mental breakdown. A fourth one followed in 1804 and he opened parliament for the last time on 15 January 1805.

GIFFARD, Mr John Giffard (1745-1819), editor and proprietor of the *Dublin Journal.* A member of the Dublin Corporation and High Sheriff in 1794.

GIFFORD, Mr John Gifford* (1758-1818), from 1798 editor of the *Anti-Jacobin Review,* an imitation of William Gifford's *Anti-Jacobin* (1797-8).

GLASSE, Revd Mr Perhaps George Henry Glasse,* (1760-1809), who was interested in Catholic charities.

GOOLD, Sir Francis (*d.* 1818) Second son of George Goold of Old Court, Cork.

GORMANSTON, Lord Jenico Preston (1775-1860), 12th Viscount.

GRATTAN,* Henry (1746-1820) In 1795 he introduced the last Catholic relief bill in the Irish House of Commons, soundly defeated when Lord Fitzwilliam was recalled. Since the Union he had been living in retirement at Tinnehinch, in Co. Wicklow. In April 1805 Lord Fitzwilliam provided a seat for him at Malton and he made his first appearance at Westminster on 2 May, in time to support Fox in the debate on the petition. He was elected for Dublin in the 1806 elections

GREEN, Mr *Clark's New Law List* shows three Greens in Gray's Inn Square: Ralph Cooper, Thomas and George Tennant.

GRENVILLE,* Thomas (1755-1846) A younger brother of the Marquis of Buckingham; MP for Buckingham.

GRENVILLE,* Lord William Wyndham Grenville (1759-1834), 1st Baron, of Dropmore, Buckinghamshire. Youngest brother of the Marquis of Buckingham.

Irish Chief Secretary 1782-3. Foreign Secretary 1791-1801 under Pitt, with whom he resigned on the Catholic question. Refused in 1804 to join Pitt's second ministry without Fox. On Pitt's death formed the Ministry of All the Talents.

GREY,* Charles (1764-1845) He acted with Fox during Pitt's first ministry and seceded with the other Whigs in 1797 but returned in 1800 to resist the Union. Refused to join Addington's ministry in 1801. First Lord of the Admiralty and then Foreign Secretary in the Grenville ministry 1806-7. His wife was a daughter of William Brabazon Ponsonby. Styled Viscount Howick when his father was made an Earl in 1806 and succeeded him in 1807 as 2nd Earl Grey.

HARDWICKE, Lord Philip Yorke* (1757-1834), 3rd Earl of Hardwicke, of Wimpole Park, Cambridgeshire. Colonel of the Cambridgeshire Militia, which he raised in 1793 and took to Dublin in 1799. Appointed Lord Lieutenant by Addington and arrived in Dublin on 25 May 1801. His field of patronage was greatly restricted by the obligation imposed on him to give priority to the 'engagements' entered into by Cornwallis and Castlereagh to carry the Union

HAWKESBURY, Lord Robert Banks Jenkinson* (1770-1828), 2nd Baron Hawkesbury from 1803 to 1808, when he succeeded his father as 2nd Earl of Liverpool. Foreign Secretary under Addington 1801-3; joined Pitt's cabinet as Home Secretary in May 1804

HAY,* Edward (*c.* 1761-1826) Although already active in 1792, as a Wexford representative at the Catholic Convention, his name does not appear in any of the records of the 1804 Committee, nor did he sign the petition. He was perhaps deliberately omitted because of his family's involvement in the Wexford rising of 1798, his own imprisonment in that year and partisan feelings revived by his history of the rebellion, published in 1803.

HELY-HUTCHINSON: see HUTCHINSON

HILL, Sir George Fitzgerald (1763-1839) Recorder of Derry and MP for the city. Related by marriage to Sir E. B. Littlehales, Undersecretary of the Military Department at Dublin Castle.

HIPPISLEY,* Sir John Coxe (1748-1825) MP for Sudbury. Involved in Catholic affairs since he had acted as a semi-official British agent at the Holy See in the previous century. His undelivered speech on the petition, published as a pamphlet in 1806, was the first of a long series of interventions in parliament.

HORSLEY,* Samuel (1733-1806) Bishop of St Asaph since 1802. His speech in the House of Lords on the second reading of the English Catholic relief bill of 1791 was generally regarded as having turned the scales in the Catholics' favour.

HUDDLESTON, Edward (1774-1852) Scully's youngest brother-in-law.

HUDDLESTON, Ferdinand (1737-1808) Of Sawston Hall in Cambridgeshire; Scully's father-in-law.

HUDDLESTON, Henry (*b.* 1772) 2nd son of Ferdinand Huddleston and brother -in-law of Denys Scully. He was admitted to Gray's Inn in 1795, received tuition from Charles Butler and became a conveyancer.

HUDDLESTON, John (1745-1835) Of Bathwick, Somerset, son of the Revd William Huddleston. He had served twenty years in the East India Company and was appointed a Director in April 1803. MP for Bridgwater 1804-6.

HUDDLESTON, General William Orchard Huddleston who was descended from Richard Huddleston, a younger brother of Ferdinand Huddleston's great-grand-father.

HUSKISSON,* William (1770-1830) Secretary to the Treasury in Pitt's administration.

HUTCHINSON, Christopher Hely- (1767-1826) 5th son of Provost John Hely-Hutchinson. MP for Cork City. He had pursued a military career on a volunteer basis, distinguishing himself at Ballinamuck in 1798 and accompanying his brother John to the Helder (1799) and Egypt (1801). Unlike the rest of his family he had opposed the Union. He spoke in support of Fox's motion on the petition and defended Scully against an attack on his 1803 pamphlet.

HUTCHINSON,* Lord John Hely-Hutchinson (1757-1832), 2nd son of Provost John Hely-Hutchinson. He was a Major-General on the Irish staff when the French landed at Killala Bay in 1798 and the defeat at Castlebar was blamed on his premature advance. When he took over command in Egypt in 1801 Lord Cornwallis trembled for 'poor Hutchinson; he is a sensible man, but no General', but he went on to capture Cairo and on 16 December 1801 he was created Baron Hutchinson of Alexandria and Knocklofty (the seat in Co. Tipperary of his elder brother, the Earl of Donoughmore). A friend of the Prince of Wales.

JERNINGHAM, Edward (1774-1822) Third son of Sir William Jerningham of Cotessy; a barrister of Lincoln's Inn. When the English Catholic Board was founded in 1808 he became its Secretary, but at this time he had no special status In 1802 he was chased by the mob for canvassing against Sir Francis Burdett and he was an ardent supporter of the French royal family in exile. He married Emily Middleton in October 1804. disappointing the hopes of Scully's sister-in-law, Jane Huddleston.

JERSEY, Earl of George Bussy Villiers* (1735-1805), 4th Earl. Made Master of Horse at the court in 1795 because of the Prince of Wales' interest in his wife. Noted for his courtly manners and described by Mrs Montagu as 'the prince of Maccaronies'. He was perhaps not at his best when Scully met him, for he died on 22 August.

KEATING, George (1762-1842) A Catholic printer in partnership with his father, Patrick Keating. When the printer J. P. Coghlan died in 1800 they had amalgamated with his firm, a nephew of Coghlan, Richard Brown, becoming the third partner.

KEATING, Mrs Frances Aylmer, sister of Lady Kenmare and wife of Roger Sheehy Keatinge, whose elder brother lived at Millicent, Co. Kildare.

KENMARE, Lady Mary Aylmer, second wife of Lord Kenmare; daughter of Michael Aylmer of Lyons, Co. Kildare by his third wife.

KENMARE, Lord Valentine Browne (1754-1812). In 1795 he succeeded his father, the seceder of 1791, as 5th Viscount, a courtesy title descending from an unrecognised creation of James II. It was not until February 1798 that he was formally raised to the peerage, in recognition of his moderating influence on the Irish Catholics. In 1800 he was promoted to an earldom for his support of the Union. Owner of a huge estate in Co. Kerry and a London residence at 48 Wimpole Street.

KEOGH,* John (1740-1817) His visits to London in 1791 and 1792 prepared the ground for the Irish relief act of 1793. In 1796 he was arrested because of his involvement with the United Irishmen, but was released and went to England, thus missing the 1798 rebellion. His home was searched after the Emmet rising in 1803. Despite his poor health he came to the fore again in 1806 as leader of the Dublin Catholics.

KEOGH, Michael Only son of Michael Keogh, Crumlin, Co. Dublin. Called to the Irish bar 1794.

KING, JOHN Undersecretary at the Home Office 1792-1806.

KING,* Lord Peter King (1776-1833), 7th Baron.

KIRWAN,* Richard Patrick (1733-1812) An eminent mineralogist, Inspector General of Mines at Dublin Castle. His eldest daughter Maria Teresa was married to John Thomas Barnewall, Lord Trimleston's son and heir.

LANDAFF, Lord Francis Mathew (1738-1806), 1st Earl, of Thomastown, Co. Tipperary, where he was a neighbour of James Scully of Kilfeacle.

LAURENCE,* Dr French (1757-1809) Regius Professor of Civil Law at Oxford and MP for Peterborough.

LISMORE, Lord Cornelius O'Callaghan (1775-1857), at this time 2nd Baron Lismore; created a Viscount in 1806. A contemporary of Scully's at Trinity College, Cambridge. An opponent of the Union.

LLOYD, Mrs Probably the wife of the Irish barrister, John Lloyd, son of the Revd Richard Lloyd of Castle Lloyd, Limerick, and brother of the Rector of Fethard, Co. Tipperary.

LONSDALE, Lady Widow of the first Earl Lonsdale.

LYNCH, Martin French (*b.* 1767) A Doctor of Law at Trinity College Dublin who was admitted to the Inner Temple in 1785 but not called to the Irish bar until the passage of the relief act of 1792, in which year he was a member of the sub-comittee directing the Catholic petition. He supported the Union and was promised a chairmanship of quarter sessions in Co. Galway. Lord Hardwicke seems to have confused him with Mark Lynch of Renmore, whose mother was an aunt of Sir Thomas French.

MCDONNELL, Mr M. I. McDonnell, a merchant of Lime Street Square, London, in partnership with J. Bushell. He was perhaps the brother of Randal McDonnell referred to by the latter in a letter of 20 April 1805 to Scully.

MACDONNELL, Randal (*d.* 1821) A partner of Edward Byrne and after his death in 1804 the leading Catholic merchant in Dublin. A magistrate in his capacity as a Conservator of the Peace for the Usher's Island district. He was a member of the sub-committee of 1792 which directed the petition to the King.

MCKENNA* Theobald (1765-1808) Son of a merchant of Carrick-on-Suir. Attended Lincoln's Inn and joined the Irish bar in 1796. Sat in the Catholic Convention but in a pamphlet of 1793 denounced the republican tenets associated with Wolfe Tone. Awarded a pension in 1801 for his support of the Union. After it he advocated a salaried establishment of the Catholic clergy and a role for the crown in the nomination of bishops. He had a brother who was a priest in Waterford and his wife, a sister of James Laffan of Kilkenny, was an aunt of the Countess of Shrewsbury.

MACMAHON, Colonel John (*c.* 1754-1817) Son of John MacMahon, a butler in the household of the 1st Earl of Leitrim, who secured for him a Comptrollership of the Port of Limerick. Going to America he was given a commission in the army by the future Lord Moira, who on his return introduced him to the Prince of Wales. Appointed Keeper of the latter's Privy Purse he became in practice his Private Secretary from 1803. MP for Alderburgh since 1802. "Formed by nature to be a courtier, wrote an obituarist, he made a most graceful and elegant bow, which he regulated in due proportion to the rank and influence of those he addressed."

MACMAHON, William (1776-1837) A half-brother of Colonel John McMahon, his mother being the daughter of a Cork merchant named Stackpole whom his father married as his 2nd wife. At this time he was a barrister in Dublin. His later promotion to the bench owed much to the influence of the Prince of Wales but he was described by O'Connell in 1815 as, after Lord Redesdale, the best equity judge Ireland ever saw.

MACNAMARA, Counsellor Daniel Macnamara (1720-1800), a Roman Catholic conveyancer who acted for several public figures, English and Irish, and had been the agent in London of the pre-1793 Irish Catholic Committee.

MAHER, Nicholas A first cousin once removed of Scully's, whose paternal grandmother was Nicholas' aunt. Valentine was Nicholas' son.

MAJENDIE, Dr Henry William Majendie*. Formerly tutor to Prince William, now Bishop of Chester.

MARSDEN, Alexander (1761-1834) Having been previously Secretary of the Law Department at Dublin Castle, he succeeded Edward Cooke in October 1801 as Under-Secretary for Civil Affairs, a post from which he was removed by the Grenville government in 1806. According to Plowden "the only merit insisted upon in behalf of Mr. Marsden, was his urbanity and politeness of manner when officially applied to."

MARSHALL, Robert Promoted by Pelham when he was Chief Secretary and taken up also by his successor, Castlereagh, who used him as a private secretary and as a go-between with the Catholics. Already Treasurer of the college of Maynooth, he was in June 1799 appointed Inspector General of Exports and Imports. In 1801 Charles Abbot, who did not continue him as private secretary, offered him the post of Secretary of the Treasury. This, according to Cooke, he prudently declined, "for the Treasury is a place of daily attendance, is only £1000, and is a confidential office, from which he would be forced out on a hostile change."

MARTIN,* Colonel/Mr Richard ('Humanity') Martin (1754-1834), MP for Co. Galway, where his vast estates gave him an influence which he had exerted on behalf of the Union. The first member of his family to be brought up as a Protestant, he was a supporter of Catholic emancipation, but when, in the summer of 1803, he agitated the Catholic question in Galway Lord Hardwicke suspected him of seeking favours from government. His military title was probably acquired when he was Colonel of the Galway Volunteers in 1782.

MATHEW, Lord Francis James Mathew (1768-1833), of Thomastown, Co. Tipperary, adjacent to Kilfeacle, where Scully's father lived. Styled Viscount as son and heir of the 1st Earl Landaff, whom he succeeded in 1806. MP until then for Co. Tipperary,

MELVILLE, Lord Henry Dundas* (1742-1811), created a Viscount by Addington in 1802. Lord Advocate for Scotland 1775-1783. As Home Secretary 1791-4 he had introduced the Irish delegation to the King. Secretary of War 1794-1801; now First Lord of the Admiralty in Pitt's second administration, but under threat of impeachment since the publication on 13 February 1805 of a report revealing irregularities in the naval accounts. He resigned on 8 April and was impeached before the House of Lords in June 1806.

MILNER,* Dr John (1752-1826) Formerly missioner at Winchester, since 1803 Vicar Apostolic of the Midland District, residing at Wolverhampton, a move to get him appointed coadjutor to Dr Douglass in London having failed. In October 1805 he was formally offered the agency for the Irish clergy but a renewed attempt to have him transferred to London (rejected by the Holy See in 1806) seems already to have been initiated by Dr Troy, the Archbishop of Dublin. His antipathy to Charles Butler and the members of the old Catholic Committee dated from their differences over the relief act of 1791.

MOIRA, Lord Francis Rawdon (1754-1826), Baron Rawdon in the English peerage 1783; 2nd Earl of Moira. As heir to his uncle, the 10th Earl of Huntingdon of Donington Park, he took the additional name of Hastings* in 1791. Served in America, where Lord Edward Fitzgerald was his ADC. Saw the English Catholic relief act through the House of Lords in 1791. Acting Grandmaster of the English Freemasons from 1790. A close friend of the Prince of Wales. Godfather to one of Wolfe Tone's sons and an inflammatory critic of the Irish administration before the rebellion. Often tipped for the post of Lord Lieutenant or Commander-in-Chief Ireland. Commander-in-Chief Scotland 1803. Master of Ordnance in the Grenville ministry 1806-7.

MOORE, Edward A merchant of Temple Street, Dublin, in partnership with Valentine O'Connor, who was married to his aunt. His mother, Anne Byrne, widow of James Moore of Mount Browne, was a friend of Scully's and like him had frequented Moira House.

MOORE, George (1773-1840) Of Moore Hall, Mayo. A barrister of Lincoln's Inn and author of a pamphlet supporting the Union.

MOYLAN,* Dr Francis (1735-1815) Since 1786 Bishop of Cork.

MUSGRAVE,* Sir Richard (1757?-1818) The author of fiery anti-Catholic pamphlets and of *Memoirs of the different rebellions in Ireland*, published in 1801.

NANGLE, James (*d.* 1811) Born in Spain, a country gentleman of Kildalky Castle, Trim. Already active in 1792. when he signed the petition to the King.

NEWBURGH, Lord Anthony James Newburgh (1757-1814), 5th Earl.

NEPEAN,* Sir Evan (1751-1822) MP for Bridport, made a baronet in 1802. Originally a clerk in the navy, he was from 1782 to 1794 an Undersecretary in the Home Office. After an interval at the War Office he was Secretary to the Admiralty from 1795 until his appointment as Chief Secretary for Ireland, where he landed on 1 February 1804. A place on the Admiralty Board then falling vacant he was pressed by the King on 6 June to accept it. From September 1804 he combined this post with his Irish appointment and when he finally left Ireland on 28 December he remained Chief Secretary until Vansittart was appointed to replace him on 23 March 1805.

O'BRIEN, Sir Edward (1773-1837) 4th Baronet, of Drumoland, Co. Clare, MP. for Clare 1802-1826. A member of the opposition and a supporter of the Catholics.

O'CONNELL,* Daniel (1775-1847) The Liberator. He had previously been involved in the Catholic question when at a meeting of 13 January 1800 (of which James Ryan was Secretary) he had urged the Catholic body to oppose the Union.

O'CONNOR, Valentine Senior and Junior The elder (*c.* 1744-1814) was a merchant of Dominick Street, married to the eldest daughter of the brewer Edward Moore of Mount Browne. The younger was his son, an importer of 37 Granary Row, Dublin.

O'CONOR, Owen (1763-1831) Son of Denis O'Conor of Belanagare and elder brother of Revd Charles O'Conor DD. Married to Jane Moore of Mount Browne. A Volunteer in 1782 and a delegate to the Catholic Convention of 1793. Became O'Conor Don in 1820 after the death of a distant cousin.

O'GORMAN, Nicholas Purcell (1778-1857) Called to the Irish bar in 1803, later prominent in the Catholic movement.

O'REILLY, Dominick (*d.* 1816) Of Kildangan Castle, Monasterevin, in Co. Kildare, a property acquired *c.* 1705 by the brothers Edward and Edmund Reilly, merchants of Dublin.

O'REILLY, Dowell (*d.* 1838) One of the East Breifne O'Reillys. His seat was Heath House, Queen's County.

O'REILLY, Sir Hugh (1741-1827) Of Ballinlough Castle, Co. Westmeath. His wife was a cousin of the Earl of Landaff and he had two brothers, Andrew and James, in the Austrian service. One of the seceders from the Catholic Committee of 1791-2; created a baronet in 1795 and given a post on the Irish military establishment as an Overseer of Barracks.

O'SHEA Probably Richard Power O'Shee (*c.* 1763-1827) of Gardenmorris in Co. Waterford, who was active in the Waterford committee of 1806.

PARNELL,* William (1780-1821) Younger son of Sir John Parnell and grandfather of Charles Stewart Parnell. He took the additional surname of Hayes on succeeding to his estate of Avondale in Co. Wicklow. Described by George Ponsonby as 'a very clever but certainly wild young man'. He had a warm admiration for the Irish Catholic clergy and published anonymously in 1805 *An Enquiry into the causes of popular discontent in Ireland.*

PELHAM, Lord: see CHICHESTER

PETRE, Lord Robert Edward Petre (1763-1809), 10th Baron.

PETTY, Lord Henry Henry Petty-Fitzmaurice* (1780-1863), MP for Calne. Went to the Lords as 3rd Marquis of Lansdowne in 1809. Chancellor of the Exchequer in the Grenville ministry 1806-7. He had an Irish connexion through his wife, whose mother was a daughter of Standish O'Grady of Capercullen.

PITT,* William (1759-1806) Prime Minister from 1783 to 14 March 1801, when he handed over to Addington following upon the King's refusal in January to sanction further measures of Catholic relief; and again from May 1804 to his death on 23 January 1806 During the King's illness in February-March 1801 he had conveyed a private assurance to him that he would not raise the Catholic question again in the King's lifetime.

POPE Pius VII Barnaba Chiaramonti (1742-1823), elected in 1800.

PLOWDEN,* Francis Peter (1749-1829) Lawyer and historian. Brother of two Jesuits and himself in the Jesuit novitiate before the dissolution of the order. His *Historical Review of the state of Ireland* was published in 1803.

PLUNKETT, Major/Colonel William (1770-1806) A younger brother of Lord Fingall who was in the Austrian service and promoted from Major to Colonel in 1804. After the refusal of the War Office to let him raise a regiment in Ireland he returned to Prague, where he died.

PONSONBY,* George (1755-1817) A younger brother of William Brabazon Ponsonby and uncle of Charles Grey's wife. MP for Co. Wicklow. He gained a reputation as an orator in the Irish parliament and distinguished himself as an opponent of the Union, but Grattan wrote of him in 1803 that "he loves his ease, and is tired of the parliamentary battle." Lord Chancellor of Ireland in the Grenville administration 1806-7.

PONSONBY,* John (*c.* 1770-1855) Nephew of George Ponsonby and brother-in-law of Charles Grey. He was briefly styled Viscount in 1806 when his father, William Brabazon, was made a baron: he succeeded him in the same year as 2nd

Baron. He had sat in the Irish parliament and was MP for Galway in 1801 but did not stand in the 1802 election. He was later to abandon politics for diplomacy, but at this time he was active as an unofficial whip for the Whigs.

PONSONBY,* William Brabazon (1744-1806) MP for Co. Kilkenny until the Grenville government made him a Baron (of Imokillly in Ireland, but in the English peerage). A staunch Whig, he had not held office since he was Joint Postmaster General in Ireland 1784-90.

POWER, Mr, of Waterford Probably the Nicholas Power who bought Snowhill in about 1808. His wife was Rachel O'Neill and their descendants were O'Neill-Powers.

PRINCE OF WALES George Augustus Frederick, later George IV* (1762-1830), whose London residence was Carlton House. Since he came of age he had been a close friend of Charles James Fox, but had also fallen under the influence of Lord Moira, who encouraged him in 1797 to urge Pitt to repeal all the penal laws and to offer himself as governor of Ireland. Since the rebellion his enthusiasm had waned and his financial difficulties made it advisable for him to keep on good terms with his father's ministers.

PURCELL, John MD (1744-1806) Grandfather of the translator of the *Rubaiyat*, his son having assumed the surname of Fitzgerald.

REDESDALE, Lord John Freeman Mitford* (1748-1830), made 1st Baron Redesdale on his appointment as Lord Chancellor for Ireland in 1802, in June of which year he married the sister of Spencer Perceval, Attorney General in the Addington administration. He carried the English relief act through the House of Commons in 1791 and had since then been Solicitor-General, Attorney-General and Speaker. Although he was admired for his mastery of the law he made himself unpopular with the Irish Catholics, particularly by initiating a correspondence with Lord Fingall in which he claimed that Catholics could not make good subjects. In 1806 he was immediately dismissed by the incoming Grenville ministry.

REEVES, Mr Probably John Reeves* (1752?-1829), the King's Printer.

RENNELL,* Thomas (1754-1840) Master of the Temple.

ROCHE, John (*d.* 1825) Eldest son of Stephen Roche of Limerick (1724-1804) and one of the leading Dublin merchants.

ROSE, George, (1744-1818) MP for Christchurch. A close friend of William Pitt, he was Secretary of the Treasury in his first administration and was now Vice President of the Board of Trade.

RYAN, Charles (*d.* 1810) An eminent apothecary of Church Street, Dublin, who sometimes took the chair at Catholic meetings in 1791 and after.

RYAN, James Probably a son or a brother of Thomas Ryan, of Ballinakill, Co. Kildare, as their names appear together at the head of the the petition to the House of Lords. He began a successful business career as an apprentice in Randal McDonnell's firm. Alleged by Nepean to have been at one time closely connected with Arthur O'Connor and Curran. Secretary to the meeting of 17 January 1800 calling on Catholics to oppose the Union. In 1806 he lost all credit with his fellow Catholics by taking advantage of his acquaintance with Fox to apply for a lucrative post involving the handling of the Irish funds. His long letter of 4 August 1810 to the *Freeman's Journal* was an attempt at self-vindication.

SCULLY, James (1737-1816) Denys Scully's father, of Kilfeacle, County Tipperary. As well as being an eminent grazier he was in partnership with his second son, James, as a banker in Tipperary town. His influence helped to carry Co. Tipperary for the Union, which he still thought would promote investment of capital in Ireland.

SCULLY, Mrs Mary (1769-1806), elder daughter of Ferdinand Huddleston (of Sawston Hall near Cambridge) and wife of Denys Scully, to whom she was married on 26 November 1801. If she did not know Scully already when he was at Trinity College Cambridge in 1794-5 she would have met him when she went to Dublin in 1799 to visit her brother Richard, who was stationed there with the Cambridgeshire militia and was befriended by Lady Moira. She was of frail health and died at Mrs Bostock's house on 17 April 1806.

SCULLY, Roger Probably Scully's first cousin, Roger (1770-1844), eldest son of Jeremiah Scully of Silverfort. He married Ellen Lyons of Croom in 1802 and resided later, if not already, at Elm Park, Limerick.

SELBY, Robert 3rd son of Thomas Selby of Biddleston, Northumberland, married to Hon. Teresa Talbot, sister of the Earl of Shrewsbury.

SHEE, Sir George (1758-1825) Of Castlebar, Mayo. Created a baronet in 1794, Surveyor General of the Ordnance and then Secretary of the Treasury in Ireland 1797-9. MP for Knocktopher 1797 to the Union. An Undersecretary in the Home Office from 1801 to 1803, when he was awarded a pension, but returned as one of the Undersecretaries for War and Colonies in the Grenville administration 1806-7.

SHEE, Joseph He and his brother Thomas, partners in a city merchant house, came from Thomastown, Co. Kilkenny.

SHELDON, William (1744-1830) A highly respected Catholic conveyancer of 3 Gray's Inn Square and Brailes, Warwickshire. Mainly responsible for the relief act of 1778 and Secretary of the first Catholic Committee in London.

SHERIDAN,* Richard Brinsley (1751-1816) The well known playwright and friend of the Prince of Wales. MP for Staffordshire. Thomas was his only son.

SHREWSBURY, Lord Charles Talbot (1753-1827), 15th Earl of Shrewsbury and Earl of Waterford and Wexford in the Irish peerage. A mathematician with an interest in mechanics. Married to Elizabeth Hoey, daughter of a Dublin printer. When they entertained it was on a lavish scale. Writing to her mother on 25 May 1805 Scully's sister-in-law, Jane Huddleston, said that she was seeing Lady Shrewsbury almost every day.

SIDMOUTH: see ADDINGTON.

SLIGO, Lady Louisa Catharine Howe (d.1817).

SLIGO, Lord John Denis Browne* (1756-1809), formerly Earl of Altamont, created Marquis in 1800 in recognition of his strenuous support of the Union. Disappointed at not getting an English peerage until February 1806. Reported regularly to Dublin Castle, both from Westport and London. Pleaded ill health as his excuse for missing the debate on the petition.

SMITH, Mr John Henry Smyth, Undersecretary (with John King) in the Home Department 1804-6.

SOMERTON, Lord Charles Agar (1736-1809), who was created Baron Somerton in 1795, Viscount in 1800, Earl of Normanton in 1806. Having been Archbishop of Cashel since 1779 he was transferred to Dublin in 1800.

SOMERVILLE, Sir Marcus (*d.* 1831) MP for Meath and a supporter of the opposition.

SOUTHWELL, Lord Thomas Anthony Southwell (1777-1860), 3rd Viscount, of Castle Mattress (or Matrix), Rathkeale, Co. Limerick.

SPENCER,* Lord George John Spencer (1758-1834), 2nd Earl. First Lord of the Admiralty under Pitt, with whom he resigned in 1801. Now in opposition, soon to become Home Secretary in the Grenville ministry.

STRANGE, Richard Father-in-law of Sir E. Bellew

TAAFFE, Baron Rodolphus Taaffe, who succeeded his grandfather in 1769, inherited the two titles of Viscount of Corran and Baron of Ballymote, both in Co. Sligo.

TAAFFE, John (1746-1825) Of Smarmore Castle, Ardee, Co. Louth, son of George Taaffe of Corballis, Co. Meath.

TEMPLE, Lord Richard Temple-Nugent-Grenville,* styled Earl Temple as the son and heir of the Marquis of Buckingham. MP for Buckinghamshire.

THROCKMORTON, Sir John (1753-1819) 5th Baronet, of Buckland, Berkshire. A leading figure in the London Catholic Committee of 1782-1791. Author of pamphlets taking up an anti-papal position and arguing for domestic nomination of bishops. His last pamphlet, of 1806, suggested that nomination by the King could be conceded if asked for. His wife was Maria, daughter of Thomas Giffard of Wolverhampton (d. 1775) by his first wife, a Petre.

THROCKMORTON, William (1762-1819) Brother of Sir John. A lawyer of 2 Lincoln's Inn, Old Buildings.

TRIMLESTOWN/TRIMLESTON, Lord Nicholas Barnewall (1726-1813), 14th Baron. Before the revolution he lived in France.

TROY,* Dr John Thomas (1739-1823) A Dominican, Archbishop of Dublin since 1784. The nephew on whose behalf he used his influence at Dublin Castle was John James Troy, who was given the post of revenue officer at Baltimore, County Cork.

TYRWHITT, Thomas (1762-1833) MP for Portarlington. He had acted as Private Secretary to the Prince of Wales until his duties were taken over by Colonel MacMahon in 1803.

UNDERHILL, Mr Revd Richard Underhill, a priest, of 52 Lincoln's Inn Fields.

VANSITTART,* Nicholas (1766-1851) He had been Secretary of the Treasury before he was appointed on 23 March 1805 to take Nepean's place as Chief Secretary for Ireland On 18 September 1805 he resigned and returned to the Treasury without ever having set foot in Ireland.

VESEY, George Eldest son of Francis Vesey of Dublin. A barrister of Lincoln's Inn, called to the Irish bar in 1785.

WELDON, John A mercer of Dame Street, Dublin.

WHITE/WHYTE, John (1752-1814) Of a Leixlip family, which was now settled at Loughbrickland, Co. Down. One of the seceders of 1791-2. Besides eight sons he had two daughters, Letitia and Margaret.

WICKHAM,* William (1761-1840) Chief Secretary in Ireland from 1802 to January 1804, when he resigned, after being in bed for three months following an accident.

WILBERFORCE,* William (1759-1833) The leader in parliament of the anti-slavery cause.

WINDHAM,* William (1750-1810) Secretary for War under Pitt 1794-1801 but now in opposition. He had been Chief Secretary for Ireland 1783-4.

WYSE, Thomas (1770-1835) Of the Manor of St. John, Waterford. Headed the list of Waterford supporters of the Union in 1799. His youngest sister was the wife of Denys Scully's brother, James.

YORKE,* Charles Philip (1764-1834) Half-brother of the Earl of Hardwicke, on whom he relied for financial support as MP for Cambridgeshire. Home Secretary in the Addington ministry from 1803 to May 1804.

SELECT BIBLIOGRAPHY
(with short titles)

UNPUBLISHED SOURCES

CISALPINE CLUB MINUTE BOOK Westminster Diocesan Archives, 16 Abingdon Road, London W8.

DIARY OF JAMES SCULLY A journal for the period 1772-1814, National Library of Ireland, MS 27,579.

DROPMORE PAPERS Papers formerly in the possession of J. B. Fortescue Esq. [now in the British Library], Add. MSS. 58,855 – 59,478.

HARDWICKE PAPERS Papers of Philip Yorke, the 3rd Earl, British Library, Add. MSS. 35,701 – 35,787.

HOME OFFICE Papers relating to Ireland in the series HO 100 at the Public Record Office, Kew, Richmond, Surrey.

HOUSE OF LORDS House of Lords Record Office, Main Papers.

HUDDLESTON PAPERS Papers of the Huddlestons of Sawston Hall, file 488, Cambridgeshire Record Office, Cambridge.

RICHMOND PAPERS Correspondence etc. of Charles Lennox, 4th Duke of Richmond, National Library of Ireland, MSS 58-75A.

SCULLY PAPERS Papers of the Scully family of Kilfeacle and Mantlehill, Co. Tipperary, National Library of Ireland. MSS 27,478 – 27,599.

TROY PAPERS File 29/9, Dublin Diocesan Archives, Archbishop's House, Drumcondra, Dublin.

WINDHAM PAPERS Calendar of Windham Papers, National Register of Archives 37,849.

PUBLISHED SOURCES

CASTLEREAGH CORRESPONDENCE *Memoirs and Correspondence of Viscount Castlereagh,* Vol. IV, London, 1849.

CORNWALLIS CORRESPONDENCE Corrrespondence of Charles, 1st Marquess Cornwallis, London, 1859.

Dropmore Papers The manuscripts of J. B. Fortescue Esq. preserved at Dropmore [now in the British Library], Historical Manuscripts Commission, 13th report, Appendix, part III.

GRATTAN, LIFE AND TIMES *Memoirs of the Life and Times of the Rt. Hon. H. G. Grattan* by his son, Vol. V, London, 1846.

HANSARD *The Parliamentary Debates from the year 1803.*

Jerningham Letters Excerpts from the correspondence and diaries of Lady Jerningham and her daughter Lady Bedingfeld, edited by Egerton Castle, 1896.

O'DONOVAN, John *The O'Conors of Connaught,* Dublin, 1891, reproducing some O'Conor correspondence in the archives at Clonalis, Co. Roscommon.

STATE TRIALS T. B. and J. T. Howell, *A complete collection of State Trials*, London, 1809-1826.

The Viceroy's Post-Bag correspondence of the 3rd Earl of Hardwicke selected and edited by Michael MacDonough, London , 1904.

THE CATHOLIC QUESTION The Catholic Question in Ireland and England 1798-1822: The Papers of Denys Scully, edited by B. C. MacDermot, Dublin, 1988.

TONE, LIFE *Life of Theobald Wolfe Tone,* edited by his son, two volumes, Washington, 1826.

WORKS CONSULTED

Army List.

Boyle's new fashionable Court and Country Guide.

BURKE *History of the Commoners*, 1834-8; successive editions of the *Landed Gentry* and the *Landed Gentry of Ireland*; *Irish Family Records*, 1976; and the *Peerage, Baronetage and Knightage.*

Clarke's New Law List.

COKAYNE, G. E. *Complete Peerage*, London, 1887 and *Complete Baronetage*, Exeter, 1900.

Dictionary of National Biography.

Encyclopaedia of the laws of Scotland, Vol. XIII.

EUBEL, Conrad (and others) *Hierarchia Catholica*, Vols. VI and VII, 1913.

HAYDN, Joseph, *The Book of Dignities*, London, 1890.

History of Parliament The House of Commons 1790-1820, edited by R. G. Thorne, London, 1986.

Holden's Triennial Directory.

HUNT, Revd. William Presidential Address delivered on 20 February 1908: *Transactions of the Royal Historical Society*, 3rd Series, Vol.II, pp.1-19.

HUSENBETH, Frederick *The life of John Milner, Bishop of Castalba*, Dublin, 1862

Irish Statutes from 3 Edward II to the Union, London, 1885.

King's Inns Admission Papers, edited by E. Keane, P. B. Phair and T. U. Sadleir, Dublin, 1982.

LECKY, W. E. H. *A History of Ireland in the 18th century*, new edition in five volumes, London, 1902.

LEET, Ambrose *A Directory to the Market Towns and Villages, Gentlemen's seats and other places in Ireland,* Dublin, 1814.

PARNELL, Sir Henry Brooke *History of the Penal Laws against the Catholics, from the Treaty of Limerick to the Union*, Dublin, 1808.

PLAYFAIR, William *British Family Antiquity*, Vols. IV, V and IX, London 1810, 1811.

PLOWDEN, HISTORICAL REVIEW *An historical review of the state of Ireland from Henry II. . . to the Union with Great Britain*, by Francis Plowden, 2 volumes, Egerton, London, 1803

PLOWDEN, HISTORY *A History of Ireland from its union with Great Britain, 1801 - 1810,* by Francis Plowden, 3 volumes, London, 1811.

Post Office London Directory

ROSE, George *Diaries and correspondence,* London, 1860.

SCULLY, Denys *A Statement of the Penal Laws which aggrieve the Catholics of Ireland, with commentaries,* in two parts, Dublin, 1811,1812.

Statutes at large, edited by Danby Pickering, Cambridge University Press, 1805.

Statutes passed in the parliaments held in Ireland, Grierson, Dublin, 1799.

Treble Almanack

WALKER, B. M. *Parliamentary Election results in Ireland, Dublin, 1978.*

WARD, Monsignor Bernard *The Dawn of the Catholic Revival* and *The Eve of Catholic Emancipation*, reprinted, London, 1970.

Wilson's Dublin Directory.

THE PRESS

The Courier
Dublin Evening Post
Faulkner's Dublin Journal
Freeman'a Journal
The Morning Chronicle
The Morning Post
The Political Register
The Times

INDEX OF PERSONS

(Names in the appendices, other than Appendix G, are included only if they appear elsewhere in the text. In some of the longer entries mere mentions are enclosed in parentheses).

INDEX OF SUBJECTS AND PLACES